SAND AND SEA

SEFTON'S COASTAL HERITAGE

Archaeology, History and Environment of a Landscape in North West England

Proceedings of the conference *Sefton's Coastal Heritage*, Formby, 15 September 2004

Edited by
Jennifer M. Lewis & Jennifer E. Stanistreet

SEFTON
LIBRARIES

2008
Published by:
Sefton Council
Leisure Services Department (Libraries)
Magdalen House, 30 Trinity Road, Bootle L20 3NJ

Cover illustration courtesy of Dave McAleavy
Sefton Council
(Leisure Services Department, Coast & Countryside Service)

ISBN 978-1-874516-16-3

9 781874 516163

Designed and printed in Great Britain
by
Mitchell & Wright (Printers) Limited, Southport, PR8 5AL

Contents

Acknowledgements

Sefton Coast Partnership's Archaeology and History Task Group extends its thanks to all those who have made this publication possible:-

- Reg Yorke whose idea it was to hold a Conference; and Ceri Jones and John Houston who chaired the event

- Sefton Council for their support and financial commitment not only to the Conference but also to subsequent publication of the papers presented

- The National Trust for a generous grant to support publication costs

- Sefton's Coast and Countryside Service for financial assistance with this project

- Formby Civic Society for holding the purse strings on behalf of the Task Group

- Lorna Lander and Sue Rudkin of Sefton Council who guided us through the administrative and technical processes of holding a Conference

- Barry Rice of Sefton Council for his expertise in the world of print

- Sefton's Library and Information Services, and particularly Mark Sargant, for fulfilling the longstanding commitment to bring this publication to fruition

- Jenny Stanistreet for continuing the role of editor in retirement and for moulding the disparate papers into a creditable whole

The National Trust

Introduction

John Houston

efton lies on the eastern shore of the Irish Sea, between the estuaries of the Ribble and Mersey rivers. Extending from Southport in the north as far as the dockland landscape of Bootle, the coastal environment is characterised by a dune landscape that undulates between the wide-ranging tidal reach of a gently sloping shoreline and a hinterland of flat mosslands interrupted occasionally by low sand-covered sandstone outcrops. Towards the south the mosslands are drained by the River Alt and the Rimrose Brook but, until the age of large-scale agricultural improvement in the 18th and 19th centuries, areas of standing water remained for much of the year.

Populated over many thousands of years, this marginal landscape has been affected by varying paces of transformation as natural agencies of climatic change, marine incursion and regression had their effect. On the one hand, wind-blown sand has concealed buildings and cultivated fields damaging – or even destroying – whole communities. At other times, old land surfaces buried many hundreds, if not thousands, of years ago can be exposed as storms and high tides erode the fragile dune face.

Some fifteen or so years ago, on 31 May 1991, the Sefton Coast Research Seminar saw the presentation of research undertaken at both local and national level and provided an opportunity for discussion with those involved in the conservation and management of our coast. This was a remarkable meeting in that for the first time in our region of north west England it brought together those concerned with understanding the natural processes of coastal development and change, and those dedicated to studies of plant and animal habitats (Atkinson and Houston 1993). Importantly, it highlighted how palaeontologists, marine scientists, geomorphologists, archaeologists and historians recognise the role each can play in understanding the

dynamics of coastal development and taking the evidence forward for interpretation, management and presentation of the coastal landscape. All the same, the published summary of the evidence for human activity in the coastal environment placed greater emphasis on historical evidence of the last 2,000 years, rather than on that of archaeology.

This was not surprising. Until the late 1970s the evidence for early human presence on the coast was known only from the occasional archaeological find – a stone axe, a stray coin. With the creation of Merseyside's Sites and Monuments Record (now Merseyside's Heritage Environment Record - HER) came the first opportunity for consistent recording and interpretation of Sefton's archaeology. Initially, this survey of the evidence – as it was found in published and archival sources, maps, museum collections and supported by targeted recording in the field – was intended for use by Sefton's planning and development control. Since then, a tightly-targeted programme of investigation into the prehistory of our coastal mosslands has produced impressive evidence for early post-glacial human presence on the coast and its hinterland, supported by an analysis of the environment in which such people survived. On the shore itself, trails of human footprints and tracks of mammals and birds imprinted in hard-baked silts deposited as sea levels rose and fell at the end of the last Ice Age captured the imagination of Gordon Roberts whose dedicated work since 1987 has brought Sefton's coast to the notice of a national audience, notably through BBC TV's *Coast* series.

Over the last twenty years the historians have been no less active in producing new work, focusing particularly on Formby, Ainsdale, Birkdale and Southport, as well as on the history of flying and the development of the coast's many golf courses. Museums at the Botanic Gardens in Southport and Little Crosby also hold important collections available for research into our coastal history and archaeology; much of the information relating to recent archaeological investigations is held in the Museum of Liverpool. In addition, Sefton's Library Service provides a rich resource for research into all aspects of the area's coastal history and activity. The Local History Collections at Southport and Crosby libraries hold a range of sources (printed works, maps, photographs), which are freely available for consultation.

The formation of the Sefton Coast Partnership in 2001 brought new impetus and opportunity to integrate the evidence of archaeology and history into the management strategies and policies of those responsible for managing the coastal resource. Under the chairmanship of Dr Reg Yorke the Partnership's Archaeology and History Task Group was established, and amongst its initiatives was a Conference to bring together specialists on topics ranging from the early post-glacial coastal environment through to 19th-century cultivation practices. Over 160 delegates attended the Conference, which was held at Formby Hall Golf Club on 15 September 2004. It is the papers emanating from this Conference that the Task Group now brings to publication.

Starting with a brief summary of human activity on the Sefton coast, the papers that follow consider in greater detail some of the archaeological and environmental evidence from many thousands of years before the first documentary material appeared following the Norman Conquest through to more recent aspects of the coast's maritime history and land use.

Human exploitation of the landscape, its flora and fauna, are seen from the perspective of both archaeological and historical material. For the first 9,000 or so years a complex combination of artefactual remains, human and animal footprints, pollen evidence and radiocarbon dating produces a picture of people living in a landscape rich with resources necessary for human survival. In contrast, with the exception of the occasional find and the knowledge that by 1066 there were established communities on our coast, the evidence for the centuries that span the Roman and Viking periods is elusive. Lessons can be learned, perhaps, from further afield. The coastal landscape at Meols on the north Wirral coast, where many thousands of artefacts have been recovered by local people and placed in museum collections over the last 100 years, provides a model on which local research can be based. Post-Conquest documentary sources inform of settlement-loss to 'sand and sea' on Sefton's coast on several occasions over the centuries suggesting that, as at Meols, significant buried archaeological deposits may yet be exposed.

Not surprisingly, as in the prehistoric period, the coastal economy of more recent centuries was based on the dual exploitation of land and sea. Though erosion and accretion may respectively have destroyed or obscured evidence for sheltered harbourage, both legitimate and illicit seaborne trade are known from the documentary sources. From the 18th century onwards the increase in shipping as the port of Liverpool developed led to measures to establish tidal markers and lighthouses; and the country's first lifeboat house was built on Sefton's coast. Fishing from the beach and maintaining the rabbit warrens that extended across the whole of the dune system were age-old practices, the latter being replaced as the dune backlands were cleared for asparagus cultivation and tree-planting.

These papers reflect only a small amount of what is known of Sefton's coastal history. They are selective and there are many other stories to tell. They are also part of a continuing story that will change and expand as new evidence emerges. Gaps in our knowledge for all periods from earliest times to the present day have recently been highlighted for north west England (Brennand 2006, 2007). Archaeologists, historians and those curious to know more about the human past – they all have a role to play in identifying and researching the missing links, and in promoting the integration of evidence for the human past into initiatives, policies and strategies of those who are responsible for managing Sefton's Coast.

Archaeology and History on a Vulnerable Coast

Jennifer Lewis

Introduction

'...Mr Aldred & I Rode to the Sea & baithed ourselves'; so wrote the diarist Nicholas Blundell of Little Crosby in August 1708 (Tyrer 1968, 181). Four years later he noted '...John Banister & I baithed in the Sea, we came home by my Snigary' (Tyrer 1970, 22). We cannot be certain that sea bathing was a regular activity but Nicholas's diaries hint at some sort of formal arrangements on the shore for, in August 1721, he went with the priest and showed him '...what Conveniency there was for him' (Tyrer 1972, 52). Can we assume that the pleasures of sea-bathing were associated with some sort of accommodation in which to change?

These details tell us that, long before the first tourists came to enjoy Sefton's seaside in the final decades of the 18th century, local people enjoyed sea-bathing. But what do we really know about life and work on the coast over the last six thousand years?

The Landscape

Sefton's coast with its wide sandy beaches backed by 'soft' mobile dunes extends for 32km between Bootle and North Meols. Towards the Ribble estuary the dunes give way to an expanse of reclaimed tidal marshes whilst, from Great Crosby southwards to Litherland and Bootle, the seafront is characterised successively by broad promenades, gardens, marinas and, eventually, an extensive complex of docklands. Whilst the frontal dunes occasionally attain a height of about 30m, to the east the landscape is one of flat and featureless peaty mosslands punctuated here and there by low sandy 'islands' and small sandstone outcrops. The mosslands, formerly dotted with meres, are now drained by canalised streams and ditches. The largest area of standing water, Martin Mere, was said in the mid-16th century to be 'the greatest meare in Lancastreshire' (Farrer 1903, 114).

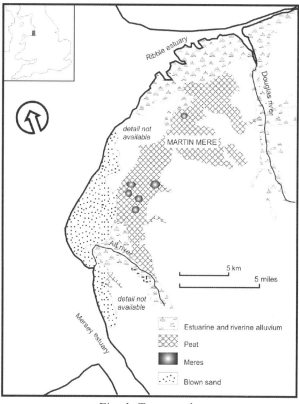

Fig. 1: Topography

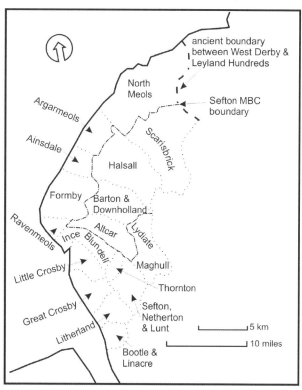

Fig. 2: Townships

To reach the drier lands above the 7.5m contour to the east, those living on the coast faced a difficult journey. Martin Mere was said by Celia Fiennes in 1698 to have '...parted many a man and his mare' and she claimed to be '...a little afraid to go that way it being very hazardous for Strangers to pass by it' (1983 ed, 214). Six years earlier an Act of Parliament had been obtained to drain the mere and work had started in 1693. A channel was cut through the embanked salt marsh and moss into the centre of the mere. However, it was ninety years until the floodgates were successfully in place though an exceptional tide in 1813 led to their replacement. As the mere was drained and land was successfully brought into cultivation, causeways of faggots covered with a thick layer of sand made good roads across the softest parts (Farrer 1903, 119-122).

Occupying the sandy landscape between the shore and the mosslands, the coastal townships were isolated from their neighbours. The mosslands were frequently inundated and extensive systems of drainage ditches were essential both for protection against flooding and to bring new ground into cultivation. In Ince Blundell the river had been 'diked' as early as the 13th century (LRO DDIn 53/2) and in 1441 action was brought for damage to lands in Little Crosby and Ince due to failure to keep the river Alt in good condition (Farrer and Brownbill 3, 1907, 83 n.9). In 1648, the rector of Sefton pleaded that his parishioners were forced to abandon their land 'having neither meadow nor pasture for their cattle' (LRO QSP 3/10). In Altcar, boats were sometimes used to get to church and, in winter, stepping stones were needed to go from one cottage to the next (Farrer and Brownbill 3, 1907, 222 n.2). All the same, deposits of mineral-rich alluvial silts were probably beneficial to the soil. Sefton's hay meadows 'that reach almost to the sea' were noted by Thomas Pennant in 1773 and it has been suggested that they were flooded systematically to encourage the early growth of grass (Maddock 1999, 67; Pennant 1801, 47).

Trackways ran along the coast either through, or just east of, the dunes (Harley 1968; Harrop, fig.6, this volume). These, perhaps, were wide, sandy lanes described as rutted by lines of cartwheels cut deep into the sand making it difficult to move across from one track to another. The mossland roads were similar but cut into peat and, unlike the sandy tracks, were sometimes impassable when wet (Jacson 1897, 150-151). The shore was probably the easiest means of moving along the coast (Harrop, fig.2, this volume). Here, boats were also beached – hazardous for those who had to avoid the mooring ropes (Tyrer 1968, 93). However, with the possible exception of Crossens where there was a boat-building yard in the 16th century (Foster 2002, 8, 76 fig. 62) nowhere are there any remains of formal harbourage; more likely, boats were beached with the tides or held in shallow water for loading. Records from the 18th century show that the shore at Crosby was used as a landing place. In April 1710, the master of the *Betty* landed near the Grange at Altcar, sending his ship forward to Liverpool; 40 years later Reverend Pococke landed at Crosby on his voyage from the Isle of Man (Cartwright 1888, 208; Tyrer 1968, 248-250). In 1787 a dying man of Formby recalled many years earlier jumping from the pierhead on to ships loading in the harbour but there must be some suspicion that this was at the emerging docks in Liverpool rather than at Formby (Hume 1866, 74). All the same, the Alt estuary may have provided some safety and a painting of 1856 shows several small masted boats beached behind a sand dune 'Near Altcar' (Walker Art Gallery, catalogue no. 1721; Bulman 2003, 39). Ballings Wharf, a sandy spit of land on the seaward side of the estuary, may have protected the creek. It was gradually reclaimed following the Alt Drainage Act of 1779 though the southerly trend of the Alt estuary had appeared by 1786 (Harley 1968). Sand was trapped by gorse faggots placed in several rows to create an embankment. Reclamation was extended and rabbit warrens had been established by 1848 (OS Sheet 90); by 1855 some 61 hectares (150 acres) had been stabilised and were available for rough grazing.

Fig. 3: Chronology of the Sefton Coast

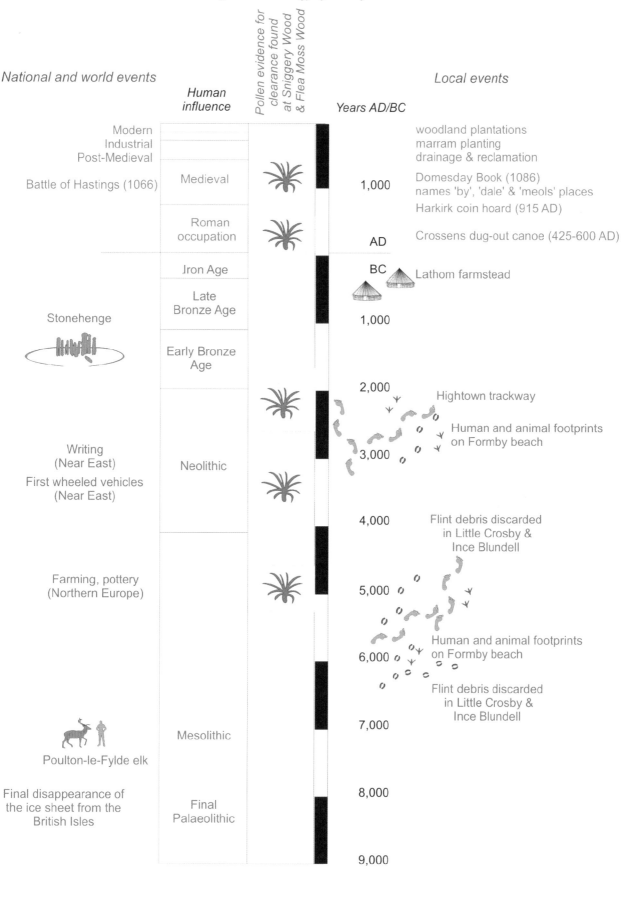

The land, however, was unsuitable for agriculture and in 1860 it passed to the 5th Lancashire Rifle Volunteer Corps as a private shooting range (Cook 1989, 9-11; Smith 1999, 59).

Sources of evidence:
Archaeology and History

Both the archaeologist (the identifier, recorder and interpreter of the physical remains of human activity) and the historian (the analyst and presenter of events, processes, demographic change and daily activities as recorded in documentary sources) are fascinated by and contribute to our understanding of how people lived on the coast over the millennia. Whilst both, however, depend upon the survival and accessibility of the material available to them, it is the archaeologist whose evidence spans many thousands of years whilst the information available to the historian dates from only the first written evidence. Over the last twenty years perception has increased as to how Sefton's landscape has been used from prehistoric times to the present day. But lots of questions remain. Could that slightly raised sandy area in a featureless field have been suitable for occupation? If so, when? By whom? Or – what does that bank and ditch represent? Where does it go? Why does it stop? What was it for? Why did it go out of use? When?

Archaeological evidence

Sefton's archaeological material survives in many guises and covers thousands of years. Human footprints associated with those of animals and birds on the beach at Formby and of stone objects at Little Crosby and Ince Blundell, show that people have been using the coast for some 6,000 years or more (Cowell, this volume; Roberts and Worsley, this volume). More recent sites such as the remains of Formby's lifeboat house, the roofless ruins of wartime buildings or foundations of failed enterprises challenge us to understand their story (Kelly 1973, 72-75; Yorke and Yorke, this volume).

Occasionally, aspects of lost farming regimes are visible in the earthwork ridges of asparagus fields and their enclosing banks and ditches (Yorke and Yorke, this volume).

Fig. 4: Ruined military building

Fig. 5: Foundations of a failed enterprise?

Subtle changes in the topography and differences in the composition, texture and colour of soils are important indicators of archaeological sites. A slightly raised sandy area surrounded by darker peaty soils may suggest the location of a long-lost archaeological site. On the shore, horizontal bands of dark organic soil exposed in the eroding face of a sand dune could represent a cultivated land surface, abandoned when it was covered by blown sand.

Objects – lost, damaged or discarded – tell of personal belongings, domestic life, trade or religious belief and, in many instances, come to notice as 'chance finds' discovered during ploughing, gardening or building works. The discovery of an artefact can hint at a place no longer visible but where people once lived, worked or worshipped. According to the material of which they are made, artefacts survive in different conditions. Stone, such as flint used in prehistory for hunting, skinning and scraping or that used for building, is not affected by the soil in which it is deposited (though plough damage is not uncommon). On the other hand, man-made objects of metal, glass or pottery survive less well; often they were broken when discarded and may be further damaged by acidity or alkalinity of the soil. Damp, peaty environments favour the preservation of organic materials, such as leather and textiles, wood, pollen and plant remains (Renfrew and Bahn 2000, 68). These can be scientifically examined for radiocarbon dating, dendrochronology (tree ring dating) and pollen analysis. The growth rings on timber can indicate a date at which the tree was felled; the rings can also tell us something of the environmental conditions under which that tree was growing. Pollen analysis may also tell of environmental change as woodland was cleared and arable or pastoral farming practices were introduced; it may also provide information about climate as species responded to colder, warmer or drier conditions (Roberts and Worsley, this volume). But to understand why an object was lost or discarded, we need to know something about the context of its discovery. A hoard of coins will elicit excitement, but the soils in which it is discovered and its association with other objects – a leather pouch, wooden container, pottery, bone – will tell us so much more.

Historical sources

Whilst archaeologists rely on the material evidence for human activity over the last 6,000 years, the historian depends on documentary records which, for the Sefton coast appear only with the Domesday Survey of 1086. Documents, historic maps and plans, drawings and paintings, together with photographs and folk memory are all helpful in considering evidence for settlement, economy, land use, communications and transport and the details of everyday life. Drawing on original documents dating from the 12th century until the early 1900s, the Victoria County History (Farrer and Brownbill **3**, 1907 *passim*) is a goldmine; its detailed footnotes particularly cast light on aspects of land use and reclamation, rights of way, field systems, fishing rights and buildings. The writings of antiquarians such as Charles Leigh (1700), Reverend Hume (1866) and Reverend Bulpit of Crossens (1908), diarists and recorders of daily life such as Nicholas Blundell of Little Crosby, travellers like Celia Fiennes (1983 ed, 114) and Dr Pococke (Cartwright 1888, 4-5, 208) and observers such as Catherine Jacson (1897) have left a legacy of detail for understanding contemporary life on the coast.

Aerial photographs show changes to the coastline and settlement pattern over the last sixty years or so and are an important source of evidence for both historians and archaeologists. At appropriate times of crop growth or soil condition they can indicate the location and form of landscape features no longer visible at ground level. For example, at Ince Blundell the pattern of medieval cultivated fields appears beneath the pastoral landscape of the 18th-century park and traces of ditches and banks suggestive of early land reclamation can be seen nearer the outfall of the river Alt (Sheppard 1978, 86-87, figs. 2, 3).

Though archaeologists and historians approach the past from different perspectives the disciplines are complementary. Each can inform the other to arrive at an understanding of how people have lived, worked and influenced the local environment on the coast over the millennia.

Settlement

The first record of settlement comes from the Domesday Survey of 1086 though Old English and Irish-Norwegian place-names cited therein hint tantalisingly of settlement and landscape in the centuries before the Norman Conquest (Ekwall 1922; Finberg 1975b). The earliest, Bootle (OE *botl* =

dwelling house), is considered to represent Anglian settlement before the 10th century. Otherwise, names of Scandinavian origin dominate. Linguistic elements such as ON *býr* tell of settlement at Formby and Crosby. The landscape is described in the sandhills of North Meols, Argarmeols and Ravenmeols (ON *melr*), the hilly topography at Ainsdale (OE *dæl* = Ægunwulf's valley) and sloping land at Litherland (ON *hlið*) (Finberg 1975b *passim*). We do not know, however, whether these places were renamed by Scandinavian immigrants in the early 10th century, or whether these people came to a sparsely occupied landscape too unattractive for permanent settlement or abandoned due to locally adverse conditions (Lewis 2002, 19). The only archaeological evidence comes from the discovery in 1611 at Little Crosby's Harkirk of a hoard of early 10th-century silver coins and ingots. Though the coins and ingots were subsequently lost, William Blundell, lord of Little Crosby at the time, made engravings of some of the coins on a copper plate (Tyrer 1953, 153-158). Analysis shows not only that the hoard was deliberately buried in *c*. 915AD but also that its coins represented Norse Viking rather than Anglo-Saxon influence (Dolley 1966, 50). The circumstances of their concealment are unknown but the early 10th century was a time of stress as Scandinavian colonists from Ireland arrived in north west England and we can only speculate that the coins were hidden for recovery in less turbulent times (Finberg 1975b, 182-183, 193; Lewis 2002, 20; *see* Philpott this volume).

The nature, form and precise location of Sefton's first settlements is not clearly understood. A complexity of ownership and control may have influenced how communities were both organised and managed. But in a landscape subject to flooding, coastal erosion and accretion people may have been forced to adapt to changing circumstances. Medieval parishes were extensive and the only parish church on the coast, at North Meols, served both that place and Argarmeols (Birkdale). The church is at the heart of Churchtown village and the arrangement of streets and buildings round the small green probably reflects the footprint of the medieval settlement. Great Crosby, an outlier of the royal manor of West Derby but attached to Sefton parish, lacked a medieval church and its 'ancient' chapel is first noted only in 1532 (Farrer and Brownbill **3**, 1907, 62, 94). However, there seems to have been a close-knit, nucleated settlement. At Litherland there was also a small consolidated settlement though again there was no parish church (LRO DDM 14/43). Before the creation of Sefton parish (in the late 12th or early 13th century) the long-lost – and possibly pre-Conquest – Harkirk at Little Crosby, first noted in *c*.1275, may have served these communities south of the Alt (LRO DDBl 50/16). These nucleated communities contrast with those such as Ainsdale, Ravenmeols and, perhaps, Formby, where loose-knit settlements and isolated farmsteads may have been more common.

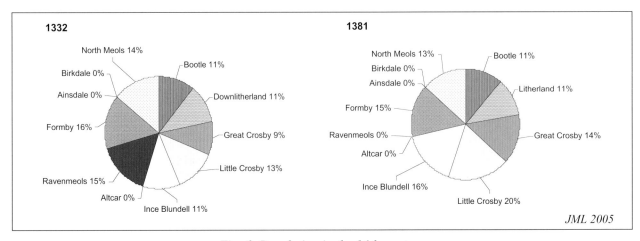

Fig. 6: Population in the 14th century

Taxation records for the 14th century, though not an accurate reflection of the actual population – and care must be taken in their interpretation – hint at a thinly populated landscape evenly distributed along the coast (Fenwick 1998, 456-478; Glasscock 1975, 149-151; Rylands 1896). There are, however, no records for Altcar and Ainsdale, probably because both places were exempt due to ownership respectively by Merevale Abbey and Cockersand Abbey. Though the people of Ravenmeols were taxed in 1332, the place escaped notice in 1381. Was this due to loss of settlement? And is the record for Argarmeols missing for the same reason?

It is generally accepted that the medieval communities of Ainsdale, Formby and Ravenmeols worshipped at a chapel at Ravenmeols, belonging to the mother church at Walton-on-the-Hill, but its existence is known only by inference to priests who held land in Formby and Ravenmeols and by a burial ground overwhelmed by sand in the early 18th century (Lumby 1939, 183-4; LRO DDFo/13/5; Lewis 1978). The Kirklake apparently was on the boundary of Formby and Ravenmeols though here there is no evidence for nucleated medieval settlement associated with a chapel. It is a mile or so from the 19th-century village of Formby and the post-medieval landscape of Ravenmeols is one of isolated farmsteads and enclosed fields.

Part, if not all, of Ainsdale was given to Cockersand Abbey and monastic records tell of a settlement associated with a formal system of named cultivated open fields together with meadow and pasture (Shaw 1956, 341-343). A well-organised farming community is indicated though not a trace has survived. However, Formby's highly organised cultivated open fields next to Downholland Brook were still farmed in the middle of the 19th century and said to be more fertile than elsewhere (Jacson 1897, 150; LRO DRL 1/40, 1845). But the location and arrangement of Formby's medieval village is

unclear and it seems to have been under stress. Migration in the 15th century is suggested by reference to 'Oldforneby' and 'Holde Forneby' and in 1532 the 'old town of Formbie' was cited (LRO DDFo 13/5; DDFo 14/2; DDIn 49/4). By 1556 fishing stalls and land for grazing at Formby and Ravenmeols had been 'ruined by sand and sea' and further evidence for loss is suggested in the legend 'heare thold town did stand' on a contemporary plan (TNA, DL 3, 73, 162 no. 12; TNA, MR2; Turner 1992).

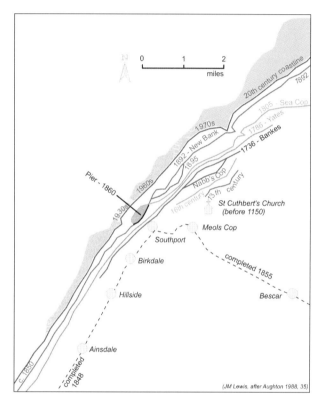

Fig. 7: Embankments at North Meols

Careful management has been needed to protect settlements and the agricultural landscape from damage. Embankments for flood prevention and land catchment survive in the vicinity of Churchtown. Land north and west of the church seems to have been particularly vulnerable and, from at least the 13th century, local people took steps to protect their landscape. The process of enclosing the marshes at Crossens has been described (Foster 2002, 25-26) and a series of embankments that run off from either side of Marshside Road mark the progression seawards as the marshes were enclosed. The oldest embankment may survive on Bankfield Lane just inside the wall of the Botanic Gardens. Though it may have been increased in size when the Botanic Gardens lake was enlarged in the late 19th century, archaeological excavation could show whether the bank was raised in the medieval period and, if so, environmental evidence from the old ground surface beneath it could provide information for the local environment 800 years or so ago.

Buildings

Churches and chapels, houses and cottages, shops and farm buildings are as much a part of the historical and archaeological record as are buried sites and artefacts. Their relationship to the street pattern and boundaries may tell us how communities have been organised over time; their form and plan may allow interpretation of their original function and status – as places of religious, domestic, agricultural, industrial or commercial use. And building materials also inform on the availability and suitability of local resources.

Until the early 17th century brick was not generally used as a building material on the coast though there are possible exceptions at Meols Hall, the so-called Old Hall at Ince Blundell and the Grange at Altcar. Stone was used where it was available in places such as Little Crosby. For the most part, until the expansion of the new seaside resorts in the 19th century, the cottages occupied by local people were thatched timber-framed, single storey structures. The roof would be supported on a series of cruck-frames, giving the appearance of an upturned boat, and the walls were made of planks or staves covered with clay daub. Nicholas Blundell notes the 'raising' of cottages in Little Crosby in 1719 and again in 1727 (Tyrer 1970, 255; 1972, 214) but suitable building timber may not have been easily available on the coast. Traditionally it is believed that many cruck-framed cottages along the coast were built of ships' timbers and undoubtedly local people would have salvaged suitable wreckage to repair or replace damaged structures (*see* Harrop, this volume).

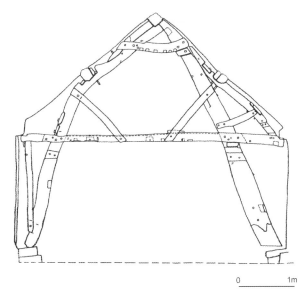

0   1m

Fig. 8: Cruck frame at 62 Gores Lane, Formby

Scattered examples of cruck-framed buildings survive all along the coast from Churchtown to Ince Blundell (Harrop 1992). The Cottage at 74 Liverpool Road, Birkdale, is a good example of a small cruck-framed house with a later box-framed extension. Tree-ring dating has shown that the timbers were felled in the period 1628-1656 suggesting that the cruck-framed element of the cottage was raised in the mid-17th century (Tyers and Groves 2000, 125). However, only a small handful of timber buildings have been surveyed archaeologically and, apart from the Birkdale cottage, none has been accurately dated.

Fig. 9: The Cottage, Birkdale

The relationship of buildings to the road pattern sometimes hints at settlement growth. On Marshside Road, Churchtown, houses set at right angles to the road – but parallel to the coast – correspond with the alignment of embanked enclosures and suggest how the village expanded westwards.

Coastal resources

Those living on the coast had access to a variety of maritime and land-based resources giving rise to a mixed economy. Hundreds of human and animal footprints preserved in muddy silts of Formby's intertidal zone have led to the suggestion that, in what was otherwise a densely wooded or waterlogged landscape, the coast was used successively from the Late Mesolithic through to the Bronze Age for hunting and gathering and cattle. Furthermore, analysis of pollen from peat deposits in Little Crosby has shown that these prehistoric people were starting to bring land into cultivation (Roberts and Worsley, this volume; Cowell, this volume; Gonzalez and Huddart 2002, 569-588).

Though the medieval landscape has long since been lost to sand and sea, the evidence from Ainsdale and Ravenmeols perhaps typifies the agricultural scene in the 13th century (Shaw 1956, 341-343). In both places land was granted in alms by members of the family of the king's chief falconer to Cockersand Abbey; but local people probably continued to farm the land from which the Abbey took an annual payment. Particularly at Ainsdale, the evidence shows a balance between cultivated fields arranged in strips and furlongs, meadows and pasture for grazing. Reference to sheep, oxen and cows, mares and sows with offspring suggests that animal breeding was a significant aspect of the local economy. Perhaps these places were part of a supply network to the royal castle at West Derby and subsequently to Liverpool itself when the place received its royal charter and the castle there was built in the early 13th century. Hides may have been processed in Litherland where the coast's only shoemaker, Adam Cordewayn, was recorded in 1381 (Fenwick 1998, 478). Personal names 'le Corket', 'le Corker' and 'Qwytlath' at the same date may hint at the jobs of people involved in tanning. By the mid-19th century Litherland had twelve boot and shoemakers and, in the 1930s, there were six tanneries here when Merseyside was the country's centre for tanning.

Fields were bounded by high banks, locally called 'cops' made from a portion of the sand, removed and carefully covered with green grazing turf (de Rance 1877, 113). Tenants were required to keep their fences in good order; in Ainsdale they had to make and keep fences between the 'inland' and sandhills and these were to be fully maintained before 1 March each year (LRO DDIn 45/4). Such fences may have separated the warrens from pastures and cultivated land, but few such cops are now recognisable though the memory is preserved in places such as Meols Cop in Southport.

The land was not easily managed and local people battled constantly against the effects of dune erosion, blowing sand and flooding. Charles Leigh commented that '...the Meales are little more cultivated than the deserts of Arabia' (1700, 63). Despite efforts to control the Alt, families in Altcar '...were frequently in such distress as to flee from home and seek refuge, and yet in summer seasons, this country is distressed for want of water, and that to a degree, as to require driving the cattle the space of a mile to drink, the springs being exhausted' (Holt 1795, 141). But this was probably an age-old problem reflected in permission given to those living in Altcar to drive their cattle from '...the King's highway between Raven Meols and Alt Bridge as far as the pasture on Alt Marsh' in 1238 (Farrer and Brownbill 3, 1907, 223). Until the 16th or 17th centuries animals were grazed in common on the dunes and, in dry periods, on the mosslands, a practice that often led to disputes between landowners and eventually resulted in agreements to enclose the lands. Grazing was strictly controlled, however, and the Court Books for Formby and Ainsdale set out the regulations for grazing sheep on the commons (LRO DDFo 15/1-9; DDIn 45/1-4, 66/17).

Perhaps a typical arrangement of land use on the coast is shown on pottery plaque of Great Crosby in 1716 (Harrop, fig.2, this volume). A zone representing the sand dunes depicts vegetation occupied by an occasional rabbit together with Great Crosby's Warren House; this is also shown on later 18th and

19th century maps (Harley 1968; OS Sheet 98). East of the dunes the land is busy with people, dogs, grazing cattle and a couple of people on galloping horses. Next come a series of enclosures with grazing animals and in the rear ground are the houses of Great Crosby with, to the left, Nicholas Blundell's six-sailed windmill built in 1709 (Tyrer 1968, 237).

Salt

A maritime environment might be expected to produce evidence for salt production; Salthouse Fields and Salthouse Moss, separated by Three Pools Waterway in North Meols, perhaps show that salt workings were in the vicinity of Bankfield Lane and Rufford Road (Coney 1992, fig. 2; Foster 2002, 5). Salt-Coal Hey, a small field on the coast a little north of Crossens, may also represent a place of salt production (LRO DDSc 151/24). The monks of Sawley Abbey, who in the opening decade of the 13th century were permitted to make a salt pit on an acre in *Ratho* (in North Meols) together with an adjacent piece of land and '…sufficient sand and turbary for all their needs there' may have been responsible for salt production and its use at the Abbey in the Ribble Valley (Farrer 1903, 8, 11; McNulty 1933, 157).

The processes of coastal salt production elsewhere in Britain have been described (Brownrigg 1748; Duncan 1812). Sand was collected on flat, sandy shores only partly covered at high tide and when the sea water had evaporated, the sand was raked up into low heaps, two or three inches high, and taken off in carts to salterns where it was laid up in large heaps. Here there were large clay-lined pits '…about 18 feet long, 4 feet broad and 2 feet deep' (c. 5.5m x 1.2m x 0.6m). Sea water was collected in little ponds (sumps) on the shore between the high and low water marks and run off through pipes to a well adjacent to the saltern. A layer of peat turfs was placed in the bottom of the saltern and the pit was filled with '…sleech to form a kind of basin'. This was filled with water that filtered through the 'mass' and turf and ran off down

a spout into a reservoir. Once the brine had been prepared it was boiled in leaden pans set on bricks over a peat fire.The tidal marshes at North Meols, and perhaps those at Altcar where also there were some 'Salt Fields' (LRO DDM 14/21) may, perhaps, be compared with those on the Wash where recent archaeological investigations have shown that evidence for salt working in the 15th and 16th centuries survived on the landward side of a series of artificial banks created from the mid-17th century onwards (McAvoy 1994, 134-148).

The use of salt as a meat preservative appears in the accounts for Bleasdale Forest in 1313-1314 (Shaw 1956, 182) though whether salt from North Meols found its way to Lancashire's royal farms is not known. But local salt was probably used to preserve fish in the early 16th century when it was noted that Martin Mere's fish house contained '52 coupel salt fishes' (TNA, DL 41/11/36).

Flax and hemp

John Holt noted that the '…culture, neither of hemp or flax, was ever carried to any great extent in this county' (1795, 70), but from Bootle to North Meols local people were involved in various aspects of textile production. With standing water on the mosslands and in worked-out marl pits, there was little need for the formal mechanics of retting pools as used elsewhere. Hemp was also grown in Formby and Litherland in the 17th century (LRO DDFo/14/7; Farrer and Brownbill 3, 1907, 97 n.8). Whether it was used locally to control the growth of couch is not known, but Holt observed that '…a crop of hemp is supposed to be an excellent means of destroying couch' which should '…never be taken from the lands whence produced, but the roots by some means there destroyed by putrefaction' (1795, 70).

Bootle's Linacre (OE *lïn,* flax) probably takes its name from a place where flax was grown (Ekwall 1922). Formby's Flaxfield was noted in 1514-1515 (LRO DDIn 51/1) and is preserved in the name Flaxfield Road; possibly, the flax was retted at a place called Scotch Lake (LRO DDFo 34/6; *scutch* – to dress fibrous material by beating, *Shorter O.E.D.* 1973). As Martin Mere was drained, flax could be grown successfully and harvested before the autumnal floods; flax retting pits have been identified on the shore of North Meols bay at Crossens (Farrer 1903, 121; Foster 2002, 32).

The process of cultivation and production in Little Crosby in the early 18th century has been described (Tyrer 1968, 1970 and 1972 *passim*). Flax grown on mossland close to the boundary with Ince Blundell, was retted in old marl pits then dried at the Oat 'kill', spun and woven. However, a distinction was made between flax used for sheets and hemp yarn used for servants' sheets and eel nets. Nicholas Blundell also bought fabric for the sails of his six-sailed windmill from North Meols and Liverpool and, possibly, Ormskirk (Tyrer 1970, 39 n.88; 1972, 47).

Evidence for flax and hemp growing has also been found at Birkdale and Ainsdale, and weavers were noted in the 18th century; but though the industrial process of producing and bleaching yarn has not been found here could Birkdale's 17th-century walkmill have been used for textile manufacture? (Harrop 1985, 88; Farrer and Brownbill **3**, 1907, 238, n.1).

Probate inventories show that many families had a spinning wheel or 'sitting-wheel' together with quantities of wool and linen yarn. However, though yarn was spun in many households it was sent to Liverpool and North Meols (if not elsewhere) for dying and weaving into cloth, and was then returned to be made up (Foster 2002, 32-33; Tyrer 1968, 171-192 *passim,* 213, 305; 1970, 7, 38-39). That this was so may be seen in 1633 when yarn, hemp and skins were carried on the *Paterick* and *Henrie* of Formbie and accounted as 'ingatt' dues to the Port of Liverpool (Moore Papers 1889, 173). No doubt the masters of these ships were Formby men but whether they traded locally along the coast or brought their cargoes from

further afield is unknown. But mechanisation of the weaving industry led to extreme poverty, particularly in North Meols where many hand-loom weavers transferred their skills to weaving silks and light cottons in the early 19th century (Foster 2002, 32).

Fish and fishing

With a lengthy shoreline and numerous mossland pools, fishing was a significant aspect of the local economy (*see* Harrop, this volume). Written records of fishing appear in the 13th century when an eel fishery on the Alt at Ravenmeols and another at Otterpool in North Meols were recorded (Farrer 1903, 12; Farrer and Brownbill **3**, 1907, 49). At both places the fisheries were associated with watermills, the former controlled by the monks of Stanlow Abbey (subsequently Whalley Abbey) and the latter by the lord of North Meols. A *piscarium* at Ainsdale and Formby was owned by Cockersand Abbey and recorded on four occasions between 1451-1537 (Farrer 1909, 1240, 1245, 1249). However, no structural remains survive to show how the fishing was organised though most likely it resembled the arrangement of stallage at Ainsdale and Birkdale, which survived well into the 19th century (Harrop, this volume).

Poll tax records for Formby in 1379 cite 26 fishermen – all apparently bachelors – of a total of 33 adults (Fenwick 1998, 461) suggesting, perhaps, that the emphasis at this time was on fishing rather than farming. However, by the mid-16th century rent could no longer be paid for stallage and grazing 'ruined by sea and sand' at Ravenmeols and Formby (TNA, DL3, 73, 162, no. 12) though the fish market at Formby seems to have recovered by 1595-6 when two barrels of herrings were bought in February on behalf of the Shuttleworth family of Smithills (Bolton) and Gawthorpe, east of Burnley (Harland 1856, 105).

Undoubtedly, the mossland meres were also an important fishing resource and from Martin Mere came eels, pike, roach, bream and perch (Coney 1992). At least 15 log boats or canoes have been recovered of which five can almost certainly be located to North Meols and the remainder were recovered from Martin Mere and its perimeter. Writing in 1700, Dr Leigh reported on the discovery of 'no less than eight canoes' whilst the mere was being drained (1700, 18, 65). Three more canoes, one set on an incline as if deliberately beached, were found between 1869-1899 (Farrer 1903, 113-114; Foster 2002, 15). The only surviving canoe, found in 1899, is now on display in the Botanic Gardens Museum in Southport (Foster 2002, 15, figs. 12-13). Radiocarbon dating has shown that the tree from which it was fashioned was felled in 1560 ±70 BP giving a felling date in the middle of the 6th century AD (about 535 AD; Beta-94788) at a time when the archaeological and historical record is otherwise silent. There is, otherwise, no evidence for settlement in the area at this time and we can only speculate that those using the mere some 1,500 years ago lived on the better drained lands on its perimeter.

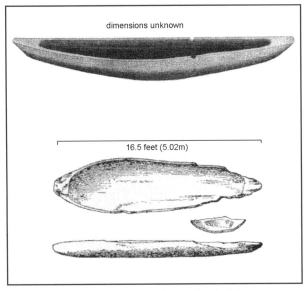

Fig. 10: Log boats from Martin Mere
(Leigh 1700, 18, 65; Farrer and Brownbill 1, 1906, 249)

Eels were speared or trapped in wicker baskets (Foster 2002, 14, fig. 11). In 1712-1713, Nicholas Blundell constructed a new Sniggery (*snig* = eel) on the western edge of his farmed land perhaps to replace an 'Old Sniggery' now within the bounds of West Lancashire Golf Club. The flow of water was controlled by 'clows', probably an arrangement of sluices, and he also raised a building of clay daub with a thatched roof, perhaps as a small fishing lodge

(Tyrer 1970, 8-80 *passim*). Here he used nets to catch eels and 'pickerells', perhaps young pike. Of these structures no trace is now visible though in Sniggery Wood a linear depression filled with dark organic soil probably defines the ditch and associated features. Here there is potential for the survival of both archaeological and environmental material. From Blundell's 'Carthous-pit' came bream, eels, carp and tench; and bream were stored in the 'Horspoole' and Blundell's duck decoy excavated in 1711 (Tyrer 1968 *passim;* 1970, 128).

Fig. 11: Nicholas Blundell's Sniggery

Warrens - Rabbits

Rabbits (coneys) were an important aspect of the local economy providing both skins and meat (Harrop, 1985, 31-37; Smith 1999, 54-55). John Holt commented briefly on the value of rabbits in the local economy claiming that greater profit could be made from them in localities less suitable for cattle and sheep (1795, 176). Not only did they breed prolifically but rabbit fur was almost as valuable as the meat. Their remains were also used to improve the sandy soils (*see* below).

The warrens were on the dunes and their considerable extent is shown on mid-19th century maps (OS Sheets 82, 90, 98). In 1666-67 Henry Blundell and Richard Formby agreed to divide Formby's warrens and created a long straight boundary from the '…Whickes and leading west through the Greenloones between GreenloonsHill and the WhyteHill to the shore' (LRO DDFo 34/1). After this '…neither could kill or capture conies with nets, dogs or ferrets within the others share' (LRO DDIn 65/42; Kelly 1973, 24-25). The boundary is still defined by a low bank and shallow ditch running seawards from Wicks Lane and set with an occasional post marked with the initials 'B' and 'F'; a post far out on the shore perhaps marks the original extent of the division.

Fig. 12: Division ditch across the warren

Fig. 13: Warren division marker posts

In 1702 Richard Molyneux of the Grange at Altcar and Nicholas Blundell of Little Crosby agreed the bounds of a warren (Tyrer, 1968, 23; LRO DDM 9/11). A 'meer' stone was set up in alignment with two others and, four years later, further measures were taken to define the bounds with stakes (Tyrer, 1968, 106). However, there is now little recognisable

evidence for formal structures relating to the warrens though a low, wide embankment on Sandy Lane in Hightown and another near the boundary between Ainsdale and Formby may represent the remains of warren walls. Warren houses survived in both Great and Little Crosby at least until the mid-19th century. That at Great Crosby is shown on the Crosby plaque and the Warren House on Crosby Marsh was used as a place for meeting and drinking (*see* Harrop, fig.2, this volume; Tyrer 1972, 18).

Wildfowling

The shore, mosslands and meres were rich with wildfowl – an important food source (Coney 1992, 59). Prehistoric footprints of humans associated with those of birds in the intertidal zone at Formby are seen as evidence for trapping wildfowl (*see* Roberts and Worsley, this volume). The method of netting birds that fed on the marshes at Crossens in more recent times has been described and, in 1803, 32 Birkdale farmers had fowling-pieces (Foster 2002, 36; Harrop, 1985, 20). In the mid-19th century shooting, of both game and wildfowl, proved an attraction to Southport's gentlemen visitors (Robinson 1848, 43).

Damage and destruction

Life on the coast was not without its hazards and the written record indicates damage by sea and sand with a consequent loss of land and livelihood particularly between Ravenmeols and Birkdale from the 13th century onwards. Half of Ravenmeols had been lost by 1289 (Farrer and Brownbill **3**, 1907, 49), probably to the sea and, in 1346, it was declared that Argarmeols (Birkdale) had disappeared into the sea and nobody now lived there (*Feudal Aids* 1904, 86). Over 150 years later, an 80-year old man said he had never known a place called *Argarmelys* but had heard that such lands had been drowned in the sea (Fishwick 1896, 24). Further south, 'Oldforneby' may have been damaged before 1442 though the circumstances are not known (see above). In 1556-57 it was claimed that revenue from lands at Ainsdale had been lost; '…there was a certain town in times past called Aynesdale …[and that] … the town time out of mind had been and still was "overflowen" with the sea "…so that there now remains no remembrance thereof'" (Fishwick 1897, 96). However, though there can be no doubt that the livelihood of local people was badly affected it is also possible that claims of loss and damage could be a useful tool in evading tax!

A period of particularly stormy weather in December 1720 caused damage and loss of livelihood along much of Lancashire's coast. Some 6,600 customary acres of land were flooded, 157 houses lost and a further 200 were badly damaged (Beck 1953; Tyrer 1972, 31-32, 79). In Sefton the worst affected places were near the Alt and Ribble estuaries. The chapel at Ravenmeols disappeared leaving only its burial ground as witness to its existence (Lewis 1978). The volatile action of wind and tides around Formby Point in 1828 ruined the landmark '…near the edge of the shore' and perhaps some 400 yards of the coastline were lost since the lifeboat house had been built 35 years earlier, though by 1839 the coastline may have recovered (Boult 1870, 246).

Stabilising the dunes

Dunes are particularly vulnerable to damage when dry weather is with high winds (Smith 1999, 26-27). The qualities of marram (*Arundo arenaria*) as a means of holding '…fast, loose and blowing sands by entangling it amongst its tough, creeping roots; and thus forming by degrees, solid banks over which no sea can break' were cited at Formby in 1725-1734 (LRO DDIn 66/17). Other plants used historically to consolidate the sand were the sand sedge (*Carex arenaria*) and lyme grass (*Psamma aminainacea*), the former being said to be one of the most powerful agents in consolidating blown sea sand (LRO DDIn 66/17).

The importance of preserving the 'star grass' or marram at Ravenmeols had been recognized as early as 1560-61 when covenants were cited in a deed of exchange (LRO DDIn 49/11). Its plantation and management were as much a part of daily life as

fishing, agriculture or rural industry. In the early 18th century, if not before, tenants in Formby and Ainsdale were required to plant 'starr', and 'lookers' were appointed to oversee the work. After the Alt Drainage Act was passed in 1779 (LRO DDBl 24/26), planting became compulsory to preserve a free flow of water draining from the Alt. Leases also forbade tenants to cut the starr (LRO DDFo 14/73). Miscreants were fined, the penalty in 1857 being 20 shillings. Furthermore, fines could be imposed on anyone found in possession of starr within five miles of the sandhills (LRO DDIn 66/39).

All along the coast, blowing sand was a constant threat; tenants had to keep their ditches scoured regularly and fines were imposed on those who failed to do so. There were disputes and disagreements over responsibility for watercourses between adjoining townships and when Nicholas Blundell excavated a new 'Grand Watercourse' it was the focus of much discussion as to whether it would help or hinder the situation (see Tyrer 1968, 1970, 1972 *passim*). Planting was used to trap the sand and prevent drainage ditches from clogging up. In Little Crosby, Nicholas Blundell used '…Cuttings of Withens in the Copp to prevent the Sand from Recking up my Grand Water-cours' together with starr, gorse, poplars, broom, 'hep-bryers', 'several sorts of young trees' and 'cooch-Grass or Quicks' (Tyrer 1970, 7-8, 11-12; 1972, 66, 91).

Soil improvement

Improvement and consolidation of the sandy soils was probably effected by a variety of practices. Efforts to improve the land in Ainsdale were made in the late 12th and early 13th centuries when permission was given to acquire the moss '…by carrying away the sand' (Farrer 1900, 588, 590). Writing more generally, and 500 years later, Dr Leigh suggested that marl, dung, lime, shell-fishes, shells, rags, the skins of hares or rabbits, 'sope-makers' ashes, sea mud, common dirt or 'putrefy'd ferns' could be used to improve the soil (1700, 55).

Marling of fine-textured soils, sandy soils and peat has been widespread in the region since the medieval period. Marl was extracted from deposits of boulder clay and provided lime and nutrients. On sandy soil it helped to reduce the effects of wind erosion. Depressions or ponds around the mossland fringes may represent former marl pits and marl was usually spread on fields adjacent to where it was dug (Hall and Folland 1967, 98-100). Records of marling next to Little Crosby's Harkirk appeared in c.1275 (LRO DDBl 50/16). In 1712 the process of extraction was described and, either to stabilise the dunes or in attempt to improve their agricultural potential, slutch was also taken from the 'side' of the Alt to be spread on the sandhills (Tyrer 1968, 303; 1970, 282-283). John Holt also described the method and expense of improving Bootle Marsh in the late 18th century (1795, 111-126).

Modern times

Though not finally completed along its full length until 1816, by 1774 the Leeds and Liverpool canal ran between Liverpool and Gathurst, then via the Douglas Navigation to Wigan (Clarke 1994, 254-5). People from Lancashire's expanding industrial and commercial centres came to the seaside via a landing place at Scarisbrick and thence by carriage to Southport. There had been a bathing house in Liverpool in 1708 and Nicholas Blundell's pleasure in sea-bathing has already been mentioned (*see* above; Bailey 1953, 235). In 1792 the first lodging house, built of timber, opened for the summer season at South Hawes (Southport) and a hotel appeared six years later (Robinson 1848, 13, 16-17). Small seaside communities at Brighton le Sands and Crosby Sea Bank were also expanding and Bootle was a '…pleasant marine village … much resorted to in the summer season as a sea bathing place' (Farrer and Brownbill **3**, 1907, 32). Crosby Seabank Company's Hotel in Waterloo appeared in 1815 and by 1825 there were seven lodging houses. On 14 August 1827 the pleasures of the seaside were described. '…Tides are now very high, quite up to the beach. … At first I tried the shower bath … I thought I should have drowned for seven or eight gallons came tumbling on my head and it was some time before I could recover my breath'. But, seemingly taking refuge in the dunes,

the writer said '…My book I can take to the sandhills' (Baines 1825, vol II, 710; Crosby Lib. C942.72P CRO.TAG).

But these new developments were not necessarily received favourably and other communities remained isolated. Farmers 'high up in the sand district' would travel three or four miles to the 'paved road' and a further twelve miles to the market in Liverpool. Formby, moreover, valued its isolation from Southport and favoured the 'extra difficulties' of the sand-hill track that were a barrier to 'ordinary communication' (Jacson 1897, 88, 151).

In 1801 there were just over 6,000 people on the coast and the largest community was at North Meols with over 2,000 people (35%) (Farrer and Brownbill **2**, 1908, 345-347). The combined settlements of Formby, Ravenmeols and Ainsdale (17%) and those of Bootle and Litherland (18%) together accounted for a further third whilst the population in each of the remaining settlements averaged out at about 360 people. In the next 40 years North Meols – or rather the emerging town of Southport – expanded more rapidly than anywhere else on the coast and by 1841 there were over 7,700 people in the town – 46% of those living on the coast.

The Liverpool to Southport railway completed in 1848 and Cheshire Lines extension to Southport in 1884 encouraged tourism and new residential development (Farrer and Brownbill **3**, 1907, 98, 234-5; Foster 1995; 2000). The railway also brought 'night soil' to feed the sandy fields encouraging asparagus cultivation (*see* Yorke and Yorke, this volume). Bootle's new docks appeared in the 1880s and, by the end of the century there was '…not a square yard of ground left that is not covered with crowded streets, railways, timber-yards, canal wharfs and … extensive docks and quays' (Farrer and Brownbill 3, 1907, 31-32). By 1901 the communities at North Meols and Birkdale (37%) and Bootle (35%) together accounted for nearly three-quarters of the population on the coast. Litherland, Great Crosby, Formby and Ainsdale (28%) were also starting to expand but over 100 years the population elsewhere had increased only slightly.

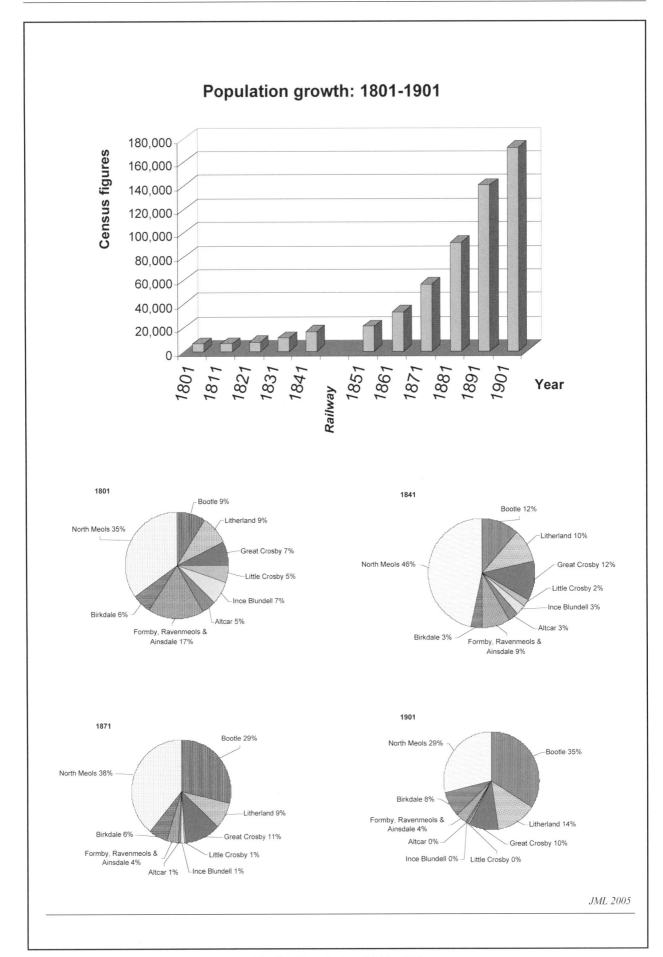

Fig. 14: Population, 1801-1901

Sport and leisure

Life on the coast had its amusements. An annual horse race on the shore between Crosby and Kirkdale was noted in 1577 when the winner received a silver bell (Barraclough 1953, 235). A longer race was run in 1714, when the course extended from Formby on a road across 'Ince Mosses' to Liverpool (Tyrer 1970, 89). Though horse racing at North Meols did not, perhaps, appear until Southport developed, an annual two-mile race was held on the shore at Marshside where the starting post was still visible in 1848 (Robinson 1848, 45-46).

The expanses of flat ground behind the dunes were used for the age-old sport of hare coursing, a favourite pastime of Nicholas Blundell and his cronies, and a century later the neighbourhood of Southport was considered to be '...the best coursing ground in the kingdom' (Robinson 1848, 47; Tyrer 1968, 1970, 1972 *passim*). Six-day meetings were held in the early 19th century at Birkdale, Churchtown and Crossens (Foster 2002, 37). The first meeting at Altcar took place in 1825 and the Waterloo Cup, on Altcar fields from 1836 until the last meeting in February 2005, attracted visitors from all parts of England.

Conclusions

Separated from its hinterland by a wide belt of mossland the region's isolation until the 19th century was not a disadvantage. Local people may not have generated great wealth and they battled to keep their lands in good condition but access to both land and sea permitted a level of self-sufficiency probably supported by seasonal working.

The historical record hints at a way of life and points us to potential archaeological survival. Can we hope that evidence for Ainsdale's medieval landscape will emerge from beneath the sand dunes? The old churchyard at Ravenmeols, almost buried by sand, suggests proximity to the lost medieval chapel, but we know nothing of its structure or the settlements it served. Are their remains buried beneath the sand only recognisable as spreads of dark, cultivated soils

are exposed along the dune front? Or were they washed away?

The damp, organic soils of the Sniggery ditch are ideal for the preservation of timber, plant and other organic remains. History tells us that the fishery was controlled by sluices and that there was some sort of thatched structure though these are no longer visible. But the ditch is recognisable as a shallow depression between low banks, and archaeological material might survive in the damp infill.

Altcar's Rifle Range reminds us of the coast's military history, but the role of derelict wartime structures is poorly understood. During the Great War troops mustered in Little Crosby. The camp was dismantled, the field has reverted to pasture and only the occasional brick or pottery sherd is recovered. What do we know of the camp and its extent? Is it possible that a military camp and its infrastructure can leave no trace?

The discovery of archaeological sites is as much one of chance, of recognition of the 'unusual', as it is of sustained research. Anyone interested in Sefton's past can look for the evidence; we can all play a part in identifying and understanding Sefton's coastal archaeology and history.

Acknowledgements

Dilys Firn for drawing my attention to the transcripts of the Lay Subsidy Lists; Audrey Coney for discussion on the evidence for salt extraction and salt fish; Joanne Jones, Keeper of Art Galleries and Museums, Sefton Council, for sight of the radiocarbon dating report on the Botanic Gardens canoe; Bob Wright for alerting me to the Great War camp at Little Crosby; Anthony Lewis for helpful comments on my text.

Coastal Sefton in the Prehistoric Period

Ron W. Cowell

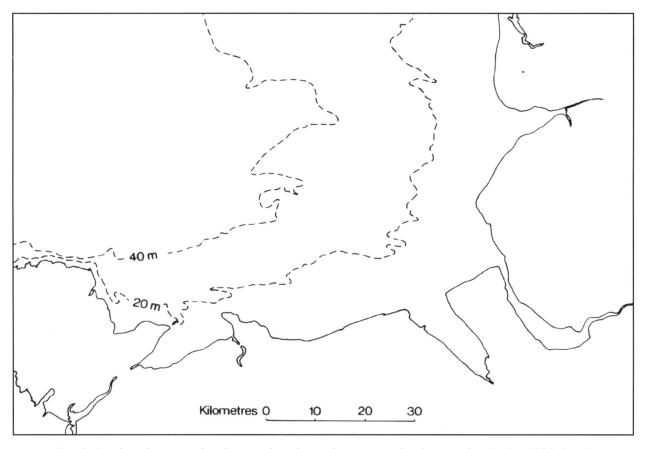

Fig. 1: Landward retreat of early post glacial coastlines as sea-level rose (after Tooley 1985, fig. 1)

Introduction

After the end of the last ice age, about 10,000 years ago, or BP (Before Present), the landscape of south west Lancashire was considerably different from that of today. At about 9000 BP sea level was 20 metres below present Ordnance Datum (Tooley 1980), producing a coastline many kilometres to the west of the present one (fig. 1). Sea level rise over the next few thousand years led to a reduction of this coastal plain so that the number of early prehistoric sites lost to the sea can only be guessed at. Evidence from the present coastal zone, which has the greatest concentration of early prehistoric sites in the area, implies that there are likely to be many. The line of the present coast was first reached, and in fact extended inland as far as Downholland Moss (fig. 2), around 7000 BP (Tooley 1982, 76) but the line of the present dune system was not roughly fixed until about 4500 BP (Innes and Tooley 1993).

In west Lancashire, a line drawn approximately from west of Hesketh Bank southwards towards Halsall and Little Crosby (fig. 2) marks the eastern edge of a large basin whose prehistoric land surface lies several metres beneath the present day ground level. This land now consists of a series of largely reclaimed mosslands such as Martin Mere and Downholland Moss. These represent former prehistoric wetlands and consist of vertical sequences, in various combinations, of peat, sand, silt and clay that have infilled the prehistoric basin. To a large extent this has been associated with the repeated onset and withdrawal of marine conditions over cycles of many centuries. The earliest inundations, from about 7000 BP to about 5600 BP, reached to the east of Downholland Moss, with marine transgressions alternating with tidal flats and saltmarsh, which at the Altmouth continued up to about 4550 BP (Gonzalez and Huddart 2002, 580).

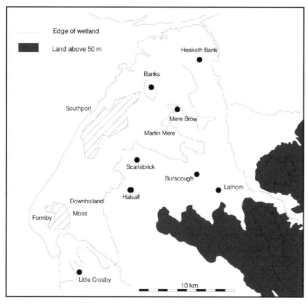

Fig. 2: Extent of prehistoric wetland deposits in south west Lancashire

Wherever the line of the tidal zone lay in prehistory, behind it inland waterlogging took place. This produced a sequence of adjacent vegetation types, so that the coastal zone might consist of intertidal flats of sand and mud, merging into salt marsh which merged into freshwater swamp and fen woodland (woodland,

such as alder, growing around the edges of swamps and pools) (fig. 3).

Beyond the influence of this wet environment, the slightly higher ground was covered in woodland (Cowell and Innes 1994, chapter 4). This gradually changed its composition throughout the early prehistoric period, from initially fairly open woodland of birch, hazel and pine to a woodland dominated by alder, oak, hazel, elm and lime after about 7500 BP, although the sandy soils of the west Lancashire area may have encouraged the lighter forest to have persisted longer and been more widely distributed than further inland, for example as was the case around St Helens.

In general though the forest became thicker and would have been difficult to penetrate during the early prehistoric period, thus making the natural breaks in this woodland, such as the rivers, the fens and the coast, places where movement was easier. Additionally, the kind of freshwater wetland environments outlined above are the second most productive sources of wild food in the world, after rain forests (Williams 1990, 22). In the Sefton coastal area these were augmented by adjacent wild resource-rich environments on the sea shore and in the forests.

Fig. 3: A prehistoric Sefton coast reconstruction for the later Mesolithic period, consisting of zones made up of a sand bar, inter tidal mud and lagoon, marsh, fen carr and dry woodland

Early prehistoric period (about 10000 to 4500 BP)

The earliest communities in the Sefton area – many thousands of years before farming was known in Britain – consisted of hunter-gatherers who, therefore, had to rely on wild resources. Because wild food is seasonal this meant that, in order to have a supply of food throughout the year, they would have had to move around the landscape to take advantage of this. Not only did the coast mark the most obvious break in the widespread forest but it was also an area where a wide variety of different predictable environments existed within a short distance of each other. Each of these environments – the tidal zone, the estuaries, salt marsh, fen, swamp and dry woodland – had their own specific characteristics that made them attractive at different seasons. As a whole range of wild resources were thus concentrated in small areas around the coast

the need for constant long distance settlement moves, to take advantage of changes in seasonal availability, could have been reduced. It is no surprise, therefore, that a large number of hunter-gatherer sites are concentrated between Formby and Crosby (fig. 4). Sites of this early prehistoric period are usually recognised by concentrations of stone tools found on ploughed farmland and other exposed surfaces (Cowell and Innes 1994). Most of the stone consists of small flint pebbles, which were deposited in clay laid down across the region by ice action. In prehistory, on many local sites the flint has often been collected from the coast.

The earliest sites in the region, probably over 9,000 years old, are found on the relatively high sandstone areas of the Wirral (around Greasby and Thurstaston) and on the Pennines (Cowell 1992, Howard-Davis 1996). There may be one similar site in our area, at Little Crosby, but that is not absolutely clear (Cowell

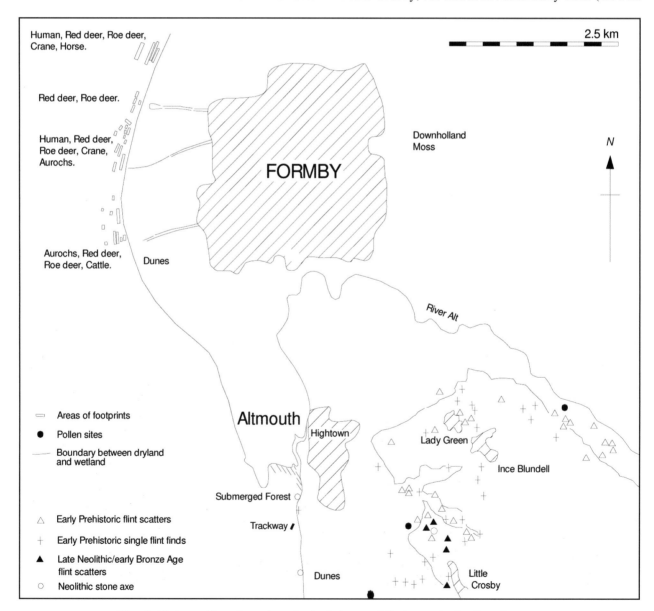

Fig. 4: Main prehistoric archaeological sites and findspots in the Formby area

and Innes 1994, 82). Many of these early sites in this area probably lie either further out to sea on land that is now lost, or else further inland, where they may have been buried by later natural deposits.

The best evidence of early occupation for the Sefton district starts a little later, probably dating to the period after c.7000 BP. At this time much of the landscape north of the present Altmouth was generally semi-aquatic, particularly between about 7000 BP and 6000 BP (Tooley 1978). However, there is evidence of these people using the coast round about this time close to Formby Point and Hightown, where early prehistoric footprints of humans and animals are found on the present beach (fig 4.; Roberts and Worsley, this volume). The area then was intertidal mud flats, which lay behind a sand barrier further out in what is now sea. The prints include those of animals such as aurochs (large wild cattle) red deer and roe deer and interspersed with these are over 200 trails of human adults' and children's footprints. Gordon Roberts has suggested that the pattern of association between some of the human and animal prints could reflect hunting or herding practices. There are also animal bones from the beach,

some of which have been dated a little later, including a red deer jawbone, a complete set of unshed antlers and a dog jawbone. The red deer antlers have produced a date of 4425±45 BP (OxA-9130) (3130-2910 cal BC) (Gonzalez and Huddart 2002), which falls in the late Neolithic (see below), while the dog jawbone came from a layer that has produced a date of 3649±109 BP (UB-3869), falling in the middle Bronze Age.

There is no direct evidence, however, that these people were living in or close to where the footprints occur, as so much of the prehistoric land surface has been covered by later sediments left by the changing coastal environment. Archaeological survey in the Alt valley, by National Museums Liverpool, shows that sites did exist on the margins of the wetlands, although it is more difficult to locate sites in the wetland areas themselves unless the overlying levels of peat or clay have been removed for some reason. There is, however, evidence for the burning of trees and swamp vegetation from charcoal that had blown into the mud flat areas in the Formby area at roughly the same time as the people were hunting and collecting on the beach there (Cowell et al 1993). This suggests that they were

Fig. 5: A reconstruction of a late Mesolithic scene in the Woodham Knoll area of Little Crosby

probably managing the swamp and woodland fringes within a kilometre or two of the present beach, and may well have been living close to the burning sites (Roberts and Worsley, this volume).

The nearest known settlements of this date to the Formby Point area, however, lie a little inland. Large areas to the south east of Formby have been archaeologically surveyed, but the area north of the Alt, surveyed by Oxford Archaeology North at Lancaster, has not been published in detail yet, so the best evidence at the moment comes from south of the Alt (fig.4). Here, about six kilometres (about four miles) from Formby Point, on low sandy ridges around Ince Blundell and Little Crosby, lie a large number of small sites that date from about 7000 to 5000 BP. At that time these people would have been living around the edges of the reed and fen swamps and woodland on the sandy higher ground that has never been inundated or, particularly in the floodplain of the River Alt, on small dryland sandy islands actually within the reed swamp (Cowell and Innes 1994).

The higher ground would have been in relative close proximity to the changing coastline during this period; sometimes, for example around 6000 BP, it would have been closer than today, at other times it was probably at a similar remove to the present line. It would not be surprising, however, for people using the Little Crosby area for short periods to also have visited the beach around Formby Point; trips of 5-10 kilometres in a day from their base would not be unexpected, from the evidence of studies of hunter-gatherer groups elsewhere in the recent past (Binford, 1983).

Fig. 6: Examples of late Mesolithic stone tool making in Little Crosby

The majority of these sites are small, made up of a not very dense scatter of stone tools, which define discrete areas. Many are likely to represent various kinds of short stay activities associated with hunting and gathering expeditions (that might include plant collecting) or perhaps fishing sites, bivouacs, hunting stands, or animal kill and butchering sites. These types of sites also occur further inland, mainly in the major river valleys flowing through the region. Sites are particularly recorded in the Alt-Ditton river system, including excavated sites at Croxteth Park, Liverpool – about 10 kilometres along the valley from Little Crosby – and others close to its confluence with the Mersey near Widnes (Cowell 2000). There are also sites in other valleys such as, in west Lancashire, the Douglas, at Mawdesley. Sometimes these valleys were visited repeatedly in a series of short stay visits. The excavations have produced small occupations, resulting in the discard of between 200-500 pieces of struck flint, often based around natural hollows probably formed by uprooted trees. The tools include a few arrowheads and implements that might have been used for piercing and scraping various types of materials, although the Mawdesley site has a much higher proportion of arrowheads, suggesting a different kind of site here. Some of the flint from the Croxteth Park site looks to have come originally from the coast, and much of the stone used at Mawdesley may have come from the southern Pennines, illustrating the mobile way of life practised by these people.

Fig. 7: Neolithic polished stone axe from Little Crosby (National Museums Liverpool)

Agriculture, and the new Neolithic culture, appeared in Britain after about 5300 BP. Pollen evidence from some of the waterlogged remains in the wetland deposits show the prehistoric environment at this time and indicate that short-lived, small clearings were made throughout this period in the surrounding woodland, presumably by the people living in the area (Cowell and Innes 1994). They also show the earliest likely evidence for the use of cereals in the region in these coastal areas, at Flea Moss Wood, Little Crosby and probably at a similar date from Downholland Moss, west Lancashire. However, as they are dated to about 5900 BP, this is still many centuries before aspects of the new Neolithic culture – artefacts and burial methods, for example –

Fig. 8: Excavation underway on the Hightown wooden structure

appeared in Britain. If this is the case, although the evidence is not totally clear, it may represent one step in the process of hunter-gatherers adopting restricted elements of the new economy, while still retaining much of their original way of life.

Even the appearance of Neolithic culture after c.5300 BP, represented by artefacts such as polished stone axes from Hightown and Little Crosby (fig.7) and an arrowhead from Ince Blundell, seems to have been introduced into a basically hunter-gatherer way of life, as settlement patterns and land use changed little for some time after.

On the beach near Hightown, a four-metre length of wooden trackway, about 1.4 metres wide, which was traced over a distance of c.60 metres, has been excavated by archaeologists from National Museums

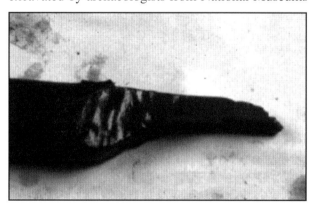

Fig. 9: A piece of wood with knawing marks left by a beaver, dating to about 5000 BP

Liverpool, and radiocarbon dated to the early to middle Neolithic (Cowell in prep). Only a short section had survived marine erosion, but there was enough to show a lower latticework arrangement of roundwood branches woven together (fig.8). The occasional split oak, and even unidentified rootstock, was also used, laid over the lower rods, perhaps as a form of rebuilding, with the final structure being over 30 centimetres deep. Eighty pieces were sampled, of which alder was most common (51%), with hazel (17%) and oak (9%) making up over a quarter of the total assemblage. Ash, elm, lime, 'hawthorn type', alder buckthorn, and birch are also present, with frequencies of less than 5%. Wood of all species is predominantly unconverted wood ('in the round'). One hundred and eighty three pieces of wood were assessed for signs of human working. Only one was unequivocally found to be so, while three others had faint traces of a single facet, one of which also had an anciently worn tip. One piece had beaver gnaw marks on one end (fig.9) and two pieces were partly charred.

There were traces of roundwood fragments in the surface of the clay in a narrow linear band for a distance of c.60 metres to the south west and better survival, partially under marine clay, for c.20 metres to the north east. The structure was laid across salt marsh (Silvia Gonzalez pers. comm.) perhaps to gain access to boats or fishtraps, for example, which might have been situated on the tidal part of the estuary, which lay lower than today's level but was still quite close by.

However, the pollen evidence suggests that around the middle Neolithic (c.4800 BP) cereal farming may have become more common in the area. In areas south of the Alt freshwater wetlands flanking some parts of the coast changed to raised bog conditions (Cowell and Innes 1994). Such areas are more acid and less productive for plant and wildlife than the swamps and fens they replaced. It is not clear if it is coincidental that cereal pollen increases in pollen diagrams in this area at about this time, or if this marks a change in the balance of land use. If the latter, then one interpretation might be that this could have compensated for the reduction in the resource potential of the former wetlands. The freshwater wetlands were still prevalent, though further to the north and north west.

Late Neolithic/earlier Bronze Age period (about 4500 to 2800 BP)

As sea-levels fell during the late Neolithic, after c.4500 BP, the rise of freshwater levels and the accumulation of *phragmites* (reed swamp) peat led to the abandonment of the Hightown wooden structure. This period saw a relatively prolonged period of low sea level, in which freshwater peat and, subsequently, deciduous forest extended to the west of the present inter-tidal zone (Tooley 1978; Gonzalez and Huddart 2002). A remnant of this process can still be seen today on the Hightown beach near the yacht club (fig. 4) where trees lie in a thin band of peat where they fell over 4,000 years ago, along with other woodland plants such as royal fern. It was a little after this time that the coast became stabilised around its present position with the accumulation of sand dunes in the Little Crosby area (Innes and Tooley 1993).

At about this time, the first hints of a change in the way people lived is apparent in the coastal areas, although people may still not have been settled permanently in what today we would recognise as farmsteads. Again, the settlement evidence is restricted to the slightly raised areas at Little Crosby (fig.4) and is represented by stone tools of late Neolithic or early Bronze Age date. The pollen diagram from the adjacent Flea Moss Wood site shows major woodland disturbance with cereal cultivation immediately post-dating 4670 ± 50 BP (SRR-2695) (Cowell and Innes 1994, 85), although it is not clear if the stone tool sites are contemporary with this particular phase of environmental evidence, as they can only be dated on stylistic grounds, which provides a broader potential date range (between about 4500 to 3300 BP).

There are only two other localities – on the lower Mersey, at Hale, and on the Wirral, at Irby – where similar sites are known (Cowell forthcoming). These sites are very different from settlements of earlier periods. They cover larger areas and have a greater density of stone tools, of a very different character from the earlier settlements (fig.10). The nature of the stone tool evidence from these sites suggests, however, that rather than being permanent settlements, many repeated visits might have been made to the same locality (Cowell, 1991). It is also highly likely that these sites are associated with domesticated animals, for which areas of wetland would provide rich grassland for grazing, perhaps at a particular season. There are also many locations in south west Lancashire where only single finds of stone tools of this period, such as flint scrapers or knives, occur (Cowell and Innes 1994; Middleton and Tooley forthcoming). These two features suggest that, even in the Bronze Age, mobility may still have been an important element of land use.

Fig. 10: Stone tools of around 3000 BP from Woodham Knoll, Little Crosby

The Late Prehistoric period (from about 3000 BP)

It is not clear if people in this area continued to use stone tools much after about 3,000 years ago; and if they did how can we recognise them, as no sites of this period have been excavated in this area. Elsewhere, by about this time settlement and land use had changed dramatically in many parts of Britain. Farmsteads as we would know them (permanent buildings with paddocks and fields) had come into existence by now. This suggests that people's concerns had probably changed, and what was most important was a defined area of farmland that could be passed down in individual families, in contrast to the looser territorial arrangements that may have been a feature of earlier periods. People's use of land had also changed now so that the best soils for permanent settlement and arable farming were valuable, although the wetland areas

Fig. 11: Reconstruction of Lathom Iron Age settlement

could still be important for a variety of resources other than food. How far people actually lived in the wetland areas is unknown, but it is likely that there is evidence waiting to be found in the region. A site in the Severn estuary may provide a comparison as there, in a prehistoric tidal zone, a rectangular wooden structure dated to the Iron Age appears to have been used on a seasonal basis (Bell 1995).

Material culture, particularly the use of pottery, is sparse everywhere during this period making it very difficult to identify where people lived; but so far no evidence has come from the local coastal area. On the Sefton coast, a final period of high sea-level is indicated in the present coastal zone, c.2300 BP (2335-120 BP (Hv 4709)), in the late Iron Age, represented by a former dune slack deposit under the present dunes at Formby (Tooley 1978). This did not cause a major transgression of the coast because of the protective sand dune barrier.

The nearest evidence for settlement of this period comes from further inland at Lathom near Ormskirk, where the earliest known farmstead dates to the period after c.200 BC (fig.11). It lies in an area of good farmland on a small area of well-drained sand, which probably includes a former spring. This is surrounded by heavier clayland and the former wetlands of Hoscar Moss. There are four adjacent roundhouses spanning the period from c.100 BC to the early Romano-British period (Cowell 2005). The largest is 10.5 metres in diameter, with a double entrance, and adjoining small fields or paddocks of probable late Iron Age date. There are also two small square granary buildings, a number of storage pits, and a quernstone for grinding corn that was made from stone from the central Pennines. There is no trace, however, of an enclosure ditch around the settlement. Although cattle bones do not survive in the acid sand subsoil, it does appear as if arable farming may be more important here than the other sites in the region, and raises the question as to whether this site type and associated economy may indicate a different social standing for its occupants.

Acknowledgements

Thanks go to Sarah Pevely for her reconstruction drawings, which have been derived from realisations by the author (based as far as possible on local archaeological and palaeoenvironmental evidence) and generated using the Vue 6 Esprit software package. Thanks also go to Annie Worsley for her advice on the images.

Evidence of Human activity in mid-Holocene coastal palaeoenvironments of Formby, North West England

Gordon Roberts and Annie Worsley

1. Introduction: Coasts and human activity in the past

In the United Kingdom there is considerable evidence for the activity of human beings in the past from a wide variety of sites. However, for the early to mid-Holocene period, which encompasses the transition from the Mesolithic to the Neolithic (c.10000–c.5000 BP), many documented sites are either inland from the coast or in the upland areas. The relative importance of the coast to populations in this time frame is difficult to ascertain and reconstructing early and mid-Holocene subsistence and settlement patterns is problematic, since many potential coastal sites have been lost to the sea (Schulting and Richards, 2002). Indeed, it is from Scottish sites that the greatest understanding of the Mesolithic coastal activity comes. This means that the story of human activity during this time period is to some extent governed by the geography of the sites so far recorded by archaeologists and by the relative rarity of remains. Archaeology has been and still is asking how, when and where did the transition from Mesolithic hunter-gatherers to Neolithic agriculturalists take place and about the role of the coast and coastal communities in this process (Raemaekers, 2003). There is evidence from south Wales for people whose diet consisted largely of marine foods (Raemaekers, 2003) but which also featured terrestrial components such as red and roe deer. What is clear is that, as more sites are investigated, the transition from reliance on coastal resources to a mixed coastal/terrestrial diet and then to a largely terrestrial system (based on the 'new' agricultural activities of the Neolithic) was not a rapid and sudden shift in practice and habit. Rather, it was a steady transition that would have taken place at different rates in different locations. The physical geography of the British Isles must have played a significant role in the

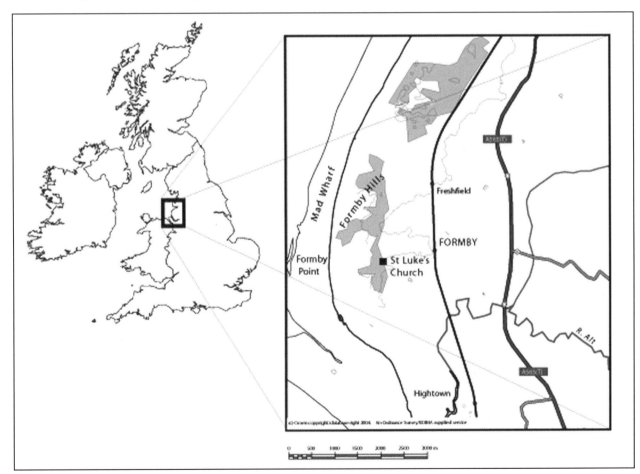

Fig. 1: Map to show the location of the study area at Formby, Merseyside, UK.

'story' of ancient populations for two main reasons. Firstly, the coastal zone would have been relatively resource-rich and secondly, the changes to sea level and climate in this period would have affected the movement of both people and the flora and fauna upon which they depended.

In this context, then, the paper examines the evidence for human activity in the coastal zone in north west England, in particular through the study and evaluation of the mammalian and avifaunal footprints at Formby on Merseyside (Fig. 1) during the late Mesolithic to the Neolithic, and it discusses some aspects of the nature of the environments in which this activity may have taken place. The paper proposes that the hunter-gatherers and neophyte agriculturalists of the time would have had a distinctive and close relationship with the physical environments of the area and their biota, and it highlights the need for further research in both archaeology and palaeoenvironmental science.

2. Formby

2.1 Historical background

Formby is reputed to have been founded in the 10th century AD by Norwegian settlers, evidence of that early habitation being its name, the Norse-derived *Fornebei*, recorded in the Domesday Survey of 1086. Its etymology suggests that it may have been 'the old BY' (i.e. 'village', 'homestead') or '*Forni's* BY' (Ekwall, 1960). Despite a wealth of archæological finds in the surrounding districts of Merseyside indicating settlement from the Mesolithic to the Iron Age, there has been an apparent absence of any earlier historic or prehistoric activity on Formby Point itself and its immediate area.

Local historian Dr Edith Kelly commented, 'The marshy state of the land must have made it unattractive to early settlers, though there is some evidence of Neolithic and Bronze Age people in the Liverpool district and some at Martin Mere... but it is not known whether or not the coastal region was ever occupied by these early settlers,' (Kelly 1982,6). This conclusion is not at all surprising. The high coastal dunes and the depth of inland blown sand continue to inhibit conventional archaeological investigatory techniques,

such as field walking and excavation. It is within this context of early philosophical speculation and learned observation, and then geological research focused on geomorphological processes and coastal erosion, that gradually the prehistory of Formby Point has emerged.

2.2 Geological and environmental background

Formby lies on the Sefton coast, a sand dune barrier coastline recognised internationally for its wealth of wildlife, broad sandy beaches and extensive dunes and it has been widely reported that, with sea level and environmental change, the present day position of the coast has not been fixed (Plater et al., 1993). Over the last 10,000 years (the Holocene) the nature and shape of the coastal zone have been altered by physical forcing factors such as climate change and more recently, during the period now referred to as the Anthropocene, by human activity. Within these changes have come observations about the varying nature of the sedimentary materials that make up the coastal zone.

Ancient remains have been emerging from the sea along the coast at various times over the last few hundred years and have been reported by several writers. In the 17th century, peaty outcrops containing tree trunks and branches were described by James (1636), Plot (1686 *see* Morton 1871) and Leigh (1700 *see* Morton 1871). At the end of the 18th century Holt (1796 *see* Morton 1871) described a 'submarine' forest at Crosby, as did Aikin (1795). Scientific and geological studies were presented from the mid-19th century onwards with work by Reade (1871), Ashton (1909, 1920), Travis (1926) and Gresswell (1953). The silt and peat deposits described in these works made no mention of mammalian imprints (although Gresswell is known to have produced sketches of deer and other animal footprints using tracing paper and pencil, rather like rubbings). This may have been either because footprints were not recognised as being ancient or because beach sedimentary and/or tidal conditions were not favourable. Indeed, until 1901, the foreshore at Formby saw considerable accretion with the High Water Mark (HWM) moving relatively westwards. Only after this date did conditions in the coastal zone change, resulting in the net removal of sedimentary materials (Plater et al. 1993). With the

Plate 1. Ridges and runnels showing, centre, an exposed sediment exposure

acceleration of this removal from the late 1960s onwards, increasing numbers of sedimentary exposures in distinctive layers began to occur along the foreshore. In 1970 Tooley reported ungulate footprints in deposits that were Flandrian (Holocene) in age[1] (Tooley 1970, 1974).

3.   The deposits
At the present time, sediments containing footprints are exposed within a 4km stretch of Formby Point from Dale Slack Gutter in the north (GB National Grid reference SD273093) to Lifeboat Road in the south (SD268063). The outcrops occur discontinuously in the intertidal zone and their appearance very much depends upon tides and conditions of the longshore currents. During periods of relative calm, sand ridges and intervening runnels (channels) develop which variously cut into the Holocene deposits (Plate 1).

The footprint-bearing deposits themselves are chiefly sandy silts or silty sands[2] (Tooley 1970; Worsley & Suggitt, unpublished data), finely laminated (layered) and interspersed with sand units, and they lie above the blue-grey marine clays of the mid-Holocene. Quite

specific environmental conditions would have been required for the deposition of these deposits and, more significantly, for the preservation of the footprints:

- the original consistency of the muddy sediments would have been semi-liquid so that animals and humans traversing the intertidal zone would have left impressions several millimetres and in some cases centimetres deep;

- the daily meteorological condition (temperature, wind) at and following the time of imprint would have been crucial to ensure that the sediment had dried out sufficiently before the impression was covered by the next tidal inundation;

- infilling would have initially been by light, very fine ($<63\mu$), wind blown materials, followed by full covering of silts and clays by the next tidal inundation;

- the tidal inundation would have been of sufficiently low energy (i.e. very little wave action) so that there was no perturbation of the surface sediments, merely a deposition to seal the print.

---

[1] The term Flandrian which refers to the current postglacial period from 10500 BP (before present) to the present day is now most commonly replaced with the term Holocene.

[2] The definition depends on the proportion of grain sizes in samples: clays are $<63\mu$; silts $<200\mu$

However, such conditions would not always have been present at the time when animal and human groups were traversing the coastal zone.

4.   The Footprints

Across the beach at Formby the tracks of human beings and animals have been identified, catalogued and investigated by Gordon Roberts since 1989 (Fig. 2).

The feeding trails are mostly straight, but at one site the overlapping, circular tracks may indicate a courting ritual being enacted. The imprints of a crane with her chicks have also been noted.

Whilst the tracks of roe deer (*Capreolus capreolus*) differ little from present-day imprints (hoof length: 4-5 cm long), those of red deer (*Cervus elaphus*) (hoof

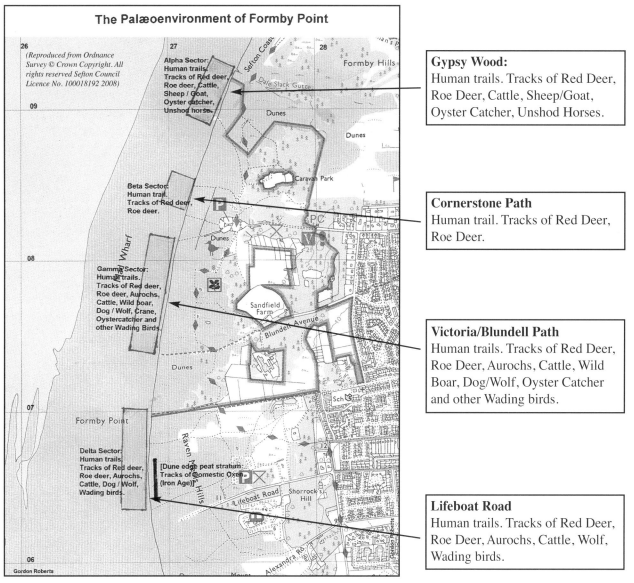

Fig. 2: Map showing the general location of Mesolithic / Neolithic Animal, Bird and Human footprint-bearing sediments

The largest number of tracks is those of wading birds which have been found in several strata. Those of the oystercatcher (*Hæmatopus ostralogus*) are the most numerous. The most impressive bird tracks are those of the crane (*Grus grus*), no doubt a summer visitor then to the marshy coastline of Formby Point as it still is today to many parts of northern Continental Europe.

length: 12-15 cm) indicate a much larger species than today's. It is possible that, as human activity increased and encroached upon the natural habitat and food supply, together with climate change, only a smaller species of red deer was able to cope, whereas the much smaller roe deer, with its more limited requirements, did not need to adapt itself to the same extent.

Other animal tracks recorded include those of wild boar (*Sus scrofa*), and unshod ponies. Occasionally *Canidae* tracks appear among the bird and ungulate imprints, but whether they are of large wild dogs (*Canis*), domestic dogs (*Canis familiaris*), or wolves (*Canis lupus*), it is difficult to ascertain, since the erosive action of the uncovering tides blurs the fine distinction necessary to make an accurate identification. At Lifeboat Road, a dog jawbone was excavated from a sediment layer which had been penetrated by alder roots that have been radiocarbon dated at 3649 years BP (Gonzalez et al., 1997).

The discovery and recording of several aurochs tracks has been very significant. The now extinct aurochs (*Bos primigenius*) was the wild precursor of domestic cattle. Palaeolithic cave paintings give some indication of its size and appearance, as do skeleton assemblages. A fully-grown bull aurochs could be 1.80m to shoulder height and 3.30m in length from the muzzle to the rump. It is thought that the aurochs was hunted into extinction in Britain during the Bronze Age, (c.2000 BC–c.700 BC) (Clutton-Brock 1986). Formby Point affords a rare, if not unique location and opportunity where one can distinctly observe its gait characteristics, with a stride of about 2 metres and the hind hoof usually registering in the impression of the fore hoof. With its hinterland fen-carr and sedge marshes, Formby Point parallels here in some respects the habitat of the aurochs in the marshy forests, river valleys and estuaries of Continental Europe described by Van Vuure (2003). When not grazing on the dune grasses, like present-day elk, buffalo, red deer and other ungulates, the aurochs may well have found some respite from the summer heat and the insects plaguing the stagnant pools of the fen-carr by wallowing in the deeper offshore mud of the lagoon. The east-west orientation of many of its tracks would seem to support such activity.

Since October 1990, 219 human footprint trails have now been recorded. Of these, 179 have provided sufficiently detailed information to enable individual stature and gait characteristics to be calculated. Using the formula applied at Laetoli by Charteris et al. (1981), modified and employed by Day (1991, and pers. comm.), and tested against both, it has been possible to estimate stature, relative stride, relative speed, velocity, stride time, cadence and speed of walking.

Determining gender has been based on a combination of height estimates and sexual dimorphism in foot shape. Research carried out by Parham et al. (1992) and Frey et al. (1993) have confirmed that males tend to have longer and broader feet than females. In addition, a woman's foot has a higher arch, a

Plate 2. Plaster cast of deformed foot with missing or fused toes and collapsed metatarsals.

shallower first toe, a smaller ball of foot circumference, a shorter length of the outside ball of foot and a smaller instep.

An earlier statistical analysis undertaken by E. J. Roberts (1995) of 75 footprint trails suggests a mean, adult male height of 1.66m and a mean, female height of 1.45m. For comparison, mean early Neolithic male and female heights from Denmark are 1.66m and 1.53m respectively (Waldon 1989). This average 8cm difference between the Formby and Danish female stature may be explained by the observation that on Formby Point those made by fully grown, adult females are rare. Gait analysis and direction of movement indicate that here it was mainly the younger women and children who were occupied in food gathering, e.g. shrimps, razor clams and other sea food from the flats, or eggs from the reed beds bordering the lagoons and creeks. Male adolescent and adult footprint trails, when not heading out into or returning from the estuary and outer coastal margins, are sometimes directly associated with red and roe deer tracks. Evidence of increased speed over the norm for the (then) soft, muddy surface, together with a deeper indentation of the toes and metatarsus, may imply hunting or some form of animal management in progress. The overall impression is of family groups being active along the prehistoric shore.

Plate 3. Deformed foot showing pronounced abduction and fused toes.

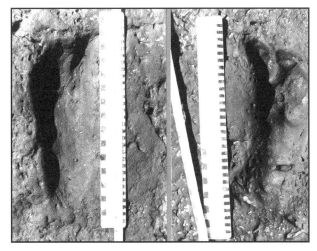

Plate 4. Deformed left and right feet displaying ectrodactyly (Split/Claw Foot).

Occasionally, moccasin-like footwear has been noted, but most of the footprint trails were made by barefooted men, women and children. This is, of course, what one would expect, given the muddy conditions. However, their foot contours, and especially the stature and age-related increasing abduction of the hallux from the second toe, indicate that the makers appear to have been either habitually unshod or that any footwear was certainly non-restrictive.

Sometimes the footprints reveal individual anatomical characteristics and apparent abnormalities:

- One young male, approximately 1.55m tall, had deformed feet where either one toe was missing or two toes had fused. A plaster cast taken of the left foot clearly shows that the metatarsals had collapsed but there seems to have been a compensatory thickening of the *peroneus longus* and the *tibialis posterior* tendons (Plate 2).

- Pronounced abduction of the *hallux* (big toe) and fused second and third toes are also clearly seen in the feet of a young female, approx. 1.46m. tall (Plate 3).

Plate 5a. Impression in silt of right foot.

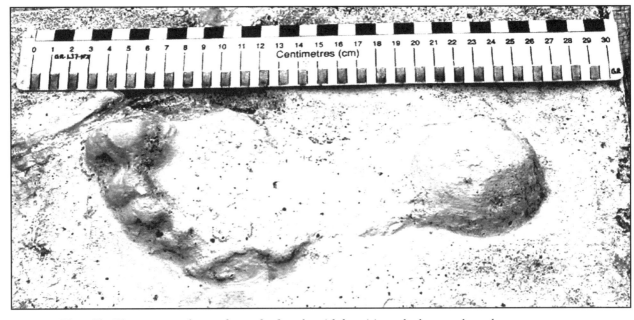

Plate 5b. Plaster cast of same foot, of a female with bursitis and who may have been pregnant or who may have been suffering from pes cavus.

- An adult female, approx. 1.67m tall, is apparently displaying indications of *ectrodactyly* (Split/Claw Foot) in both feet. (*Ectrodactyly* may also be accompanied by a similar abnormality in the hands.) She was moving at approx. 3.24kph/2mph (Plate 4).

- There are the footprints, too, of an adolescent female, approx. 1.40m tall, with indications of

bursitis. She also appears to have been walking awkwardly, her weight firmly on her heels, her feet arched and her toes curled under, talon-like, striving to maintain her balance and posture as she slowly made her way across the slippery mud. Such gait characteristics may have been caused by pregnancy (Jackson, pers. comm.). Alternatively, her arched feet might also signify *pes cavus* (hollow foot), an

Plate 6. Healthy foot of young male showing pointed toenail 'drag'.

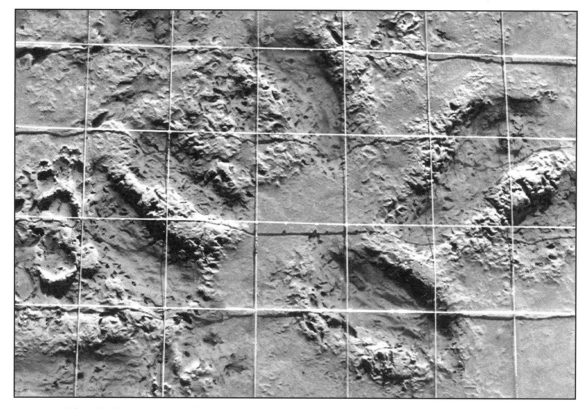

Plate 7. Footprints of playing children. (Each square of grid measures 10cm x 10cm)

indication, for example, of diabetes, or motor neurological disorders such as muscular dystrophy and Friedreich's ataxia. On the other hand, she may simply have been carrying a heavy basket of seafood slung in front of her (Plates 5a and 5b).

These examples, however, are the exceptions. Almost all of the footprints observed display no medical defects at all. Interestingly, however, one imprint of a young male, approx. 1.33m tall, clearly shows the pointed 'drag' caused by uncut toenails! (Plate 6).

- And at one site, a turmoil of tiny, sun-hardened footprints evokes the poignant image of a small group of children, stomping around in the cool mud – quite literally 'mud-larking' – while their elders foraged for shell food nearby, one mud-baking day, five thousand summers ago (Plate 7).

5. Investigating the palaeoenvironments

5.1 Environmental change and the Formby coastal zone

The last glaciation ended about 10,000 years ago and by 9500 BP the climate of Britain was at least as warm as it is today. Temperature rise continued until the climatic optimum was reached between 8000 and 5000 BP, with average summer temperatures in Britain being 2–30C higher than at present. During the last major glaciation, global sea levels had been some 120 metres lower than today's (Fairbanks 1989) but now, as the ice melted, huge quantities of water were released into the oceans.

The rising sea waters flooded across the Mesolithic landscape of what is now the Irish Sea towards the present coastline, continuing then to inundate the low-lying north Merseyside landscape to the east. Although the sea level, in general, then began to fall and to reach its present position about 5000 years BP, the Sefton coastline nevertheless fluctuated on a cyclical basis during the late Mesolithic and early Neolithic. Indeed, Tooley (1978a) identified four long-term marine incursions or transgressions between 8000 and 4545 years BP, with possibly a fifth transgression around 2335 years BP.

It has been suggested that for much of the Holocene there was a north-south trending coastal barrier (Pye and Neal, 1993a, 1993b; Neal, 1993; Huddart, 1992) and that the earliest dunes in the region, which formed between 5800 and 5700 BP, may have originated on an emergent offshore sand bank which was already in existence by 6800 BP. Prior to this dune barrier development, the area had been characterised by an extensive, intertidal sandflat to the west and mudflats and saltmarsh to the east. Now, the earlier saltmarsh was replaced, first by freshwater marsh and then by wooded fen-carr. Areas of active saltmarsh may, however, still have existed on the fringes of the proto-Ribble and Alt estuaries.

The west, intertidal muds and sandy beach deposits may then have been capped by low, emergent beach bars or islands. These would have deflected and reduced wave energy, thus allowing the deposition of muddier elements in their lee, as well as continuing to supply sand for the nascent coastal dunes. Intertidal muds may also have accumulated on the seaward side of the beach barrier in response to a reduction in wind/wave conditions and a slight fall in sea level. Thus, between the island(s) or beach bar, a reed-fringed intertidal lagoon and mudflats evolved and this was the environment in which the imprints were made.

The character of the coastline changed after 3250 years BP. Barrier progradation continued westwards in response to the continuingly abundant sand supply to the nearshore and dunes, and the earlier muds and sediments were overwhelmed. From 2300 BP there was extensive dune stabilisation which persisted up until the early Middle Ages.

5.2 Age of the deposits

Until the age of the Holocene sediments themselves could be ascertained, the footprints were initially placed, tentatively, into a prehistoric, temporal context by referring to earlier geological and environmental research and the Carbon-14 dating of any organic matter associated with the geomorphology of the coastline.

Plate 8a. Sediment exposure and 'stooks' of alder roots.

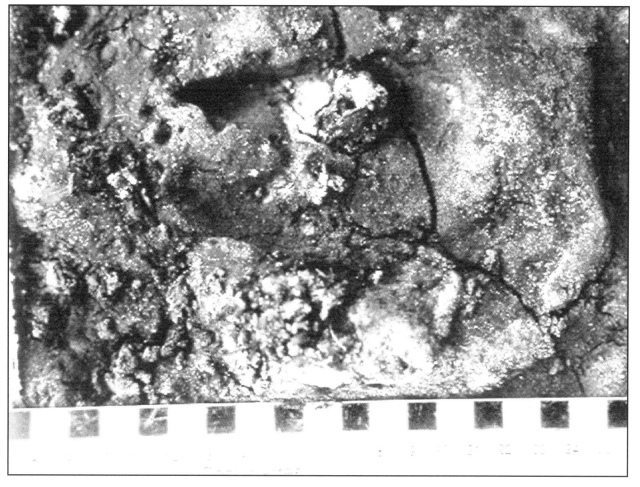

Plate 8b. Alder roots piercing a red deer imprint.

In 1970 Tooley demonstrated that the date of a dune-edge, woody detrital peat stratum at Lifeboat Road was 2510 +/- 120 14C years BP with a compatible date (2333 +/- 120 14C BP) obtained by Pye and Neal (1993b). The hoofprints identified in these deposits as domestic oxen by Jewell (pers.comm.) were therefore Iron Age in provenance. At some locations, principally at Lifeboat Road but also at Blundell Avenue, alder (*Alnus*) roots were observed following and growing down into ancient desiccation cracks in the sediments and sometimes, even, penetrating ungulate imprints (Plates 8a and 8b).

At Lifeboat Road, three sets of dates had been obtained for them: 3230 +/- 80 ^{14}C years BP (Pye and Neal 1993b), 3333 +/- 83 ^{14}C years BP (Gonzalez et al., 1996) and 3649 +/- 109 ^{14}C years BP (Gonzalez et al., 1996). At Blundell Avenue, Carbon-14 dating carried out on *Alnus* roots growing into imprint-bearing sediments there gave a similar age: 3575 +/- 45 14C years BP (dated in 2001, Roberts 2007 unpublished).

The dates for the *Alnus* roots established, therefore, that the underlying silts and the animal, bird and human footprints they contained were *older* than the Bronze Age (Cowell et al., 1993, Roberts et al., 1996, Gonzalez et al., 1996 and Huddart et al., 1999a, 1999b).

Two sediment samples from Blundell Avenue submitted by Gordon Roberts were next dated by Optically Stimulated Luminescence at the Research Laboratory for Archæology and the History of Art, Oxford (1998). At this site, the erosion process had enabled both human and red deer (*cervus elaphus*) imprints to be observed in 'stepped' strata. The overlying sand was cleared away from a parallel location about three metres to the east in order to uncover the surface of the, as yet, unexposed sediments. Samples of sediment were then taken at depths of minus 30cm and minus 10cm, to correspond with the near-by, previously exposed strata 'steps'. These were to give dates of 6650 +/- 700 years BP (for -30cm) and 5750 +/- 600 years BP (for -10cm) (Lab. Ref. 1528b).

Because of its substantially wider age range, luminescence dating usually gives poorer precision than Carbon-14 dating (Aitken, 1990). However, even if the most recent dates are accepted for the sediments and the imprints they contain, this would indicate an age of at least 5950 years BP for the lower sample and at least 5150 years BP for the upper sample. These indicated deposition between the Late Mesolithic and the Early to Middle Neolithic periods and verified the earlier assumption, based on the radiocarbon dates of the *Alnus* roots, which had suggested that the sediments were laid down before 3,500 BP.

More accurate, corroborating dating was obtained following the discovery and excavation in 1999 of a complete red deer antler set out of hoofprint-bearing strata at Wicks Path. This gave a date of 4450 +/- 45 14C years BP, confirming a Neolithic provenance for the upper silt strata (Ref. OxA-9130, 2000).

The imprints can therefore now be placed into a more accurate chronological, temporal, sedimentary and prehistoric context. They date, approximately, from 5000 BC to 100 BC, i.e. from the late-Mesolithic through to the Iron Age.

5.3 Recent work

In 2004 further samples were obtained from the imprint-bearing sediments following exposure by tidal activity. They were taken from freshly dug sections approximately 1-2m away from the eroding exposures, as the sedimentary layers could be easily traced eastward (inland). The samples were subjected to a suite of analyses including palynological investigations (to determine the pollen and spore content of the sediments) and charcoal counts. Pollen and spores from plant species are unique in shape and sculpturing. Their outer coats (exines) are extremely resistant to decay; only oxidising conditions will completely destroy grains. Normally the older the deposit the less likely perfectly preserved pollen and spore grains will be evident. However, under certain conditions grains may last for many thousands of years. Each species can be identified, if well preserved, because of a unique combination of overall morphology (shape, of which there is a large variety) and exine sculpturing (some grains are smooth, others look rather like crazy-paving; again, there is considerable variety) and so it is possible with care to elicit the proportions of different species present within a sample once it has been carefully prepared.

Samples were prepared at Edge Hill University (ECRU – the Environmental Change Research Unit in the Department of Natural, Geographical and Applied Sciences) following standard analytical techniques described by Moore and Webb (1978), which were adjusted to compensate for the high quartz content of the sediments, the mean grain size and the relatively poor preservation of organic matter. (Treatment includes boiling in Hydrofluoric Acid, Hydrochloric Acid, and washing and boiling in Sodium Hydroxide). Counting of the pollen grains (using a Leica ATC 2000 light microscope, at magnifications of x400 and x1000) was problematic given their poor quality (in wholly terrestrial deposits, such as peat, grains are well preserved; here in coastal margin deposits, preservation is variable); however, suitable, countable material was obtained from 6 distinctive layers. A count of around 300 grains was obtained for each sample, which necessitated repeat preparations from selected samples, and from these raw data, percentage values for each species were calculated.

The results from the pollen/spore counts are presented in this paper as summary diagrams of percentages for selected species only:

Layers FP (Formby Point) 3 and FP4 are the human footprint-bearing deposits, though all the other layers, with the exception of FP6, contained animal and bird footprints.

The percentage of unidentified species (grains that were broken, crumpled or had their outer coat degraded) is high, and highest in the older sediments, reflecting the nature and status of preservation in the sands and silts. However, it is apparent from the diagrams (Fig. 3) that many species were clearly identifiable.

Alnus (alder) and *Corylus* (hazel) (Fig. 3a) reflect the regional abundance of fresh water fen marshes and waterlogged ground. Indeed, both pollen types are found at sites where there is clear evidence of marine transgression, which will have produced a relatively slow rise in sea level generating conditions eminently suitable for the spread of both species.

The presence of *Quercus* (oak) and *Tilia* (lime) (Fig. 3a) pollen suggest that the climate at the time of deposition was relatively warm and wet, in particular the highest values of *Quercus* in FP4, reflecting the climate regime of the mid-Holocene. *Tilia* especially, is a thermophilous species, requiring relative mild conditions and its easily identified pollen grains have been found around Britain in sediments from the warmer mid-Holocene.

Pinus (pine) is present in all the samples. It is well represented in the palynological records of Britain, largely because it is produced in large quantities and it can travel for very long distances. It is most likely that this represents either somewhat distant woodland or small stands of pine growing at the margins of raised mires and other wetlands (fens) or where these areas were beginning to dry out.

Pollen grains from the family *Ericaceae* (Ericales) are found in sample FP1 (Fig. 3b). In coastal zones Ericaceous pollen is derived from coastal heathland, itself often found in the later stages in sand dune successions. In Psammoseres (sand dune ecosystems) dunes and slacks often give way to heath vegetation or scrubland with greater distance from the sea (currently dune heath exists at Freshfield close to the A565). In some British pollen records heath pollen is also ascribed to the Neolithic farming practices of forest clearance on the lighter soils of southern England or the uplands (Godwin 1984). However, given the close proximity of the Formby samples to the marine margins i.e. coastal lagoons, small estuaries and sand dunes, it is highly likely that the Ericales found here represent dune heath communities. Although not displayed here, Ericales pollen is also found in much older samples from below the marine silts and clays of the climatic optimum (c.5-6000 BP) and again, this most likely represents the presence of older, stable dunes and hence sand dune ecosystems much earlier than hitherto reported in the literature. This is supported by the early presence of natterjack toads and sand lizards on the coastline, from which Smith (1999) infers that a suitable sandy habitat may even have been in existence from about 9500 BP.

The presence of ericaceous pollen may also be significant, because where it appears in other records associated with Neolithic activity, it often goes hand in hand with charcoal remains and has thus been associated with the clearance of vegetation using fire. Indeed, in most parts of upland Britain today heath is maintained by carefully managed periods of burning. This suggests that people were not only harvesting flora and fauna in the coastal zone but they may also

Figure 3 (a–c). Pollen diagrams from footprint-bearing sedimentary layers at Formby Point.

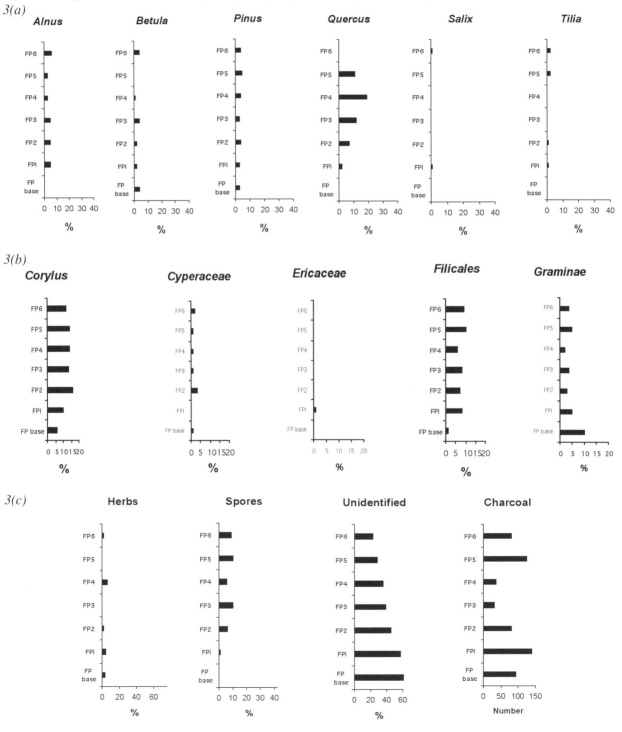

have been actively managing the vegetation communities there. This is supported by the presence of charcoal fragments in all the samples, but it is most notable in FP1 and again in FP5. Interestingly, the nature of the charcoal in the samples differs somewhat; the fragments found in FP1 are mostly very fine (less than 10μ) and rounded, whilst those found in the other samples are much larger and more angular, ranging from 14μ to more than 75μ. This suggests that the FP1 charcoal may have derived from burns at higher temperatures than fires producing the charcoal fragments in other layers. More angular charcoal pieces are likely to have derived from low temperature burns, probably from small-scale events such as campfires in the local vicinity, maybe as close as several hundred metres. The very fine charcoal fragments are most likely to have derived from larger scale, higher temperature events at some distance (up to several kilometres) from the site of deposition. There exists the intriguing possibility that such carbonaceous particles were produced by proto-industrial activity such as smelting.

Salix (willow) (Fig. 3a) does not preserve well, being a fragile and delicate grain, but its presence here (sample FP1) suggests the existence of well developed and semi permanent dune slacks. Although it is very difficult to distinguish between *Salix* varieties, the location of the sample sites and the nature of the sediments in which the pollen have been found support this view. In addition *Salix* pollen is usually unrepresented, making the sample count even more significant. *Salix repens* (the creeping willow) is the variety most common in the dunes and slacks of the present day Sefton dune system and so it is highly likely that the fossil *Salix* found in FP1 represents the close proximity of large, mature, wet dune slacks.

Another genus that is represented (Fig. 3a) in all but one sample layer (FP5) is *Betula* (birch). This tree produces an abundance of easily recognized pollen, although it is difficult to differentiate between species, particularly in samples such as these from Formby. Because of its abundance it can be over represented but it is nevertheless important within the

context of this research. Birch, along with alder, represents a significant part of the fen hydrosere and consequently is often taken to represent that kind of wet environment. However, it is also found as part of the mature stages of a psammosere (sand dune succession) growing happily either in or near dune heath or in dune scrub.

The family *Cyperaceae* (Fig. 3b) includes species of sedge that are found in both wet dune slacks and marshlands, both freshwater fens and estuarine salt marshes. Their pollen is difficult to distinguish, more so when the quality of preservation is compromised. Values are highest in FP2 but without more work it is impossible to be sure which environment the fossil remains are representing. However, it is more likely that they indicate the freshwater conditions found in large, well developed wet slacks or on fen marshes, simply because estuarine – salt marsh conditions often reduce the chances of preservation.

The 'herb' group (Fig. 3c) includes pollen from the *Compositae* family; C. tubuliflorae (e.g *Bellis perennis* - daisy) and C. liguliflorae (e.g. *Taraxacum officinale* - common dandelion) have highly distinguishable and well preserved pollen grains. The many different species within this family have been grouped together, though in most pollen diagrams the liguliflorae and tubuliflorae would be separated, since they are, in dune ecosystems, representative of groups of herbs found chiefly on the drier dune slack and dune ridges. Other families are also grouped here, again to represent the drier and mature dunes.

Gramineae (Fig. 3b) are the grasses. Easily identifiable when well preserved, the pollen is extremely difficult to differentiate when conditions have been less favorable, simply because the grains crumple, fold and degrade. However, percentage values are reasonably high in spite of the poor preservation, and this is indicative of, and representative of, large 'open' landscapes such as those found in dune systems.

Finally, the *Filicales* group (Fig. 3b) includes the spores of ferns which are found in woodlands and freshwater fens. Interestingly, all the samples contained these spores, which often are well preserved because of their bean-like shape and tough outer coat. Even when crumpled, these grains are often identifiable. Another group included in the diagrams (Fig. 3c) is the 'spores'. Included here are grains produced by mosses which were most likely to have been growing in the mature ('grey') dunes, much as they do today.

5.4 Discussion

The pollen data enable us to reconstruct a landscape characterized by a variety of coastal and terrestrial environments. The well documented research by Tooley and others has recreated palaeoenvironments in the region. This work has examined the fossil remains from samples that contain a wealth of footprints and so it allows us to describe the kinds of environments that were being exploited by the human and animal populations at the time.

The data confirm the highly varied and mixed nature of the environments in the coastal zone such as dunes and freshwater slacks, lagoons, scrubland, heath, freshwater marshes and woodland. It is highly likely that the mixture of coastal environments was always within 'striking distance' of the mature woodlands, the 'Wild Wood' of the mid-Holocene.

This paper proposes that over the period of significant footprint activity, coastal environments changed markedly, though it is most likely that the various environments listed above were present in differing proportions or at variable distances from the sampling site. As with modern coastal environments, the variability implied by the pollen data is a measure of the richness and variety found within rapidly changeable and responsive systems. Such diversity, producing a wide range of natural resources, would have been attractive to both people and animals.

The presence of *Salix* (willow) in FP1 and FP6, together the herbs and grasses, suggest two periods of established dunes with slacks and ridges, FP1 having dune heath, which means that the dune system was extensive. Since FP1 also has the most charcoal – charcoal fragments that are very small and more rounded – it is possible that the dune heath may have been fire controlled. Evidence of mixed woodland in samples FP2 to FP5 suggest that the dunes may have been further away from the sample sites; either breached by tidal inundation or degraded and replaced by lagoons and creeks and with woodland much closer (higher *Quercus* values). Interestingly, the lowest and oldest sample (FPbase) has the highest proportion of *Gramineae* pollen, which may indicate either dune grasslands or high marsh.

Figure 4a: Phase 1

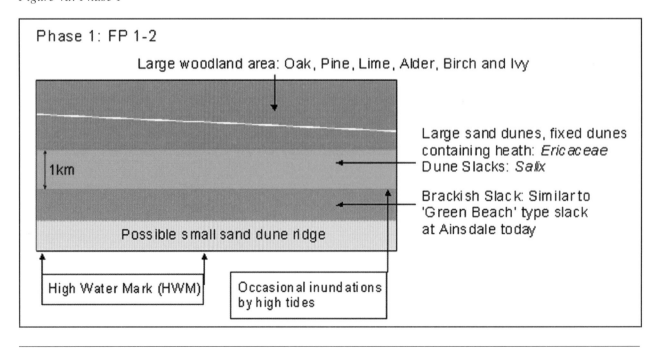

Figure 4b: Phase 2

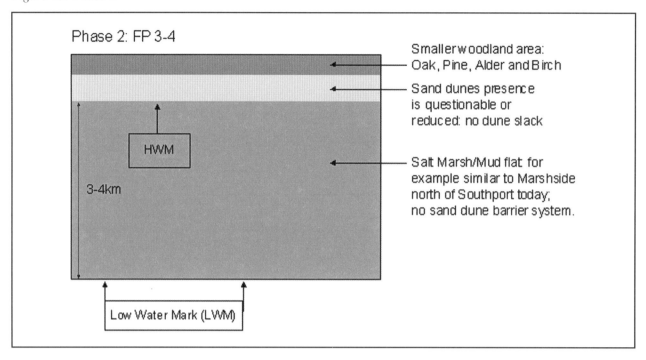

Figure 4c: Phase 3

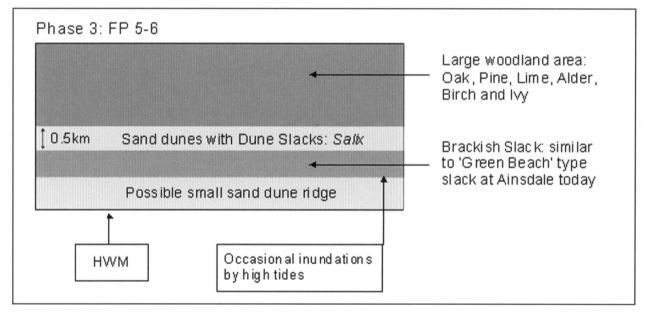

Figures 4a – 4c are schematic representations of all the pollen data. By combining the percentage values of the flora known to be indicative of a particular environment it is possible to describe the environmental change around the sample sites as a series of phases.

Each phase includes two of the FP layers and they enable us to 'visualise' the way in which the coastal zone changed over time. At each phase the coastal zone would have been characterised by areas that would have been resource rich with a remarkable

variety of plants and animals. Such diversity and abundance would have 'earmarked' the area for exploitation. Groups of people may well have tracked across muddy lagoons, sand dunes and marshes in the search for organisms that would have provided much to support their needs.

It is exciting to consider that the very shores we now enjoy provided bounty for people 5,000 years ago.

Searching for Lost Settlements - the example of Meols

Robert A. Philpott

Introduction

A cursory glance at the map might give the impression that the coast of north west England is a fixed and unchanging line. In fact the soft coastline of the region is far from static but is a dynamic zone of continuously changing shape and position. Two stretches of that coastline either side of the Mersey estuary, in Sefton District and north Wirral, share a number of common features. Both have a lowlying coastal landscape protected against incursion of the sea by an extensive zone of sand dunes of some antiquity, backed by extensive mossland. Both have experienced a complex sequence of marine regression and transgression which has led to the repeated deposition then inundation of a series of land surfaces. An important characteristic of both coastal zones is the dune belt which has developed over earlier land surfaces, sealing a buried landscape beneath the sand, and shifting over time. The processes of shifting sand dunes and changing sea level, coastal erosion and deposition have in turn had an impact on human settlement and activity along the coast. In both cases coastal erosion has occurred in recent centuries. The Sefton coast at Formby Point has suffered marine erosion since 1906 with a 5 km stretch of the coastline affected; over 400 m of coast has been lost to erosion in the 20th century, at an average rate of about 4 m per year (Smith 1999, 24).

A map drawn by Charles Eyes in 1792 and updated in 1847 (MDHB Records, NML Archives) (fig.1) shows that the Wirral coast lost a strip of land up to 450 m wide between the 1770s and the late 19th century when the completion of the sea defences largely prevented further erosion. In the case of the north Wirral coast, the erosion during the 19th century produced a rich yield of archaeological finds, largely from the Meols-Hoylake area. This paper will examine briefly the evidence for Roman and later settlement of the north Wirral coast in the light of a recent study of the Meols artefacts and the sites from which they came. It will also consider the rather less well known archaeology of the Sefton coastal landscape and assess its potential in the light of the evidence from north Wirral.

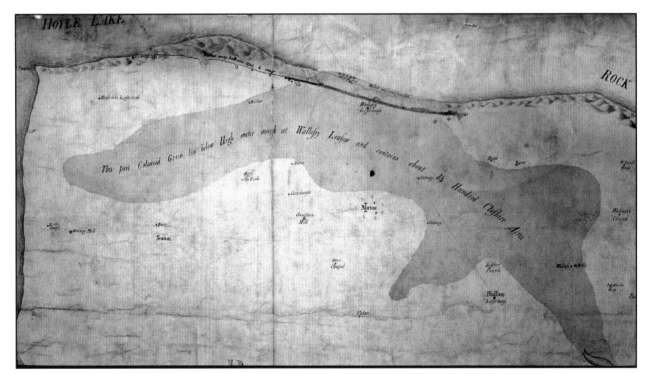

Fig. 1: Detail of Charles Eyes' map (1792) of the north Wirral coast, annotated to show extent of erosion to 1848 (courtesy of Trustees of National Museums Liverpool)

The North Wirral Coast: Meols

In 1846 Reverend Abraham Hume visited the parsonage in Hoylake and noticed a group of objects on the mantelpiece. Enquiring where they were from he was told that they had been picked up by an old man who had since 1828 amused himself by collecting objects he noticed on the shore (Hume 1863, 47). Hume published an account of the early finds in 1847 and, once the antiquarians became aware of the rich deposits of finds, they and their local contacts regularly scoured the beach for artefacts. Other antiquarians such as Henry Ecroyd Smith from the 1850s and Charles Potter from the 1860s began to collect either by visiting the shore in person or buying from local people. As more material came to light Hume followed up his initial study with a remarkable work, 'Ancient Meols', published in 1863, which illustrated no fewer than 350 objects, and represented an erudite study of the finds then available from his own and others' collections. The material came to light through the rapid erosion of the north Wirral coast during the 19th century, which exposed and then removed a series of buried land surfaces which underlay the coastal sand dunes. Out of these eroding occupation deposits were washed several thousand objects which were then deposited on the shore at Great Meols. Over the course of about 60 years, nearly 20 individuals amassed collections, numbering from a handful to many hundreds, or even thousands, of finds (fig. 2). Active collecting continued until the early 20th century but the yield of the 'produce of the Cheshire shore' was then in serious decline, in part no doubt due to the embankments preventing further erosion.

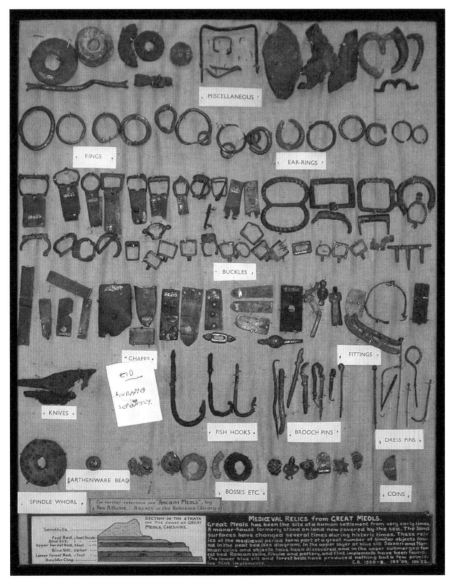

Fig. 2: Display board from Warrington Museum and Art Gallery showing a range of Meols finds

Estimates of the total range upwards of 5,000 objects. In 1867, admittedly 'an unusually propitious' year, no fewer than 906 objects were found on or near the sea-beach (Ecroyd Smith 1868, 126), while in the seven-year period from 1862 to 1868 a total of 1,968 objects of all dates were found. The objects themselves ranged in date from the Mesolithic period to the 18th century in date; although the great majority, including over 2,500 of the surviving pieces, belong to the later medieval period, that is from the Norman conquest to about AD 1500 (Hume 1863) (fig.3), and there was a swift decline in finds from the early 16th century onwards. Some classes of medieval objects are present in huge numbers. There are for instance over 800 belt fittings, 119 brooches, 127 knives and over 50 keys, but the assemblage includes a wide range of finds including leather shoes, pilgrim badges, personal seals, domestic equipment such as candleholders, military or hunting equipment such as arrowheads, crossbow bolts and chain mail, and agricultural tools such as shears and hoes.

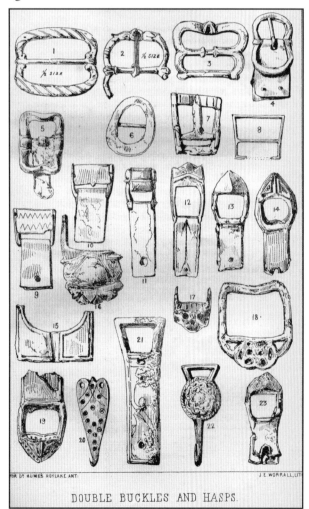

Fig. 3: Plate IX from Abraham Hume's 'Ancient Meols' (1863) illustrating medieval finds

About 3,000 of the finds from Meols survive in museums today. A recent study, co-ordinated by the writer with Dr David Griffiths of Oxford University and Dr Geoff Egan of the Museum of London Specialist Services (Griffiths et al. 2007), together with a team of nearly twenty specialists, aimed to document and catalogue all the finds. This has involved examining surviving objects as well as using illustrations or descriptions of those which are now lost to reconstruct the finds assemblage and to re-assess its significance in the light of modern scholarship. The project has also examined the information on the findspots and the circumstances of recovery to cast light on the early use of the coastline and the settlements that grew up there.

One of the significant characteristics of the Meols finds was the way in which objects of different periods tended to concentrate in different sections of the shore. Although the sparse Iron Age finds were not recognised as such at the time and their locations were not distinguished in most cases, material of later periods tend to cluster together in discrete zones. Romano-British finds occurred on the east side of the Dove Point promontory, early medieval items (Anglo-Saxon and Viking) came from about a mile to the west, while the later medieval finds were largely concentrated between the two. One important implication is that there was not a single 'site', but rather a sequence of sites or settlements, and these appear to show a steady drift along the coastline. Although we cannot currently reconstruct in detail the shoreline and the Hoyle Lake from the Roman to medieval period, it appears likely that the complex relationship between the various factors – changing sea level, shifting off-shore channels, the presence of a deep water anchorage, protective sand bars and the coastline – has led to a shift in the location of sites chosen for settlement and the zones of the shore used at various times.

The Sefton Coast Dunes

Like the north Wirral shore, the Sefton coast has a dune belt of some antiquity. The '-meols' place-names, derived from Norse 'melr' meaning sand bank, indicate the presence of sand dunes on the

Sefton coast by the Norse period, and studies by Innes and Tooley show that the dunes have a much earlier origin. Blown sand deposits are found sealing peat as early as 4510±50BP at Sniggery Wood near Little Crosby (Innes and Tooley 1993, 36). An initial period of sand migration and dune building occurred on the Sefton coast between about 4600BP and 4000BP; the suggested mechanism is that a fall in sea level provided a large reservoir of intertidal sandy deposits which became destabilised on drying and blew inland, creating a barrier system (Innes and Tooley 1993, 39). Furthermore, there is evidence that sand-blows eventually overwhelmed the mossland at Downholland Moss and Sniggery Wood.

Another phase of dune stability occurred after about 2500BP when soils developed and peats accumulated in the dune slacks (Innes and Tooley 1993, 39) and hoof prints of domestic oxen were contained in a dune slack soil. This layer was associated with an oak stump with a radiocarbon date of 2510±120BP (Plater et al. 1993, 29).

Later periods of dune stability are suggested by analogy with areas close to Liverpool Bay, although no direct evidence has come from the Sefton coast. At Ansdell on the north shore of the Ribble organic horizons and peat intercalating sand have been dated to between 1795±240BP and 1370±85BP; pollen of mixed oak woodland and cereals were evident. The latest is found at Lytham broadly in parallel with north Wirral where Kenna's work indicated dates on 'soil bed' and deposits and peaty bands in the dune system of the north Wirral. These latter ranged in date from 925±50BP to 540±40BP, containing typical dune slack pollen flora (Kenna 1986).

Early, though undated, soil layers have been identified under the Sefton beach dunes from the late 18th century onwards, when an early ground surface up to 4 inches (10 cm) thick buried under as much as 2 feet (0.61 m) of sand could be seen on the coast at Formby (Holt 1795, 8; cited in Lewis 2002, 9). Similar layers of buried soil deposits have been noted in recent times exposed through tidal and wind erosion (Smith 1999, 35-6; cited in Lewis 2002, 9).

Fig. 4: Dove Point, Meols from the air (R. Philpott, courtesy of NML)

A Comparative Survey

A brief chronological survey of the settlement evidence along the coastal zone from the late Iron Age to the later medieval period will attempt to draw out areas of similarity and divergence between the Wirral and Sefton coasts. In particular the recorded archaeological discoveries of Meols in Wirral will be used as an example to illuminate the potential of the Sefton coast.

Iron Age and Roman Meols

At Meols one of the most important features of the coast was Dove Point, a triangular promontory which projected from the northern Wirral shore. Close to the promontory and just off shore was a deep channel protected by sandbanks from the wind and tides. The channel, known as the Hoyle Lake, is recorded in documents from the medieval period (fig. 4). A deed in the Chartulary of the Abbey of St Werburgh mentions the 'lake of Hilbre which is called the Heypool' [*lacum de Hildeburghey que uocatur le Heypol*], *c*. 1245-83 (Tait 1923, 298). The Hoyle Lake silted up quickly during the post-medieval period, probably in part due to the canalisation of the Dee which altered the flow at the mouth of the estuary. Captain Greenville Collins shows between five and seven fathoms of water on his chart of 1689 (fig. 5),

but by 1847 the Lake had largely silted up, with only a chain of isolated pools no more than a fathom deep along the former channel, and by the end of the 19th century it had virtually disappeared.

The coastal location combined with the excellent natural harbour of the Hoyle Lake had made it an attractive location as a port from the middle Iron Age through to the medieval period, when it was one of a series of ports along the Dee coast of the Wirral peninsula towards Chester. Finds at Meols date from the 5th century BC and include late 3rd century BC coins from Carthage and 1st century BC coins struck by the Coriosolites tribe of Brittany and the Channel Islands, demonstrating the distant destination of the long-range trade route along the west coast of England and Wales. Cheshire salt is one of the traceable commodities which may have been shipped out from the port during the mid and late Iron Age. The Cheshire Stony VCP (Very Coarse Pottery) containers which can be traced to the brine springs of the Middlewich to Nantwich area show a distinct coastal distribution around North Wales and even extend as far as the Severn estuary (Morris 1985; Matthews 1999). The significance and strategic potential of the port was recognised by the Roman army in the mid 1st century AD. Meols saw activity in the early Roman period, as a remarkable group of pre-Flavian finds (dating to pre-AD 68) testifies. These include coins of Augustus (fig.6), Claudius and Nero, a military belt-buckle, a rim from an imported samian dish and brooches of mid 1st century AD type.

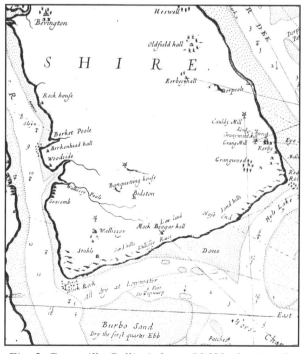

Fig. 5: Greenville Collins' chart of 1689, showing the north Wirral coast and the Hoyle Lake

Fig. 6: Four Roman coins of Augustus found at Meols (donated by Mr K. Herd to NML; acc.no. LIV.2005.34)

The explanation for such a group of very early finds, virtually unprecedented in north west England, suggests that the existing port at Meols was used by the Roman army in offensives against the Brigantes to the north and against the Druids of Anglesey in north west Wales. Significantly Meols lay on a wedge of territory of the Cornovian tribe who appear to have been one of the tribes that surrendered to Claudius after the invasion of AD 43 and remained friendly to the Roman administration after the conquest of south eastern England. Of critical importance for the Roman troops was the location of the existing harbour.

With the foundation of the legionary fortress at Chester in the AD 70s, and the permanent occupation of the region by the Roman army, Meols may have lost some of its initial strategic importance. Nevertheless, the finds show that the port remained in use throughout the Roman period. Finds include a substantial collection of over 120 Roman coins, 70 brooches, an exceptional group of over 30 Roman ear-rings and other material, though relatively little pottery – but they serve to show that the port acted as a market place, and probably also retained some military significance. One role may have been as a port of transhipment for minerals from north Wales where vessels unloaded cargoes from sea-going to river barges for Chester, as well as a refuge port on the important west coast trading route. The port remained active until the end of the Roman period, the latest coin dating to Magnus Maximus, AD 383-8. The discovery of a late 4th or early 5th century military belt buckle plate at Meols hints that its strategic location on the northern tip of Wirral may once again have lent it a military role in the late Roman period. At that time pirates in the Irish Sea threatened the coast and appear to have required the construction of defences in north Wales (at Segontium and Holyhead) and at Lancaster, all sites facing the Irish Sea.

The hinterland of the port in north Wirral has also begun in the last decade or so to produce evidence of Romano-British settlements on the dryland fringes of

the large lowlying mossland area behind Meols itself. Finds of Roman material at townships at Bidston, Moreton, and Newton within 3km or so of the shore may derive from a series of rural settlements in the hinterland of the port.

Sefton in the Roman Period

In the Iron Age and Roman period the particular location of Meols, on a promontory close to two major river estuaries, and at the margin of territory of three different tribes, and close to the mineral resources of north Wales made it something of a special case, its importance determined by the conjunction of tribal boundaries and favourable physical geographical location during the invasion and occupation phases. This being so, it is worth examining briefly areas of similarity and difference between Meols and the Sefton coastal zone.

F. W. Walbank observed half a century ago, that, '…in general, South-west Lancashire west of the road north from Warrington – an area of thick wood and marshland – is still a blank space on the map of Roman Britain' (1953, 219). However, within this wider area a combination of aerial photography, chance finds and systematic fieldwork has demonstrated that the Romano-British population of the lowland north west was considerably higher than could have been imagined even 20 years ago. To give just one example, an archaeological survey of the metropolitan district of Knowsley in the early 1980s (Cowell 1981), covering all known sources of information, produced just three widely dispersed Roman coins. Intensive research, largely in advance of development and in particular of the construction of the A5300 road, has transformed that picture. By 1997 the district had produced an Iron Age enclosure with structures which was reused in the Roman period at Brook House Farm, Halewood, an unenclosed Romano-British settlement at Brunt Boggart, Tarbock, a Romano-British tile manufacturing site at Ochre Brook, Tarbock, used by contractors to produce roof tile for the rebuilding of the legionary fortress at Chester (Cowell and Philpott 2000), and an unenclosed settlement with over a dozen Romano-

British buildings at Court Farm, Halewood (Adams and Philpott, forthcoming). In addition, fieldwalking has produced Roman pottery from a site at Rainhill, while a sherd of pottery at Prescot hints at Roman activity on the hilltop. The transformation in understanding has been achieved by concerted research, fieldwork and excavation.

In the Sefton coastal zone the generally flatter and lower-lying topography, prone to flooding and inundation, suggests that a high priority for settlement would be the areas of slightly raised, and therefore better drained, ground. The dryland islands which were so important in prehistory (see Cowell this vol.) were equally significant for later settled populations and we might expect topography to constrain the location of settlement within the lowlying marshy environment in the Iron Age or Romano-British period as it did in the selection of medieval sites in Sefton and West Lancashire.

The same constraints operated upon the Romano-British population, though the evidence is rather limited as yet, and may have depended upon such factors as differences in the overall sea-level at various periods. Support for this view is found in one township, Ince Blundell. The place-name is British in origin, and first appears, in the Domesday Book, as *Hinne*, from *Inis* meaning island, in recognition of its slight elevation in a generally lowlying landscape (Ekwall 1922, 118). It is possibly no coincidence that one of the few pieces of evidence of a probable Romano-British settlement is found in the township. A small rectangular enclosure with a clearly defined entrance, observed as a cropmark, is almost certainly a farmstead. Although the site is technically undated, a dispersed group of Roman objects found by metal-detecting in the vicinity is likely to represent stray finds lost near the farmstead.

Elsewhere in Sefton district, finds of Roman material do occur on either side of the dune belt although nowhere in great quantity. The coast between Blundellsands and Crosby has produced a thin scatter of Roman material. An *antoninianus* of Claudius II (AD 268-70) was found on the shore at Blundellsands but there are no more details of the findspot. Other coins include a bronze *sestertius* of Julia Mamaea (AD 222-235) about three yards from the sand-dunes about 4 inches (10 cm) down at Formby and a bronze *antoninianus* of Tetricus I (AD 270-3) about 200 yards west of the dunes at Formby (Liverpool Museum records). The Crosby shore has also produced a coin of Nero dated AD 64-66 (OS Record Card). More concentrated are a possible Roman needle, an 'ornament', and two fragments of mortarium at Altmouth, which were given to Liverpool Museum but were lost in the war. In about 1866 near Formby village were recovered a coin of Constantine I or one of his sons dating to the first half of the 4th century and a Republican silver *denarius* of Sergia (Ecroyd Smith 1868, 90-4). In the late 1980s and early 1990s two further Roman coins (one of Hadrian; the other of the 4th century AD, possibly of Constantine I or II) were found on the shore near Formby Point (PAS Database: N. Herepath pers. comm.; J. Lewis pers. comm.).

There is some evidence that small tidal creeks were used elsewhere in the Merseyside area during the Roman period. Two coin hoards at Otterspool, one late Roman, the other possibly Anglo-Saxon (Ecroyd Smith 1866a; 1866b), a hoard of five Roman coins deposited c.320 in the upper end of the Pool of Liverpool (Gladstone 1932, 8), and the position of the Iron Age enclosure at Brook House Farm, Halewood next to a tidal inlet of Ditton Brook, which was also occupied in the Romano-British period (Cowell and Philpott 2000), all point to the exploitation of these significant topographical locations in the Roman period. They may have been local havens for vessels though their very existence suggests they may have attracted settlement at various periods in the past. This receives its most graphic demonstration in the choice of the tidal pool for the creation of the royal borough at Liverpool in 1207 by King John. Clusters of finds, as well as small numbers of known enclosure sites, demonstrate the existence of rural settlements close to the estuary shores of the Dee and the Mersey.

The coin finds at Formby village and scattered finds along the coastline are likely to represent settlements rather than casual losses. The mouth of the Alt might have seen some activity as part of trading along the west coast route during the Roman period. The apparent concentration of Roman finds in the vicinity of Formby Point suggest a further possible focus of activity, perhaps connected with the 'Wicks Wood Gap', a buried channel which has been tentatively interpreted as a possible former outlet of Downholland Brook or 'Formby's lost harbour' (Huddart et al. 1999b).

Further Roman finds are known from the slightly raised ground east of the main mossland belt which extends from Scarisbrick to Altcar, largely within West Lancashire. Jennifer Lewis has collected the evidence for these. There are records of coins from the Birkdale side of Halsall Moss, before 1949, which include a *denarius* of Hadrian now in the Botanic Gardens Museum, Southport (Darley accessions 1949, no. L.H.1: info from a list drawn up by J. Lewis), and others including 'some' of Vespasian, whose present whereabouts are not known. According to a label in the Botanic Gardens Museum, the silver *denarius* is one of a number found from time to time in the same locality by different workmen. These finds, which extended over many years, included coins in various states of preservation, but some of Vespasian (AD 69-79) were almost in mint condition. Roman coins are also recorded as 'found on the surface of the marshland' at Great Crosby (Reade 1881, 439), but once again the precise spot is not recorded. A coin of Vespasian was found in about 1899 at Martin Mere (North Meols) (Blundell 1924, 207). Other finds of Roman material at North Meols are reported to have been discovered before 1860 by Thomas Brookfield. They consisted of 'a number of sepulchral silver urns and coins from the time of Vespasian'; the urns were said to be 'ranged like mugs on a buttery shelf' (Bulpit 1908). The report would carry more conviction if the word 'silver' were attached to the coins rather than the urns.

Moving further inland, the higher ground of the Halsall area has also produced a number of Roman coins of 2nd-4th century date, as well as a Greek bronze coin of Seleucus III of Syria (225-223 BC) which was found on Halsall Moss; and there is an unverified report of another Greek bronze found a couple of fields away. Although the Greek coins could be modern losses of souvenirs brought back by soldiers serving in various Middle East campaigns, the possibility that they are ancient losses cannot be totally dismissed. It is perhaps worth noting that the port at Meols produced three Carthaginian coins of almost exactly the same date. The Roman coins, however, appear much more likely to represent settlement on the drier and better drained land overlooking the moss than either Iron Age trade or modern introductions.

In the past such speculation over the extent and location of Romano-British settlement in the Sefton coastal district could have been dismissed as no more than that. The coastal zone is not an easy environment in which to identify sites. The extensive dune cover cloaks the landscape and gives little opportunity either for cropmarks to develop or chance finds to come to light. The recovery of large numbers of finds is not in itself likely given the low level of material culture of the population of the time. However, we are on much more solid ground now with analogy from adjacent districts, and we may be able now to identify a series of locations where coastal activity might be expected, as well as inland areas as the focus of settlement. The reporting of every stray find or metal-detected coin is of considerable value in building up a picture of the extent and date of settlement, and allows the identification of potential concentrations which may indicate settlements or other activities. Continuous monitoring of eroding faces of the dunes or of development or other groundworks within and behind the dune belt will be needed to ensure that fugitive traces of early settlement are recognised and investigated appropriately.

The Early Medieval Period (AD 410-1066)

Anglo-Saxon Meols

The nature of the site at Meols in the early medieval period is difficult to determine. It may not even have taken the form of a permanently occupied settlement, instead perhaps operating as a seasonal beach market. Nevertheless the port continued in use into the post-Roman period. Imports include a group of penannular brooches of 5th and 6th century date recorded by Hume and representing perhaps local or regional trade while long range Mediterranean contacts appear to have been maintained with the Byzantine empire from here as elsewhere in western Britain and Ireland (Harris 2003, 143-54). Finds include a pottery pilgrim flask from the shrine of St Menas near Alexandria in Egypt and three 6th and early 7th century Byzantine coins from Meols and nearby Moreton (Thompson 1956; Philpott 1999). These indicate that the west coast trade route continued in operation throughout what is generally an archaeologically impoverished period. For the 8th century a variety of finds, including two Frisian sceattas, suggests contacts across the Irish Sea and the continent (Metcalf 1992). Once again the peripheral coastal location of Meols, on the outer limit of Mercian territory, but easily accessible from the Isle of Man, Wales and Northumbria, was an important factor in its continued success as a port (Griffiths 1992).

Sefton

As elsewhere in the north west of England, the Anglo-Saxon period in Sefton remains elusive in archaeological terms. The early medieval period in Sefton has been discussed in detail by Lewis (2002) and little can be added here. Place-names such as Melling and Bootle indicate the general location of Anglo-Saxon settlements, though nothing has yet been found to pinpoint these sites archaeologically. A Northumbrian *styca* of Aethelred II dated to AD 844 found on Formby beach represents the only direct artefactual evidence of Anglo-Saxon activity. Such coins are not rare in Cumbria and Lancashire and fall into a pattern of evidence for local coastal trade (Metcalf 1992, 96).

One unusual class of find from the wider region has a bearing on the use of waterborne transport during this archaeologically virtually invisible period. Early medieval logboats, of a type suitable for use in inland waterways and estuaries, have been found at several locations. One at Martin Mere was radiocarbon-dated to the 6th century AD (Beta-94788 1560±70BP), while no fewer than nine logboats found in a 20 km stretch of the Mersey (especially around Warrington) have been dated to between the 9th and 12th centuries (McGrail and Switsur 1979).

Viking settlement

In the Norse or Anglo-Scandinavian period the Irish Sea coastal regions of both south west Lancashire and north Wirral saw settlement by Norse from Ireland and perhaps the Isle of Man. The origin of the settlement may lie in expulsion of Norse from Ireland in AD 902 (Finberg 1975a), although Norse settlement in Wirral in the early 10th century may have reinforced existing settlement rather than being wholly initiated by Aethelflaeda's grant of 'lands near Chester' to Hingamund, the leader of the Viking group which was expelled from Dublin. Fellows-Jensen has argued on place-name evidence that the Wirral and south west Lancashire settlers may have come from the Isle of Man rather than Ireland, while the prevalence of '*by*' names suggests a Danish component (1992, 39). Concentrations of Norse place-names demonstrate the extent of the settlement (fig.7), while in each case what were effectively enclaves of Viking settlement appear to have been defined formally, with Raby in Wirral and the etymologically identical Roby near Prescot forming the boundaries (*ra-by*, ON boundary farm or village). Each enclave also has a Thingwall, or 'field where an assembly meets', providing a physical focus for these self-governing communities (ON *þing-vollr*: Dodgson 1972, 273).

Meols appears to have acted as a beach market where trading took place on the beach or shore nearby at recognised times, such as fairs, out of the jurisdiction of officials (Griffiths 1992). Norse finds include a fine series of nearly 20 ring-headed pins, a larger

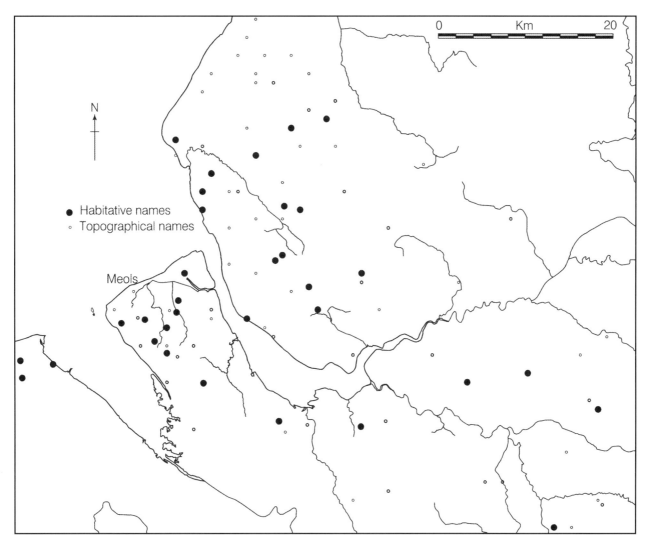

Fig. 7: Distribution of Norse place names in Wirral and south west Lancashire (after Fellows-Jensen 1992)

collection than the important *burh* and trading settlement at Chester, for example, and the largest group known outside Dublin; there are also strap-ends, buckles and mounts; a stirrup mount bears a 10th-11th century Ringerike design. The market function is attested by over 20 Anglo-Saxon coins of 10th and 11th century date, from mints as diverse as York, Canterbury, Winchester, Shrewsbury and Chester, and including one of perhaps only two Hiberno-Norse coins found in England (Griffiths 1992). Objects of characteristically Hiberno-Norse style such as the ring pins demonstrate that the direction of trade was aligned largely towards Ireland. The variety of finds, which include Irish pieces, is not typical of a small fishing and agricultural settlement. The role of Meols in the 10th and 11th centuries formed a contrast to the highly regulated port at the

burh of Chester where the Domesday Book indicates tight control over shipping and goods by the later 11th century. By contrast Meols was a trading settlement at the northern end of a separate political entity, the northern Wirral Viking enclave and, as David Griffiths has suggested, served the needs of this separate community (1992, 69). Higham has suggested the estates of the Scandinavian lords in both south Lancashire and Wirral were purchased by King Edward in AD 920. From then they formed part of the Mercian Kingdom, and would have allowed Edward to retain control over the Mersey crossings and to extend his authority northwards as far as the Ribble (Higham 1992, 28). South Lancashire and Wirral may have passed to the direct control of King Edward in his accord with northerners in AD 920 (Higham 1992, 28).

Place names of Norse origin along the Sefton coastal zone reflect the existence of a distinct Scandinavian enclave, with a preponderance of Scandinavian place names. The Norse settlement extended from the coast inland as far as Knowsley and, like Wirral, had an assembly mound at Thingwall and a Raby (here named Roby) on the enclave boundary. Amongst the concentration of Norse names, two distinct types of names can be discerned. Habitative names ending in –by such as Formby or Crosby point to places characterised by settlements, while toponyms were names bestowed on topographical features. Several places such as North Meols, Ravenmeols or Argarmeols containing the element meols from Old Norse melr, sandbank, sandhill (Ekwall 1922, 15), demonstrating that sand dunes were already a dominant topographical feature of the coastline by the 10th century. Ekwall notes in the Cockersand deeds of the end of the 12th and 13th centuries that many place names or field names in Ainsdale, are Scandinavian in origin, containing Norse elements such as hou, skarth, slet and storr (1922, 250), often referring to minor features of the landscape. As Norse personal names also survive by this time, it is clear that some names could have been bestowed on the landscape or fields after the Norse period proper, once words had passed into the local dialect.

Whilst the place names and field names point to a distinctive Norse settlement and go some way to determining the area of such settlement, the physical evidence for such settlement is much harder to find. The only substantial Viking-period find, discovered in 1611 is the Harkirk coin hoard, buried c.910 at Little Crosby, consisting of over 80 coins as well as some ingots, and dating to the first generation of Viking settlement (Edwards 1992, 52-4). The coins are now lost although reputedly some were melted down and made into a pyx which was used in Little Crosby chapel. We know nothing directly of the Norse settlements along the Sefton coast. However, elsewhere in Scandinavian regions the settlement pattern is dispersed, based on the individual farm or estate, rather than nucleated villages. The population was almost certainly not dense – the parishes, which

were probably founded by the 11th century, were large, usually an indication of a low population density; and much land such as the moss was lowlying, poorly drained and unattractive to settlement. It has been suggested by several writers that the Norse settlers occupied uninhabited or unoccupied land in the lowlying coastal zone by contrast with Anglian settlements which tended to occupy the higher and better drained land further inland (discussed by Lewis 1982, 26-7). Slight evidence from Wirral suggests that Norse settlement occupied discrete farms. The excavated site at Irby produced a distinctive bow-sided building form, found in a sequence later than Romano-British roundhouses but earlier than medieval rectangular structures (Philpott and Adams, forthcoming). Only one datable artefact was directly associated with structural evidence, a distinctive 10th-12th century spike lamp deposited in a building foundation gully, but is sufficient to open up the possibility that this is Norse-period occupation at this township whose name itself points to Norse settlement by Irishmen (Irby = ON 'farm of the Irish': Dodgson 1972, 264).

The intervisibility of the Sefton and Wirral enclaves suggests Meols could have served as a major port in the Irish Sea for both communities. The largely coastal settlements of Norse communities – each self-governing with its own 'thing' and defined boundaries – are in any event likely to have maintained strong mutual contact, linked by ties of common language, kinship and commerce. Communication overland involves a protracted journey and their historic seafaring tradition suggests there must have been constant traffic on the short sea journey across the mouth of the Mersey estuary between the two adjacent Norse communities. Such connections by water inevitably raise the question of where a Norse-period harbour might lie in the Sefton coast. One obvious answer is the mouth of the Alt, a river name of British origin in an area of relatively dense Scandinavian settlement, although the tidal mouth of the Crossens Pool, north of the early settlement of Crossens, offers another potential harbour further north. This may have also benefited from the proximity of Fairclough's

Lake, a safe tidal anchorage off the North Meols coast which, as Fearon and Eyes's chart of 1738 shows, survived until the 18th century (J. Lewis pers. comm.; Aughton 1988, 75-7). Jennifer Lewis has summarised the evidence for the use of the mouth of the Alt in historic times as a harbour (2002, 8-9). There is an early 13th century reference to 'Skypul' at Altmouth (Hulton 1847) and a possible landing place by the early 18th century opposite Alt Grange on the north bank. However, changes in the river mouth may have obscured the original channel. These early ports need not have permanent installations such as quays or piers for unloading vessels. Boats could be beached and unloaded by carts at low tide with no need for permanent infrastructure (McGrail 1997, 65-70). Their use as ports may be inferred from documentary references allied with concentrations of finds, although it is common for many types of goods passing through a port to leave no trace of their passage, particularly in the case of perishable organic cargoes.

Later Medieval Meols

For the later medieval period (roughly 1066-1500), in many other respects, Meols is far from an exceptional settlement. At that time, there is little in the documentary record to suggest that Meols was anything other than a minor coastal village. It was a rural township in the parish of West Kirby, possessing neither a parish church nor even a chapel of ease. It did not support a large population and the basis of its economy was in part agricultural, supplemented (by the post-medieval period or earlier) by fishing, as the large collection of fish-hooks demonstrates. Little is documented of its activities; yet this small coastal village has the distinction of producing an assemblage of medieval finds which, for many classes of object such as dress accessories, is second only to London in size and scope, and in some cases surpasses it.

The size of the assemblage requires some explanation. In part the distinctiveness of Meols lies in a chain of coincidence which led to the preservation and subsequent discovery of such a large quantity of finds. What set of circumstances produced such a vast assemblage of finds from such an undistinguished settlement? First it seems likely that some material was lost or discarded by the existing population of the village at Meols, including a worn leather shoe found *in situ* in a midden. In addition, there is some evidence that the inhabitants were manufacturing some items, the best evidence being a buckle with casting sprues still attached. The total amount of metal and other items may have been swelled by the presence of locally manufactured items in the village, and perhaps stock of objects for resale. Furthermore, the longstanding port of the Hoyle Lake seems to have operated as a hidden market. One of its attractions as a port in the later medieval period is that it lay on stretch of coastline which fell outside the jurisdiction of the two medieval port authorities of Chester and Frodsham, which covered the Dee and Mersey shores respectively; thus effectively it was unregulated (J. Laughton pers. comm.). This introduced a trading element to the settlement, with more material circulating in the village than was used solely by its inhabitants. Items such as coins were probably lost during trading; the medieval coins contain a high proportion of the tiny cut half or quarter pennies, which were legitimately subdivided to create small change, but once dropped were difficult to find. While this might account for the presence of a large quantity of objects in use or circulation than at an inland rural settlement of comparable size, it still fails to account for that amount of material being available to be found. In medieval England metal items were almost invariably recycled once broken beyond repair. The extremely low volume of finds at the few excavated rural settlements in the north west is testament to the efficiency of that process. But these by themselves are still not enough to account for an assemblage nearly as large as that of London.

A further step in the process of the creation of this large assemblage may be postulated. The large number of medieval artefacts from Meols may result from the settlement being engulfed on more than one occasion by shifting sand dunes. Ray Kenna's work on the dunes produced a radiocarbon date of 550BP from the soil bed under the dunes and argues from this that they had formed by the 12th-13th centuries (1978, 29). The decisive argument for this is the discovery in the 1890s of medieval building foundations, with timber posts and clay in an excellent state of preservation. The buildings emerged from under sand dunes as these were eroded away. The process by which the deposits were revealed is described by Edward Cox, '…as the fretting of the sea removes the blown sandhills, there appears, a few inches above the level of the spring tides, an ancient surface, showing traces of cultivation. Upon this the remains of mediaeval and older houses are continually washed out, together with ploughs, spades, and other agricultural implements; showing that this was arable land' (Cox 1895, 43). The existence of a medieval road running east-west was observed on more than one occasion. Charles Potter recorded a visit to the shore:

'…When visiting the shore in the company of Messrs. Edw. W. Cox and W. Fergusson Irvine, in the spring of 1892, we came across the uncovered patch of an old track, or road: its direction was E. by W. On this were deeply-impressed wheel marks, 5 feet apart, the breadth of the wheels being 9 inches. The horses had been shod with the very broad mediaeval shoes, and the driver with the sharp-pointed shoes of the same period, which left an impression 11 inches in length, by 4½ inches at their greatest width. There were also the foot-prints of cattle. In my collection I have leather pointed shoe soles, and broad horse shoes so similar that they might possibly have formed these very impressions. The marks were deeply impressed in the soil, and as sharp and fresh as if made within twenty-four hours previous to exposure' (Potter 1893, 243).

Thus the medieval settlement which had been buried by sand finally emerged through coastal erosion in the late 19th century, while the washing away of the occupation deposits revealed the associated artefacts.

The sandy coasts of Britain and north west Europe suffered what has been described as a '…long epidemic of disasters' from the 13th century to about 1800 when great storms inflicted serious damage on

coastal areas ranging from Brittany to Denmark (Lamb 1982; 1991). The effects of major storms on the landscape included '…blown sand, the formation and movement shifting of dunes sometimes forming a continuous coastal barrier, the scouring of sand or dry soil and spreading of drift-sand into nearly flat expanses' (Lamb 1991, 3). Considerable shifts in dunes occur at times when exceptionally low tides coincide with high winds so that a large expanse of sand is dried and loosened by the wind and blown inland.

Numerous examples can be cited in Britain for the serious effect of great storms on coastal places. Blown sand could overwhelm agricultural land and even whole settlements. A storm of blown sand on 19 August 1413 obliterated the centre of the medieval town of Forvie, Aberdeenshire on the east coast of Scotland, while at Newborough, Anglesey in 1331, 186 acres (75 ha) were destroyed for ever by the inflow of blown sand (Lamb 1991, 4, 18; Roberts 2002, 35). Equally devastating was the encroachment of a line of great sand dunes, which obliterated the port of Harlech on the west coast of Wales around 1400 (Lamb 1982, 183-5). At Kenfig on the south Wales coast, sand dune movements created a lagoon, about 1316, which closed the medieval port there; while a later storm there in 1573 carried a line of high sand dunes 3 km inland (Lamb 1982, 183; 1991, 18-19). The repeated movement of dunes or influxes of blown sand resulted in the progressive covering of agricultural land in the Breckland of Norfolk and Suffolk, probably as a result of three major storms in the period between 1570 and 1668 (Lamb 1991, 39-40). In the Sefton dunes, in historic times, there are records of the encroachment of the dunes on agricultural land and houses. Sylvia Harrop (1985, 28) cites the case of the Lost Farm, a cottage on the boundary between Birkdale and Ainsdale, which was progressively covered by blown sand by the early 19th century.

Sand-blows and encroachment of dunes may have occurred at different times with varying degrees of severity. The experience of other places on the west coast suggests that on occasion these may have affected limited areas, but at other times substantial areas of land may have suffered, either from the shifting of dunes or covering of land by blown sand. The burial of a settlement could be sudden and unexpected and in these circumstances the rapid inundation by sand meant that possessions could not be retrieved. This might be akin to a blanket of snow, perhaps collapsing the houses, and hiding from view vast numbers of personal belongings. Thus the settlement may have experienced the loss of a wide range of objects, domestic items, agricultural tools and personal possessions, dress fittings, shoes and so on, through sudden inundation by sand. No documentary record exists of such an engulfment, but in view of the poverty of medieval references to Meols that is by no means a decisive argument against it. Furthermore the finds suggest that such a catastrophe may have occurred more than once in the medieval period. The sudden engulfment may be detectable as peaks of material of contemporary date, and there appear to be two such episodes, one in the 12th century and another in the late 14th-early 15th century (G. Egan pers. comm.).

The village of Meols appears to have changed location probably in the late 15th or early 16th century. Hume in the 19th century recognised from the findspots of coins that the village had shifted some way inland. His argument was supported by the date of coin finds from two distinct locations; coins of Elizabeth I (1558-1603) and later monarchs come from the modern village of Meols while the earlier coins came from eroding shore line some way to the north (1863, 92). Potter confirmed that the findspots of later coins were geographically separated from the earlier finds. '...On close enquiry, I have found that every coin I possess of these later reigns [Elizabeth, later Scottish kings including James I of England, Charles I and II, James II, William and Mary], and the relics left of William's army, have come from the higher and cultivated lands of Great Meols, or westward from Great Meols to Hilbre and West Kirby' (Potter 1876, 138). This reinforces the argument that the present village core of Meols, set around a small green, with at least one probable 17th

century cottage on the edge of the green, shifted to its present position in the last decades of the 15th or first decades of the 16th century.

Added to these factors are two further links in the chain of circumstances that has led to the survival of so many artefacts. First, the waterlogged conditions have ensured that fragile organic materials have survived, so that leather shoes and straps, wooden knife handles and bowls – as well as the metal alloy of lead and tin common in the later medieval period but which was highly susceptible to corrosion in most soils – have all been preserved at Meols. The final stage in the process is the circumstances of retrieval of the finds. Effectively a large volume of occupation deposits from the settlements was filtered and sieved by the sea washing away the soils but depositing the dense metal items on the beach. Thus a large quantity of material was exposed to view over the course of half a century of collecting.

The history of Meols and recovery of finds suggests that the enlargement of the north Wirral sea wall in the 1860s had an impact on the pattern of erosion and reduced the quantity of finds (*cf.* Potter 1876, 140-1). In addition the sea wall potentially also sealed behind it a substantial volume of material that would have eroded away in time.

Lost Medieval Settlements in Sefton

The case of Meols has perhaps its greatest relevance to the Sefton coast for the medieval period. The Sefton coast has a number of recorded 'lost' settlements, which are rather better documented than in north Wirral. Several settlements suffered loss of territory through sand or sea inundation. The following owes much to Jennifer Lewis's work on the Sefton coastal townships (Lewis 2002).

Argarmeols

Argarmeols, the precursor of Birkdale, is recorded in the Domesday Book as Erengermeles, when it was occupied by Wigbert with 2 carucates of land worth 8s. Argarmeols had disappeared by 1346 when it was claimed '*que villa modo adnichilatur per mare et est ibi nulla habitacio'* (Feudal Aids 1904, 86, fig. 1.8c). In 1503 John Shirlok, aged 80 years, deposed that 'he never knew of any place called Argarmelys, but that he had heard that there were such lands, which had been drowned in the sea. The place of them was unknown to him' (Ekwall 1922, 125). The lords of the manor continued to plead its loss until the 16th century (Lewis 2002, 41). Birkdale was formerly part of Argarmeles (Ekwall 1922, 125).

Ainsdale

The place-name Ainsdale is probably Norse in origin, from *Einulfr* a personal name and *dale* (Ekwall 1922, 125) or possibly OE 'Ægenwulf's valley' (Mills 1986, 54). There were two ploughlands at Domesday (Farrer and Brownbill 1907, 50), and a large number of grants were made to Cockersand Abbey at the end of the 12th century. However Lewis notes that the focus of such activity is unknown. '...Ainsdale appears to have suffered a similar fate to that of Argarmeols though perhaps not quite as drastically by the 14th century' (Lewis 2002, 42). By 1555-6 it was claimed '...there was a certain town in times past called Aynesdale ...[and that] ... the town time out of mind had been and still was "overflowen" with the sea so that there remains no remembrance thereof now' (Fishwick 1897, 96, cited in Lewis 2002, 42). By the 19th century Aindsale's field systems, which formed the subject of the medieval documents, had not survived; the population was sparse with a small nucleation at the east of the township near the mill (Lewis 2002, 42).

However, there is good evidence from the 12th and 13th centuries to show that the community at Ainsdale was associated with an organised system of open-field cultivation. Shaw (1956, 341-3) discusses the Ainsdale field system at some length, using 13th century deeds for land in the possession of the Abbey of Cockersand. He notes the existence of cultivation on the 'usual strip system', with a series of townfields containing selions arranged between a number of small hills called *knots* or *hows* and intervening *dales*. The selions were closely subdivided into strips, with scattered ownership amongst the strips. The townfields lay around what may have been a nucleated village. The location of the field system cannot easily be correlated with surviving documents and maps, the earliest map surviving only from the 19th century.

Deeds of the late 12th-13th century also refer to structures within the township. Charters of the period 1190-1213 indicate the grant of a toft in Ainsdale with a garden and meadow nearby, which lay between two other tofts, again suggestive of a nucleated settlement (Farrer 1900, 578); Richard de Ainsdale granted a *sheal* [shepherd's or herdsman's hut] in a place known as Stardale (Farrer 1900, 577). A sheepfold and shepherd's house are also mentioned in 1190-1216 as situated on the eastern side of the town (Farrer 1900, 569). A revealing deed, dated to 1213-20, notes that the canons of Cockersand were granted all that they could acquire of the moss from Siward's boundary eastwards to Blakemere, by carrying away the sand; the implication of removal of sand from the moss to extend the area under cultivation or pasture (Farrer 1900, 590). A further grant makes it clear that this area lay near to their houses, which were in turn close to the marsh (Farrer 1900, 588-9). Although these are not located, they do indicate that encroachment of sand on mossland had occurred by the 13th century, and that this was fairly close to the houses. The deeds in addition refer to elements of the settlement which have archaeological potential. Apart from the messuages or houses, a barn belonging to Cockersand Abbey is mentioned in a deed of 1190-1213, in or next to Atefield (Farrer 1900, 581).

Ravenmeols

The Domesday Book of 1086 shows that Ravenmeols [Mele] was occupied under King Edward by three thanes in three manors and assessed at half a hide worth 8s. The existence of a chapel of ease at Ravenmeols of the parish of Walton on the Hill, at least as early as the late 12th century can be inferred from deeds of Cockersand Abbey (Farrer 1900, 565-66), and continued as the parochial chapel of Formby Chapel in 1650 (Fishwick 1879, 82). However, storms and sand incursion in the 1730s led to its abandonment, and a new chapel dedicated to St Peter was built further inland in 1746. The old site remained in use as a burying ground and a new church, St Luke's, was built on the site in 1855 (Lewis 1981).

The settlement pattern of Ravenmeols and the adjacent township to the north, Formby, is unclear. Although they were separate townships, as Lewis notes, the boundary becomes blurred and the distinction lost by the 16th century. Much of the land of Ravenmeols appears to have been destroyed by sand and sea before the 16th century. As regards the field systems associated with the settlement, grants of the early 13th century in the de Hoghton Deeds indicate many parcels of land held in strips within named fields such as Midelpulmershe, le Mekes and the Solacres, each with multiple tenants in the fields (Lumby 1936, 140-1), demonstrating the existence of an open field system within the township. The medieval field names and topographical features indicate a lowlying landscape where marsh and pools (e.g. Toxlepol, Langebacpol) were prominent, ditches marked field and township boundaries and 'islands' of raised ground were denoted by Norse *holm* names. The presence of an open field system is usually associated in the region with a nucleated settlement or village. This receives some support in slight hints in documents of a nucleated settlement when in 1240-47 John del Lee grants to Richard son of Henry de Meols a toft between the houses of William son of Edwin and Brun son of Roger, demonstrating a row of at least three houses. However, the existence of what may be outlying houses is suggested by a later 13th century deed. This records a messuage and toft next to 'le Forde' and may indicate an isolated house next to the Alt (Lumby 1936, 141).

The location of the core of the settlement, if indeed it were nucleated, is uncertain. However, once again the existence of the chapel from at least the 12th century may provide a clue. Lewis notes that the chapel which stood within the boundary of Ravenmeols was actually called 'Formbye Chapel' on Saxton's map of 1577, Ravenmeols having lost its independent status by then. The chapel may however have acted as a focal point for a small nucleated settlement in the medieval period.

There is very little in the way of artefacts that might hint at settlement of this period. A cut silver penny of Henry II, minted in London 1180-89, was found near Formby Point; but by itself it adds little to the picture as it may be a casual loss, or connected with coastal trade rather than associated with a settlement itself (PAS; Nick Herepath pers. comm.; J. Lewis pers. comm.).

The Sefton coast has certainly suffered within the recent past from major sand-blows and coastal inundations. Nicholas Blundell's diary records the great inundation of the Lancashire coast in a storm of December 1720; '...the four next days very wet and extreamly windy the like scarce ever known and never so high a Tide known as was these four dayes especially the 18th & 19th chiefly at the Meales, Alker, Alt-Grange & towards Lancaster; never so much damage done by High Tides in these parts as now' (Tyrer 1972, 29-32). Over 660 acres (267 ha) of land were flooded and many houses destroyed. The inundation extended as far inland as Martin Mere and up the Douglas, and damaged the floodgates at the mouth of the Alt. In 1739 a great sandstorm blew large quantities of sand up to 1.5 km inland from the coast at Ravenmeols and Formby (Jones et al. 1993, 11; Smith 1999, 52). From the 17th century there was a change in the management of dunes, towards consolidation (to prevent the sand-blows which had resulted from unmanaged use of the dunes) by measures such as planting marram grass and the creation of rabbit warrens.

The Archaeological Potential of Sefton's Lost Settlements

The similarities between the north Wirral and Sefton coastlines in their history of coastal inundation, coastline change, dune building and movement, suggests that the kinds of evidence of ancient settlement that have survived at Meols may also be present along the Sefton coastal zone.

The example of Meols provides a model for assessing the archaeological potential of the buried medieval and earlier settlements of the Sefton coast. Discoveries at Meols demonstrate that in lowlying, waterlogged or anaerobic soil conditions, the survival of organic remains can be of exceptionally high quality. Not only were timber building foundations preserved, but also the clay floors and the base of upright posts were clearly observed and described, although it is unfortunate that there are no known photographs or drawings of these remains to permit a modern re-assessment to be made of their form. Middens were discovered intact beside buildings, and in the early 1890s the whole medieval village street, complete with imprints of human and animal feet, were visible, eroding from under the sand dunes. Stake alignments of outbuildings and pens were noted and, as both Hume and Ecroyd Smith observed, elements of field systems such as butts or heaped up strips of land were also evident under the sand dunes (Hume 1863, 10). It was not only medieval structures which were well preserved. Although the Roman site at Meols appears to have been largely or wholly lost to coastal erosion, a group of circular buildings observed eroding from under the sand dunes in the later part of the 19th century is likely to represent the preserved remains of a late prehistoric – probably Iron Age – settlement, even though its precise location cannot be determined.

In this lowlying waterlogged landscape, the possibility that timber foundations survive in as good a condition as those seen at Meols would offer a remarkable opportunity to study the physical remains of structures which on dryland sites survive only as negative features such as post-holes and beam slots. The preservation of structural remains, such as the foundations of timber buildings, would enable details of construction techniques and carpentry to be examined, while enabling the acquisition of precise felling dates for timbers through dendrochronological sampling. This in turn could provide important new evidence for the vernacular architectural traditions of a region where medieval structures are little understood, and very few have been excavated. The exposure of such structures on the shore today, if subject to proper archaeological investigation, could yield much valuable information on little understood questions of prehistoric, Romano-British and medieval settlement and structures.

Not only did the buildings and the fields survive exceptionally well, but also the peculiar circumstances of soil conditions at Meols ensured that the artefacts were remarkably well preserved. This included not only organic items of bone, textile, wood and leather, but also metal objects, and particularly those in lead-tin that are highly susceptible to decay in most soil conditions. Medieval artefacts were also found some way inland in a distinctive 'artificial soil' layer, evidently a cultivated soil. Depending on the nature of the inundation of the settlement, whether it occurred by sand-blow or sea incursion, there is potential for artefacts to survive *in situ* in the buildings, middens and occupation layers. The lowlying nature of the coastal zone and the burial of the occupation surfaces by sand deposits suggest that we might expect good preservation of organic artefacts through burial in waterlogged or other anaerobic conditions. These might include items such as leather, wood, textiles, and sensitive metal alloys, such as lead-tin, which would provide invaluable information on types of artefact which have been lost through decay at most dryland sites. There is also potential for recovery of more durable artefacts such as metal or ceramics, where little evidence so far has been recovered from this part of the region. This might yield information on the manufacture and trading of pottery, evidence of imported goods and coastal trade. Together these circumstances might offer the potential for a remarkable insight into ancient society and economy.

Another fundamental benefit of deposits sealed under sand dunes is the lack of disturbance to deposits through recent agricultural or construction activities. Such intact land and occupation surfaces may permit the elucidation of sequences of occupation or other activity which elsewhere are frequently truncated by recent disturbance. Such deposits would be highly valued in their ability to contribute to obscure questions such as the origins of medieval settlement and the question of continuity from earlier periods. Well-preserved occupation deposits might yield important data on the date of the origin of nucleated villages, as well as potentially providing evidence for the date of inundation or burial itself.

A modern-day 'Meols' would also have vast potential for environmental studies on preserved plant, insect and animal remains, using scientific analyses that were not available in Hume's day (pollen analysis, plant macro-fossil evidence, crop production and processing, insect remains and so on). The experience of Meols suggests that middens could survive intact, presenting the opportunity to recover evidence of animal bones to contribute to questions over the nature of diet, butchery practices, and the health and breed of livestock, as well as the use of resources such as food from the wild, e.g. fish from preserved fish-bones.

Potential of the Coastal Zone

The potential for continued recovery of archaeological and environmental remains from the Sefton coastline is high. Not only have others outlined some of the important discoveries such as the late Mesolithic trackway at Altmouth and the footprints at Formby Point (R. Cowell this vol.; G. Roberts and A. Worsley this vol.), on the Sefton coast itself, but the example of Meols demonstrates the potential for recovering evidence for settlements lying on or close to the coast.

The erosion along the shore of early sediments and exposure of sediments and land surfaces along the Sefton coastline, whilst it represents the loss of land and of habitat, could present a remarkable archaeological opportunity if the coastline is monitored in such a way as to recover the fragments of evidence that may be revealed. The observation of an Iron Age land surface buried under the sand dunes at Formby Point provides a rare opportunity to monitor an early datable horizon as it is exposed through dune movement and erosion. The location of finds, especially where there are clusters such as in the vicinity of Formby Point, may indicate the location of settlement or trading activity. Of equal importance is the continued monitoring of building work and development within the broad dune belt on the landward side of the coast. Such monitoring has the potential to recover information on the medieval and earlier settlements.

The scope of such a programme should ideally extend beyond just the Sefton coastline to embrace the whole of the Dee-Ribble coast from Blacon near Chester to North Meols. This is a fragile yet rich environment for traces of past settlement and activity. Recent discoveries include a series of 30 wattle fences on the intertidal zone at Leasowe near Meols, which may be fish stalls, and a pit exposed in eroded coastal cliff at Speke containing burnt cracked stones and charcoal. Elsewhere footprints have been observed recently in silts off Red Noses near the north west tip of Wirral by Christine Longworth, while some years before 1895 a circular building was observed in the intertidal zone at New Brighton (Cox 1895, 44, 47).

The final lesson from Meols is the way in which the site or sites were first discovered by chance and subsequently monitored over a period of half a century by antiquarians. Without Hume's initial observation and recognition of the significance of the finds, the site may well have gone unnoticed. The continued diligent collecting and observation of the finds by Hume, Ecroyd Smith and Potter – and their subsequent publications – have left a legacy not only of important collections available for study today, housed in no fewer than five institutions, but also their observations on the position and stratigraphy of the deposits which modern study can use to create a greater understanding of the site. This makes possible reinterpretation of the stratigraphy and development of the coastline and its settlements in the light of subsequent scientific developments, and the study of the artefacts in the light of increased understanding of their chronology and function, together with application of types of scientific analyses such as X-radiography and XRF analysis of metal alloys to the early collections.

Careful collecting of material and observations along the shore made over half a century or more has led to the accumulation of data on the shoreline development and the settlements as well as the superb artefact collections from Meols.

Monitoring and Recording the Coastline

The length of the coastline as well as the width of the Sefton dune belt and wide expanse of exposed beach at low tide make monitoring the huge coastal zone a daunting task. Rapid changes in the disposition of sands and silts can reveal deposits or layers overnight and as quickly obscure them. Nor is there any predictability in the time or place where significant deposits will be revealed by coastal change, as the work of Gordon Roberts in monitoring the prehistoric footprints has shown. Erosion of the various periods of settlement at Meols occurred over perhaps a century or more and only ceased when the sea wall fixed the line of the coast.

The movement of coastal deposits is variable in intensity and extent, with some areas experiencing continual erosion, and in these locations monitoring needs to be regular and frequent. Accurate surveys of the coast are needed to record the deposits as they are exposed and to map their profile. As the coastline recedes or deposits are exposed, continuous monitoring can start to build up a three-dimensional model of the terrain represented by the strips of exposed soil. Monitoring is thus a long-term process, not a single event.

Ensuring that the archaeological potential of the coastal zone is not lost requires co-ordinated action. The involvement of people on the ground is critical, drawing on the enthusiasm and local knowledge of those who understand the local tides and deposits and can work safely in a difficult environment. Key players in such a programme are the Sefton Rangers who know the coastline and work there, as well as local people who have an interest in history of their locality. The example of Gordon Roberts's remarkable work on the Sefton coastline, recording deposits of international importance and ensuring their preservation through record, and that of Abraham Hume a century and a half earlier in Wirral, illustrate how vital is the role of the people on the ground. Not only does this require a network of people on the spot but also it demands that they have the knowledge to recognise the significance of what is there and the skills to be able to record it.

A model for such a programme might be the Shorewatch initiative in Scotland that has harnessed the interest, enthusiasm and local knowledge of volunteers to monitor and record archaeological features along the Scottish coastline (Fraser et al. 2003). Working in a zone between Low Water Mark and 50 m beyond High Water Mark, local volunteer groups undertook site surveys to establish a monitoring baseline, followed by continued monitoring for signs of erosion or accretion, and disseminating data to appropriate bodies including the local SMR or HER. Issues that arose concerned professional advice and guidance, as well as training for volunteer groups to raise awareness and levels of knowledge. Coastal areas subject to the most rapid change were identified and received more frequent monitoring visits.

An ideal model of the process might involve the creation of at least one liaison post for a professional archaeologist who should be experienced in the understanding and recording of coastal environments, employed to work alongside local volunteer groups, local societies, schools, colleges and universities. They would provide training in archaeological survey and recording techniques, would help to define and implement programmes of survey and monitoring, and should be capable of an informed professional judgement on the significance of discoveries. Furthermore they should have access to appropriate scientific expertise to ensure the maximum yield of information is extracted from the observations by those familiar both with the stratigraphic context and the formation processes of the deposits. They should be based in an organisation which can provide a supporting infrastructure and resources. This would enable the project archaeologist to transfer the data derived from the project to the appropriate archives and sources such as the local Merseyside HER and local government departments concerned with planning and shoreline management. Feeding the data into a GIS-based database such as the HER, or a dedicated but compatible system, ensures that the results can inform the development control process and management plans for the coastal zone as well as provide high-quality information for archaeological or local history research. Once they are stored centrally in a secure, maintained environment the data will represent an archive of great value to planners, coastal management departments, specialist researchers and interested non-specialists alike.

Conclusions

Meols has many lessons for those interested in coastal environments, opening our eyes to the great and largely untapped potential of the historic coastal zone of Sefton, and beyond. The similarities between the deposits and landscapes of north Wirral and Sefton raise the possibility that for certain periods in the past the Sefton coastline may have similar potential. It also serves as an object lesson in the importance of continued monitoring of the coastal zone. The importance of the successive sites at Meols was recognised in the 19th century only through the application of accumulated local experience and observation. Such experience, allied to professional expertise and the use of rapidly developing technologies, will enable the preservation by record of what will inevitably be hidden through accretion or destroyed through erosion.

Acknowledgements

The assistance of Sarah-Jane Farr (Merseyside Archaeological Officer) and Mark Hart of the Merseyside Archaeological Service, and Nick Herepath (Finds Liaison Officer, Portable Antiquities Scheme) based in National Museums Liverpool, is gratefully acknowledged for information on Romano-British and other finds. Dr Geoff Egan (Museum of London Specialist Services) provided valuable material and discussion through his work on the Meols project. Ron Cowell of National Museums Liverpool – as ever – gave freely of his experience and insights in discussion of various points. Above all, Dr Jen Lewis provided valuable discussion of many points, and drew on her own unrivalled and extensive knowledge of Sefton district to guide me to a wide range of references and leads. To all I am very grateful.

Sea, Shore and Everyday Life in the 17th and 18th Centuries

Sylvia Harrop

This article concentrates on the northern part of the south west Lancashire coast, and is based very largely on research done by members of the Birkdale and Ainsdale Historical Research Society. In the 16th and 17th centuries, there were four topographical influences on the people of this part of the coast and the way they lived. From east to west these were: reclaimed agricultural land – the heys; the sand dunes – the hawes; the shore; and the sea (Harrop, 1985, chs. 2-4). This article deals with the last two of these.

THE SHORE

Apart from getting from the dunes to the sea, what did the shore mean to the local inhabitants of Birkdale and Ainsdale?

Travel

First, it was an important highway. The condition of roads in Lancashire during this period was generally poor, and particularly across marshland. There were no major roads near to the coast, a situation not remedied until well into the 19th century. (fig. 1).

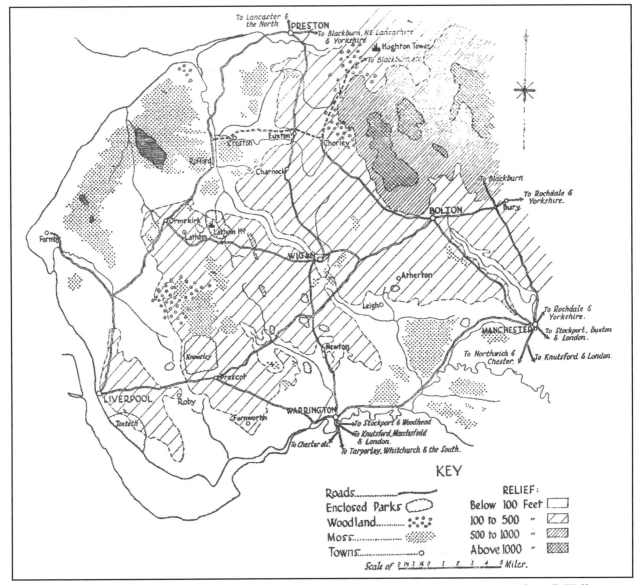

Fig. 1: South west Lancashire: roads, towns, topography, etc. prior to the 18th century (from F. Walker "The Historical Geography of Southwest Lancashire before the Industrial Revolution", 1939, with permission of the Chetham Society)

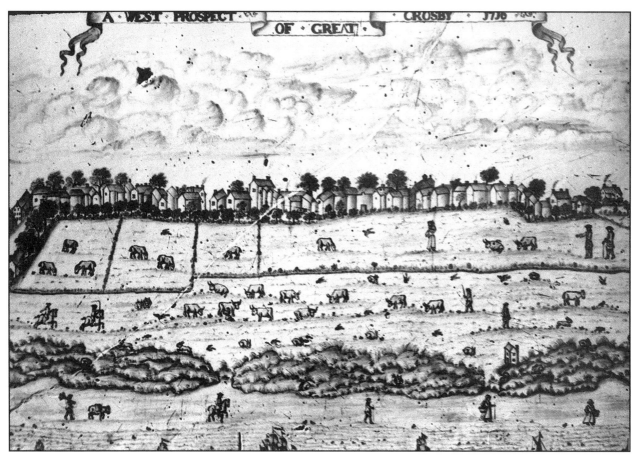

Fig. 2: Plaque of Great Crosby in 1716 (from J. E. Stanistreet & A. Farthing "Crosby in Camera: early photographs of Great Crosby and Waterloo", 1995, with permission of Sefton Libraries)

The mossland between the sea and the higher land made travel very difficult from east to west and north to south, particularly in the winter (Crosby 1998, 60). For example, the route from Ormskirk to North Meols over Ottersties Moss was said to be so worn out and decayed in the 17th century that it was impassable in wintertime

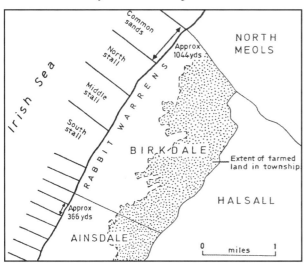

Fig. 3: Plan of Birkdale and Ainsdale showing the layout of the fishing stalls (from S.A. Harrop "Old Birkdale & Ainsdale", 1985, with permission of the Birkdale & Ainsdale Historical Research Society)

(LRO DDSc 149/12). Along the coastal strip, such tracks as did exist were on soft sand, making travel very slow. So many people used the shore: the 'perfectly smooth and hard beach', 'of immense extent' (as it was described in 1805), was much easier to walk or ride on (Bailey 1955, 44); and the journey was quicker in time, despite the fact that the distance was considerably greater and journeys were dictated by the state of the tides. For centuries the shore was a main public highway from Liverpool to Bootle, Crosby and North Meols (Tyrer 1972, 246; LRO DDIn 55/189, 13; Higham 1998, 31). Nicholas Blundell of Little Crosby, the diarist, regularly travelled along the 'shore road' from Crosby to Liverpool, and he and his wife rode to North Meols, presumably along the sands (Tyrer 1968, 97, 249). Rare visual evidence existed in a Liverpool delft pottery plaque of 1716 (fig. 2), showing people travelling along the sands by Great Crosby, some on horseback, others walking, aided by sticks or driving animals. (This plaque was unfortunately destroyed in the Second World War, but fortunately illustrated in a book published in 1871 (Mayer 1871, 4; Stanistreet and Farthing 1995, 3).

Fishing

Fishing was an important activity for those living along the coast, providing both food and a source of income. It is interesting that for Birkdale and Ainsdale there is so far little evidence of fishing from boats on the sea, compared with further north around Marshside. (In 1800, for example, North Meols had a fishing fleet of 13 trawl boats (Bland 1903, 71)). The people fished from the shore, governed by an unusual system of 'fishing stalls', dating from the mid-16th century at least, whereby the whole shore from Birkdale to Formby was leased to tenants by the lord of the manor, who held the rights over the shore between high and low water. By the beginning of the 18th century there were four large equal stalls in Birkdale, of approximately 1,044 yards each north to south: and 26 smaller, equal stalls in Ainsdale and Formby, of approximately 366 yards (fig. 3).

What explains the different sizes of stall from north to south? The fact that the Birkdale South Stall was worth twice as much as the other Birkdale stalls suggests that the fishing was more prolific and, therefore, profitable, along the shore to the south.

Indeed, the difference in values soon led to disputes among the tenants of the North, Middle and South Stalls; so a scheme was drawn up in the 1740s, dividing each stall equally into three, so that all had a share of each. This arrangement was to last until all the lives in two of the leases had expired, and then each lessee was to have sole use of his own stall (Harrop 1982, 161).

Defining the boundaries of these stalls was difficult, and led inevitably to disputes. The east and west boundaries were from the sandhills or high watermark to the low watermarks, allowing for a 16 foot (that is, a neap) tide. It was the divisions from north to south, marked out with stakes across the shore, that caused trouble: markers decayed, were easily removed or were washed away by high tides; and then great difficulty arose in fixing the correct line. The boundary between the North Stall and the Common Sands, for example, was set by lining up the 'perpetual landmarks' of Ormskirk church steeple and a stub 'set on a hill'; but by the end of the 18th century the stub had disappeared, and with it the agreed boundary (Harrop 1982, 162).

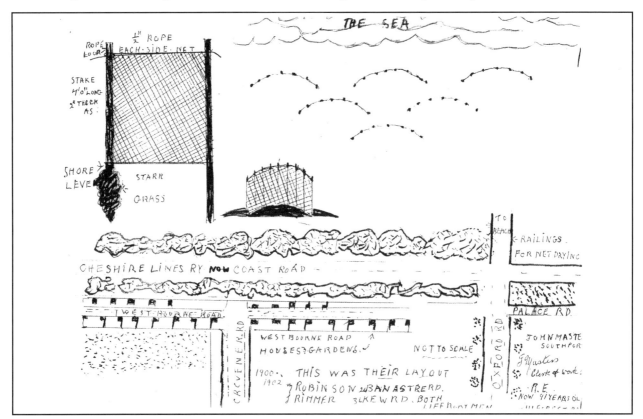

Fig. 4 : Plan showing the system of fishing on Birkdale beach in the early 20th century, by Mr J. Masters (from S. A. Harrop "Old Birkdale & Ainsdale", 1985, with permission of the Birkdale & Ainsdale Historical Research Society)

Tenants usually fished with stake nets – a system which survived until the early 20th century, as shown by this plan (fig. 4) drawn from memory in the early 1980s by an old resident of Birkdale. Stakes were driven into the sand, leaving about four feet above the surface, and on to these they lashed nets. As the tide receded, fish were caught in the nets, and were then gathered into hampers and carried away, some for local consumption, but most for sale, presumably at the local markets of Ormskirk, Preston and Liverpool. The majority of fish caught were cod, whiting, plaice, sole, fluke and ray. It is interesting that, though cockles were to be found on the Formby and Marshside beaches, there were none at Birkdale and Ainsdale; and there appear to have been no shrimps at that time.

The Common Sands stall was always leased separately. The other Birkdale stalls were leased along with property, land and warrens, and were normally let with specific holdings. Stalls appear to have been a good investment. It is reported of one man, Peter Hodges, that in 1709 he built himself a cottage and while it was being built he caught enough fish to pay for it (Bland 1903, 55). In the mid-1980s I was told by a part-time fisherman using night lines off the Birkdale shore that, in a good season, a net costing £60-£80 would pay for itself in a week. Since the Birkdale stalls were so large, they were sometimes divided or, more often, shared with or sublet to other members of the tenants' families or to neighbours, bringing extra income to those holding fishing leases. It is important to note that these tenants were also permitted to take wildfowl as part of their leases, providing another source of food and income (Harrop 1982, 162-163). This method of fishing was also largely danger-free – unlike fishing from boats, which claimed a number of victims from Birkdale and from further north around North Meols (Cheetham and Sparke 1934, Burials). A particularly tragic incident took place in 1799, when three brothers and a cousin, all of Birkdale, drowned when returning from a fishing trip. The irony of this was that the boys' father, William Hodges, had only recently leased the North Stall for fishing (Harrop 1985, 20-21).

Flotsam and Jetsam

The sea was a very powerful and important part of local life and, as will be clear from other chapters in this volume, (especially those by Barbara and Reginald Yorke) this was a treacherous coast. Whole settlements had been washed away in the Middle Ages, including Argarmeols, probably situated on the coast south of North Meols, around the end of the 14th century; Arnoldesdale or Aynesdale, near Birkdale, only a very long memory in 1555 (Fishwick 1897, 93-96); and Ravenmeols, near Formby (Farrer and Brownbill 1907, 45). There was very good reason for the new settlements of Formby, Ainsdale and Birkdale to be situated at least half a mile inland. In 1720 there was another great inundation of the Lancashire coast in which the coastal areas of North Meols suffered badly. On 18 and 19 December 1720 there was a sudden and violent storm which resulted in petition on behalf of over 130 local people, '…Inhabitant[s] Rack tenants Sufferers by a Dreadful Inundation of the Sea within the parish of North Meols and the Townships of Hesketh-cum-Becconsal Tarleton and Martin Mear'. Land was flooded, houses were washed down, nine people were drowned and 100 families almost ruined and without homes. Very fortunately, however, the inundation did not reach to beyond the Birkdale township boundary, so Birkdale and Ainsdale escaped (Beck 1953, 95-98).

In bad weather many vessels were wrecked on the coast, and valuable items came ashore. In a 1662 court case witnesses remembered recovering barrels of tallow, a sail yard, and a cockboat, that is, a small ship's boat, as well as masts and planks, which provided valuable building materials in an area where wood was in short supply. The right to possession of any wreck coming ashore was an extremely important and valuable one, and the witnesses in the court case were agreed that it was always the landowners of Formby, Birkdale and Ainsdale who received the wreck (Gibson 1876, 121-123). Nevertheless, its ownership continued to be a cause of arguments between landowners, and in 1671 Lord Molyneux, who held some ancient rights to wreck from the Crown, and Henry Blundell, the lord of the manor, tried to sort it out. They agreed that Blundell was to have '…all goods and chattels called Floatsam,

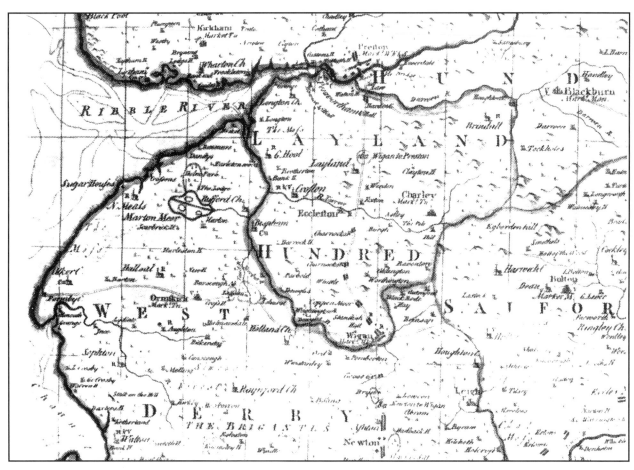

Fig. 5: Portion of Bowen's map of Lancashire, 1760

Jetsam Lagan and wrecked goods cast up or wrecked upon the seacoasts' of his manors for 300 years in return for an annual rent of 12d (LRO DDM 16/9). 'Floatsam' was wreckage found floating on the surface of the sea, and if it was between the high and low watermarks it belonged to the lord; 'jetsam' were goods thrown overboard to lighten a ship in distress; and 'lagan' were goods or wreckage lying on the bed of the sea (Harrop 1985, 17).

There appears to be no evidence of wreckers, that is, people deliberately luring vessels on to the shore, but 'Wreck lookers' were appointed by the Manor Court to look out for wreck, impound it and report it to the lord. The Blundells of Ince, the lords of the manor, lived a good distance from Birkdale and Ainsdale, so there was little to prevent the local people, on the spot, from moving quickly and helping themselves to useful items cast up on the beach. During the second half of the 18th century there were only two years, 1771 and 1783, when anyone was brought before the court and fined for carrying away wreck. It is unlikely

that these were the only people who ever helped themselves to the wreck; and it is perhaps significant that in 1788 the Wreck lookers were given one quarter of any wreck for their trouble (Harrop 1985, 17). There was perhaps some kind of working, but unwritten agreement, whereby local people were allowed to take some items from the beach so long as the lord received the major part. Wood – masts and planks – appear to have been sold on behalf of the lord: certainly, timbers from wrecked vessels were used as roof trusses and beams in local cottages (Gibson 1876, 121). Other items were often very welcome: Nicholas Blundell of Little Crosby records that word was brought to him that a ship loaded with butter had suffered damage in the night, '...Some of it was brought up to Great Crosby and [Ellen Rigby] bought us three Muggs of it' (Blundell 1952, 186).

It is important to note that a treacherous coast and wrecked vessels also meant many drownings. The coroner regularly rode over to see bodies washed up on the shore. The coroner's account for 24 March

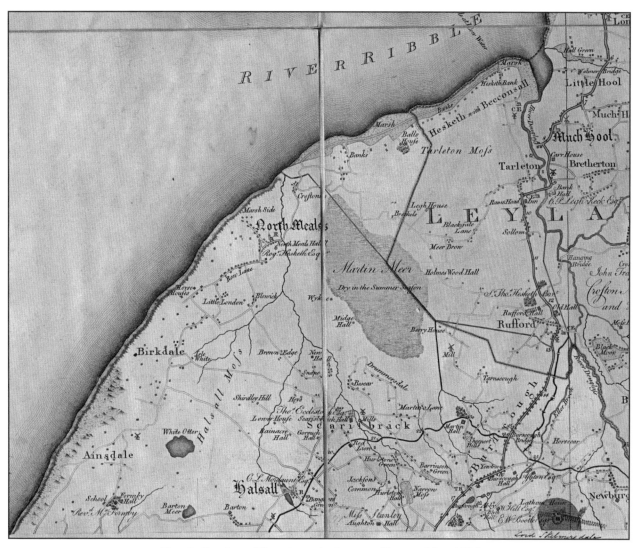

*Fig. 6: Portion of Yates' one-inch map of Lancashire, 1786
(courtesy of Liverpool Record Office, Liverpool Libraries)*

1757 is typical: '…At Birkdale on viewing of the body of a seafaring man being found dead upon the shore at high water mark and supposed to belong to some ship or vessel swept away by the violence of the winds and waves which had been very stormy' (Harrop 1985, 16). For the period when the perceived cause of death was entered in the North Meols burial registers, almost 6% of the deaths were caused by individuals being drowned. From 1730 to 1799, 75 cases of drownings were recorded. These were from both wrecked and local vessels (pers.comm. P Lynch). In the 1790s alone there were 17 recorded wrecks on the North Meols coast (Booth 1947, 14).

THE SEA

To the outside world, early maps of Lancashire show no sign of settlement on this coast between North Meols and Formby. Saxton's well-known map of 1577

just shows a belt of yellow sand dunes. The only addition made by Speed in 1610 was to name the dunes 'The Mosse'; and though many more maps were issued in the next 150 years, Birkdale and Ainsdale still did not appear – largely, it has to be said, because cartographers tended to copy one another. (fig. 5).

It was not until 1786, when Yates published the first properly surveyed map of the county, at the scale of one inch to the mile, that the two villages at last made their appearance (Harley 1968, 25) (fig. 6). They had, of course, been in existence for more than seven centuries, and Ainsdale appears in Domesday Book. So, the maps showed little sign of settlement; the mosses were difficult to cross, especially in wet weather and in the winter; there were no roads to speak of; and as late as the 19th century topographical works described the area as an 'uncultivated waste'

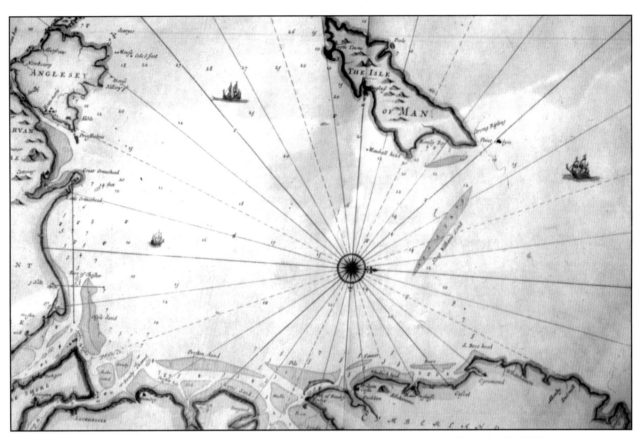

Fig. 7: Portion of Captain Collins' chart of the north west coast of England, 1759

(Bland 1903, 39). An account of 1849, speaking of the Birkdale and Ainsdale foreshore, said that during high water small vessels of light draught might traverse the beach, but that this was very rare. '...There are ... no places for loading and unloading vessels ... the whole line has remained unused and deserted' (LRO DDIn 55/189). The longstanding reputation of this part of the coast as treacherous for shipping suited the local people very well because, for more than a century, the most valuable and exciting activity along the shore was not fishing, but something that by its very nature must be clandestine, and carried out in quiet or deserted places. It was, of course, smuggling.

The south west Lancashire coast does not at first sight appear to be likely smuggling territory, since this is normally associated in the public mind with small coves, surrounded by high cliffs, where boats could run in unseen. Nevertheless, from the mid 17th century smuggling was rife along this coast: so that by 1715 Customs officials could describe the north west coast of England, and particularly the Lancashire

coast near the Ribble estuary, as '...A place of the greatest smuggling in the country' (Jarvis 1954, 6-7). Overall, the total amount of goods smuggled into England along the Lancashire coast was almost as great as that which was illicitly landed on the coasts of Kent and Sussex. The key to this situation was the coast's proximity to the Isle of Man (fig. 7).

In 1523 the famous decision was made that the Isle of Man formed '...no part of the realm of England' (Moore 1900, 738-739); and from that date to 1765 the island remained independent of the British crown, owned by the Stanley family, Earls of Derby who, since the 15th century, had ruled as Lords or Kings of Man. It is likely that there had always been some trade between the island and parts of the Lancashire coast; but from the mid 17th century onwards, trade increased considerably for two main reasons. First, the seventh Earl wanted to increase his revenues by increasing commerce with and from the island. As the island was independent, it was decided that it could frame its own tariffs, and that any goods imported into the island could legally be resold: that is, Manx merchants could buy goods from any country, store them and then resell them. Equally, '...the Commissioners appointed by Royal Letters Patent to manage the Customs of the Kingdom had no competence in the Isle of Man, ... [and] the King's writ did not run there' (Jarvis 1945-46, 246).

Fortunately for the Earl and the Manx merchants, this decision coincided with increasingly heavy taxes imposed by the Stuart kings on a number of goods, especially tobacco and wine. For example, James I, who particularly disliked the growing habit of smoking, raised the tax on tobacco from 2d to 6s 6d per pound. His son, Charles I, relied heavily on taxes, including Customs and Excise duties, to pay for his government. After the 1688 Revolution, which resulted in the accession of William of Orange, England was drawn into war with France, and it was necessary to maintain a large army in Ireland to prevent an invasion by the deposed James II (Jarvis 1945-46, 248). To pay for these military expenses, heavy duties were imposed on all luxury goods, including silks, lace, wines, brandy and spirits; and especially heavy duties were laid on French goods, which by 1695 were taxed at 25%. The more taxes were increased, the more profitable smuggling became, and the Manx trade entered its most prosperous period. The Excise duties were resented by all sections of the population; illicit landings were made all round the coast; and the unique situation of the Isle of Man made it a centre for the storing of contraband goods. Merchants from Liverpool moved to the island and formed groups to buy ships and goods for trading (Jarvis, 1945-46, 250). It must be stressed, however, that the trade between the Isle of Man and the Lancashire coast was regarded as perfectly legal by all participants (though not the English Government!). The island was independent; the Earl had decreed that any goods imported into the island could be legally resold; and the people along the coast believed that any interference with the trade was an attempt to take away the hereditary right of the Earl of Derby. Their consciences were quite clear on the matter.

There was also a change in the design of ships towards the end of the 17th century. The introduction of the fore and aft rig enabled '...a revolution in sailing technique', which had '...immense influence upon the methods of illicit trade by sea.' The newly rigged vessels were much more manoeuvrable than the square-rigged ships, '...able to come into almost anywhere, with the wind in almost any quarter, and having discharged her cargo, could leave its dispersal to someone else, and could get away, whether there were an off-shore wind or not' (Jarvis 1945-46, 247-8). Smuggling boats were also specially built for the purpose, and could come in at low water, whereas the Customs sloops could only do so at very high tide. Moreover, the crews on smuggling ships knew the whole of the Irish Sea and were '...the best sailors and watermen in the world' – much superior to those of the Navy, many of whom had been pressed (Wilkins 1992, 55, 21, 70). A letter of 1750 stated that: '...I believe that the running trade from this island is doubled since I was here last, and all the ships and wherries employed by the Government do not catch one in fifty, as a merchant of this place assured me himself' (Moore 1900, 437).

So it was that wine, brandy, rum, tea, tobacco, spices and sugar were landed on the west Lancashire coast. Flat-bottomed, shallow-draught vessels, specially built for the trade, could come close inshore, at night. They chose 'the darkest and roughest nights' (Atholl Papers 40B/24); and folklore in Formby speaks of cattle in the sandhills with lights fixed to their heads – surely a reference to the days when contraband regularly came ashore. It is also likely that they were guided by a light from Ainsdale Mill (Harrop 1985, 62). A report by Customs officials in the mid 18th century gives a very clear account of the trade on the coast since the beginning of the century. At first, the goods were buried in the sand or taken to a safe hiding-place and customers sought; but soon the trade became more organised, specific items were brought over to order, and the participants on land were ready for the ships: '...The dexterity of the smugglers is so great that in fifteen minutes the cargo of a boat can be unloaded and placed on horseback and galloped off into the country.' The riders quickly vanished across the sandhills and through the treacherous marshes to their destinations: '...where no Troops, but light horse, can possibly pursue, and overtake them' (Atholl Papers 40B/24).

Where did the goods go? By the very nature of the operation, details of local smuggling are limited, but there is enough evidence to show that many of them found their way into the houses of the local gentry. In the 1680s, the lord of one moiety of the manor of North Meols, Barnaby Hesketh, was himself practically involved in trading smuggled wine, brandy and tobacco from France. He and his brother, Bartholomew, boarded a ship that came into North Meols in 1686, to supervise the unloading of contraband for their use. The brandy was safely stowed at Widow Jump's cottage and at Meols Hall, where it joined '...great quantities of prohibited and uncustomed goods' (LRO QSP 653/45).

Nicholas Blundell was also housing smuggled goods at his home, Crosby Hall. At no time does he describe in his diaries, which he kept very safely hidden, exactly how the landings were made; and he gives no clues about any arrangements for the trading – but that he received smuggled brandy and claret is clearly stated in his entries over many years. In December 1721 he states: '...In France, according as our News Papers constantly give us an Accont; there the plage has Raiged violently this Year' (Tyrer 1972, 63). By an act of Parliament of 1720 French ships were banned from all English ports (Smith 1980, 58-9). A proclamation was made in Ormskirk and several towns to say that watch must be set on the coast to see that '...all persons come by sea perform quarantine'. There followed a list of the places on the coast where watch must be kept in case Frenchmen landed, including Birkdale, North Meols, Ainsdale, Formby, Crosby and Bootle. Nineteen pounds were set aside for maintenance of watch in each of these areas – a very large sum, indicating that the possibility of French sailors landing at any of these places was considered seriously by Ormskirk magistrates; and that each of the places named was, at least, suspected of illicit trading with French vessels (LRO QSP 122/21,1724).

In the event, no reports of landings were made, and no quarantine was needed – but Nicholas Blundell was certainly handling contraband French brandy early in 1720, whether direct from France or via the Isle of Man. First, in February, he purchased an 'Act against Runing goods 10d.' (Tyrer 1972, 6 n.1). This did not deter him from what followed:

23 February 1720 'William Thelwall set me a good New Lock on my Seller Doore.'

27 April 1720 'Mr Thomas [the Customs officer] cerched the West-Lain-hous and a deale of the Out-Housing at this Hous for Brandy as he heard was conceiled here, Thomas Marrow our Cunstable and Henry Williamson were with him.'(Tyrer 1972, 10).

It is clear that Mr Thomas had reason for searching for brandy but, unsurprisingly, found nothing. Houses used for hiding forbidden Roman Catholic priests could easily hide contraband; and one can be pretty sure that the constable and Mr Williamson, whom the next entry in the diary shows to be a wine cooper, made sure that the Customs officer did not get too close to the hiding place. Indeed, it seems evident from the entries that the contraband was not in the outhouses, but in the cellar, and well hidden under straw. The diary tells us what happened next:

30 April 1720 'Mr Williamson the Wine-Cooper came hither and Ordered two Kasks of Clarett for Thomas Howerd'.

5 May 1720 'I mixed about eight Gallons of Frensh Brandy with water ...'

27 May 1720 'Charles Howerd botled off some Clarret, Mr Aldred had some of it and I had above eleven gallons of it.'(Tyrer 1972, 11, 13)

Less than a year later, on 3 February 1721, he wrote: 'This Night I had a Cargo of 16 Larg ones brought to Whit Hall'. The next day:

4 February 'William Carefoot [his groom] covered the Cargo very well with Straw'.

10 February 'Charles Howard brought me a good provision for Acqua Coelestis, I showed him his goods well stored in Whit-Hall.' (Tyrer 1972, 3, 36). (Charles Howard was Nicholas's tailor; he and his brothers were his confederates in the smuggling enterprise (Blundell 1952, 201-2)).

It is obvious from his diaries that Nicholas Blundell was providing cellar space for the forbidden goods in what he rather provocatively calls 'Ye Whitehall'; and that he was sharing the wine, not only with some of his trusted tenants, who were also part of the whole operation, but also with friends among the neighbouring gentry. In June 1720, for example, both Mr Scarisbrick of Scarisbrick Hall, inland from North Meols, and Mr Molyneux of Mossborough Hall, Rainford, sent their servants for some claret (Tyrer 1972, 14).

Twenty years later, in 1740, tea and brandy came in on the North Meols coast, smuggled, it was alleged, by several people living in Kew Lane, North Meols. In a consequent court case it was alleged that two brothers, John and Thomas Rimmer, with Thomas Aughton and James Taylor, had at the beginning of the summer carried several casks of brandy and chests of tea on horseback from the coast to the house of Mr Cross of Crosshall, near Chorley, some 20 miles inland. The informant, Henry Ball, stated that he had helped to carry the goods and that they did not see Mr Cross, as the family '…were busy eating and drinking in the house and could not tell what passed out of doors'. The goods were left in some outhousing (LRO DDSh 12/4).

Smuggled goods were probably also enjoyed by people lower down in the social scale than the gentry. It is rare to find evidence other than probate inventories for such people but fortunately for historians of south west Lancashire, the very full household accounts of Richard Latham, a yeoman farmer of Scarisbrick, four miles inland from North Meols, have survived. Covering the years 1724-1767, they include quantities of spices, treacle, dried fruit, wines, spirits and tobacco (though no recorded tea or coffee) – some, at least, of which are likely to have come, untaxed, over the water from the west (LRO DP 385; Weatherill 1990).

Who then was involved in the trade? Examples have already been given of the gentry's involvement; but practically everybody appears to have had a part to play. A contemporary document states that: '…the least appearance of danger from [Customs officers] is conveyed to [the smugglers] by signals, which at the same time inform them to what parts they may with safety steer'(Atholl Papers 40B/24). This document further reports:

'That upon the west coast of Britain, the Farmers, their servants Men and Women, and the lower class of people in general are artfully engaged by the more substantial smugglers to be adventurers, in proportion to their respective means, in the illicit practice of smugling from the Isle of Man, as the most certain pledge for securing their assistance on all occasions, the pernicious effects of which are too evident by their conduct, being always ready to assemble, obstruct, assault and deforce the officers of the revenue in the execution of their duty, and by the great neglect of their proper, usefull and necessary occupations in the Country' (Atholl Papers 40B/24).

It is difficult to say how much of this account applies to any single locality, but available evidence indicates that the people of Birkdale and Ainsdale were very much involved in the trade. The likely scenario when a 'run' was expected was that a lookout was stationed on the coast to see that all was clear before the ship came ashore. It would have been very easy to see the whole of the coastline from a high sandhill or from the tops of the Ainsdale and Birkdale windmills (the latter after 1750) (Harrop 1985, 60). In addition, the many manorial duties tenants had to perform such as 'Wreck lookers', 'Lookers to the star (marram) grass', 'Hawslookers', 'Lookers that no persons dig, get, lead or carry off any sand within the Manor' (Harrop 1985, 66-67), as well as working on the fishing stalls, meant that many of the tenants had perfectly legitimate reasons for being on the shore at any time. If an Excise officer came along, people could provide proof that they were going about their lawful business. The above account states that the assistance of local people in the trade was secured by engaging them to be 'adventurers', that is, people who undertook or shared in commercial adventures (SOED, 29). In other words, they had a stake in the whole enterprise. How this was organised is not known: there does not appear to be much sign of conspicuous consumption in Birkdale and Ainsdale in this period – though a number of Birkdale and Ainsdale homes did contain unusual and precious items in the 18th century (Harrop 1985, 85-86). Payments made to all who assisted in the trade could well, however, have been used for draining land, improving farm buildings or buying livestock, which would not attract outside attention. Nor do we know how payment for goods was arranged, but once they were brought to order, payment was possibly sent back on the boats delivering the cargo – and could well have been, at least partly, in barley for the Manx breweries and hides for the tannery (Atholl Papers 1765, 40B/24).

The account also stresses the treatment that those involved in smuggling handed out to the officers of the Revenue: obstructing, assaulting and preventing them from carrying out their lawful duties. One would expect the Commissioners of the Revenue to say this, but there is plenty of evidence to back up their statement. It is easy after this space of time for smuggling to take on a romantic aura, with a battle of wits between the smugglers and the authorities of the Crown. In fact, the trade was often dangerous – on both sides – and violent. In the episode mentioned above, involving Barnaby Hesketh of North Meols in 1686, the local Customs officer, William Blake, was at hand when the ship arrived. He boarded the ship and attempted to do his duty, to arrest the captain and crew and seize the prohibited goods, in this case wine and six runlets (casks) of brandy. He claimed that he was himself detained and offered a considerable sum of money not to board the ship. A couple of years later, Blake again attempted to board the same ship. This time, he claimed that one of the crew stabbed his horse; that as the tide was coming in, he and Bartholomew Hesketh cut his whip and saddle girth so that he fell from the horse again as he tried to remount; and that he was then badly beaten up by the ship's captain and crew, so that he was '…sore wounded, one of his ribbes being broken and breast ill bruised and hurt'. Further assaults followed. It took two years from the original assault for the case to

come before the Ormskirk magistrates, and then all the accused were discharged (LRO QSP 653/45).

There appears to be no evidence of anyone on the Lancashire coast being successfully prosecuted for smuggling. The comment of a Customs officer on the Isle of Man, reporting back to London, was equally true of the Lancashire coast: '…notwithstanding the laws provided to restrain them, they are effectually secured against the punishments justly due' (Atholl Papers, 40 B/24). How did this happen? On the local side, we have seen that everyone living on and near the coast knew about the trade, and many were actually involved in it, from the gentry downwards. It was, of course, the gentry who, as Justices of the Peace, sat on the bench at the quarter sessions and heard any cases involving those accused of smuggling – so it is not surprising that there were no successful prosecutions against them. Furthermore, the letter books of the port of Liverpool contain evidence of smugglers being sheltered and protected from arrest by local Customs officials; and, if actually caught and sent to gaol, being assisted to escape. They also state that sheriff's officers will not arrest any of the smugglers with writs out against them (Jarvis 1954, 52-53). It is interesting that in the Blake case, mentioned above, Blake sent for the constable to assist him against the smugglers, and the constable refused to come (LRO QSP 653/45). The account of the case in 1740 against a group of North Meols men accused of smuggling tea and brandy also shows how confused the evidence was from witnesses (possibly, or even probably, deliberately). In addition, the main accused, Henry Ball, had 'been sheltered and protected by the Collector of Preston', with whom he was on drinking and 'business' terms. There is no wonder that the case was dismissed (LRO DDSh 12/4).

There was also another crucial factor in the trade's success: the effects of government policies over the period. The increasingly heavy taxes on luxury goods that gave rise to the trade have already been discussed. The total failure of successive governments then to impose their law on the consequent illegal trading was an equally important factor. Up to the late 17th century, there was no organised Customs and Excise service. The Stuart kings relied on Customs duties for more than half their revenue, but the right to collect them was 'let' out by the Exchequer, which 'farmed' them to outside persons. The person who took out the 'let' paid a sum of money to the Exchequer and reimbursed himself by collecting the tax. The Crown was not really interested in whether the duties were collected, so long as the value of the income from them was not diminished (Smith 1980, 22-3). Thus, no real attempt was made to enforce the law. As smuggling grew, however, the Crown decided to assume direct management of the Excise, and appointed Commissioners in 1671 (Jarvis 1945-46, 245-46). In Liverpool, many existing staff were replaced by new appointments (Jarvis 1954, xix). By 1688 there were officers in all the ports, who began to exercise some control over illicit trading. In the following year, however, William of Orange assumed the throne and in February 1689 issued an order that there would be a 'cessation of all offices until their beneficiaries were authorised to act by fresh powers', thus changing the officers once again (Smith 1980, 26). William Blake was probably one of the Customs officers removed from the service in 1689. There were complaints that the Excise was full of Jacobites, supporters of the deposed King James II, and many officers were removed for real or perceived disloyalty to the new monarch (Smith 1980, 32). This was especially likely in Lancashire, with its strong Catholic adherence; and the question of religion and loyalty continued to be important. In 1716, the year after the attempted invasion by the Old Pretender, the Board of Commissioners wrote to the Collector at Liverpool as follows:

'We being informed that William Purchase, Waiter and Searcher at Meals, his wife is a roman catholick and that he suffers his children to be educated in the same religion, you are to examine and report to us the truth thereof with your opinion.' (Jarvis 1954, 10).

The evidence is overwhelming that the job of the Customs officers on the spot was all but impossible.

Attacks of the type reported in 1686 seem to have been rare on this coast, unlike the extreme violence that was common on the south coast – possibly because the officers became wary of challenging smugglers; but the officers had to live in an atmosphere of continual unhelpfulness and hostility (Smith 1980, 44). The local people made life as difficult for them as possible; and if they needed assistance, no local enforcers of the law would help them. In 1725 Customs officials on the Isle of Man, reporting on the Lancashire coast, said that if the vast frauds continued, then it would be necessary to station officers within sight of one another, with troops to assist them, as no help in apprehending smugglers could be expected from any local people (Jarvis 1945-46, 252). Twenty-five years later, another report said that the officers on the coast could do nothing, as they were single-handed and placed five to six miles from each other (Jarvis 1945-46, 260). The Customs letter books of the port of Liverpool give a graphic first-hand glimpse into the life led by Mr Clough, the Waiter and Searcher at North Meols, that is, the Customs officer appointed to search ships, baggage or goods for dutiable or contraband articles (Jarvis 1954, 172; Wilkins 1992, 9). Early in 1739, he was in trouble with his superiors for not keeping a horse, thus disabling him '...from performing his duty as he ought to do'. A letter of 20 February 1739 gives his response:

'You will please to observe that he acknowledges the charge, but endeavours to extenuate the crime by alledgeing there was noe hay to be bought there and therefore he was obliged to hire a horse by which he has done his duty; but we must beg leave to observe that the excuse he pretends to make of the want of hay is a very lame one and must be entirely false, for it is notoriously known that there has not been soe great a pleant [plenty] of hay nor soe cheap in this country these 20 years, and the said surveyor informs us that he does not perform his duty by rideing his district as often as he ought but neglects the same and pretends he walks it some times by which it appears plainely in our humble opinion that he is very culpable' (Jarvis 1954, 52).

Not only did Mr Clough not ride round his district as he ought, but he lived some way from the shore. Two months later, his superiors decided to do something about this unsatisfactory situation, proposing to remove him to Crossens, '…which is close by the water side, and where he will have a much better prospect both of the sea and of the river Ribble and be capable of making better observations than he possibly can where he now resides …' (Jarvis 1954, 52). The picture is of an officer doing his best to keep out of the way of any smuggling activity. In June 1740 four extra officers were sent to assist Clough '…in apprehending and taking some of the smugglers that there was warrants out against, which we are obliged to send our own officers to execute, for the sheriff's officers will not arrest any of the smugglers' (Jarvis 1954, 53). The transcript of the case brought in 1740 regarding the smuggling of goods from North Meols to Crosshall shows Mr Clough trying very hard to assemble evidence, but no one questioned would admit to anything that would stand up in a court of law (LRO DDSh 12/4). There is little doubt that Customs officers were entirely on their own, 'foreigners', despised and disliked by the local people among whom they had to live, and charged with carrying out an impossible job – not helped by being constantly bombarded from Whitehall and left short of the necessary resources to do the job.

Local action could be positive as well as negative. In the growing port of Liverpool, Customs were laxer than anywhere else in the country, and Customs officers frequently bribed to admit goods free of duty (Nash 1991). Furthermore, in the late 17th century, someone arranged for Liverpool Customs officers to be picked up by the 'press gang' for service with the Navy. The comment of the Commissioners in London summed up the position neatly – in something of an understatement, '…it was felt by the Treasury that this was gravely prejudicial to the safeguarding of the Revenue' (quoted in Smith, 1980, 22). Those officers lucky enough to escape impressment were likely to find themselves called up for jury or inquest service at the very time that a 'run' was expected. It was not until 1786 that officers of the Customs and Excise were protected from service on juries and inquests; and this exemption from jury service still applies today.

Throughout the first half of the 18th century, Customs and Excise officials from Ireland and Scotland did their utmost to arouse the officials in London to the extent of trading which was taking place, not only on the coast of Lancashire, but also along all the western coast of Britain – but with scarcely any response (Carson 1972, 70-72). The situation grew steadily worse: in June 1750, for example, the Commissioners for managing and causing to be levied and collected his Majesty's Customs wrote to the Right Honourable the Lords Commissioners of his Majesty's Treasury, enclosing a letter they had received from the Comptroller at Whitehaven regarding information that: '…there has been within the last three weeks the greatest importation there [the Isle of Man], of brandy, teas, East India and other high duty goods ever known, all which are intended to be run upon the coasts of Great Britain and Ireland' (Atholl Papers X14-14). By 1764 it was estimated that the loss to the Revenue on Customs duties as a result of the 'trade' from the island was around £350,000 (Atholl Papers 40 B/24). The traffic had reached 'enormous proportions' and something had to be done. The British Government decided to put a stop to it by the only effective means – by seeking to revest the island in the British Crown. Pressure was put on the Duke of Atholl, who had become the owner of the island on the death of the tenth Earl of Derby in 1736, and in 1765 he offered to sell to the Crown for £70,000. This was accepted, ratified by act of Parliament, and statutory powers taken immediately to suppress the smuggling that had been such a problem for almost a century (Jarvis 1945-46, 263-65). Contrary to some sources, the trade did not stop almost immediately (Wilkins 1992, 99-119); but we found no evidence of further activity on this coast. Within 20 years of the sale of the island the Collector at Liverpool reported that, '…There has not been any information received of an avow'd smuggler coming within the limits of this port since the Isle of Man was annexed to the Crown' (Smith 1980, 46-7).

So a source of adventure, income and luxury and untaxed goods came to an end – an activity which was only a sideline, an adjunct to local people's daily occupations, and regarded by them as quite legitimate. Tea in the afternoon, claret to accompany the rabbit pie, a pipe or two of tobacco, a glass of brandy, all these now had to be bought at normal prices – though in 1784 William Pitt the Younger, the Prime Minister, reduced tea duty from 125% to 12½%, thus making smuggling tea unprofitable and increasing greatly the sales of legal tea (Smith 1980, 94).

What were the effects of nearly a century of smuggling? Intoxication? Perhaps cheap drinks at the inn? It was said of the Isle of Man that, 'There are few shops, and not many houses occupied by the lower orders, where spirits are not sold either in large or small quantities. The Smuggling trade introduced habits of intoxication, which still prevail [in 1816] to an extent the most lamentable.' (Bullock 1816, 278). (Drunkenness – and immorality – were believed to result from smuggling in the south also (Gaskell 1857, 30)).

Did it stimulate the growing of barley in greater quantities, to supply the Isle of Man breweries malting free of duty? In the 18th century, breweries were established on the island, '…which are more than sufficient to consume all the barley they can collect from the west parts of Great Britain, and from Ireland' (Atholl Papers 40B/24). There is certainly a tradition in Whitehaven, on the Cumbrian coast, that Cumberland Rum Butter was concocted by local smugglers in the 18th century (Whitehaven Leaflet).

By the end of the 18th century, as Liverpool was growing rapidly and Preston developing as a port, and with the movement of the coastline to the west (Harrop 1985, 27), Birkdale and North Meols were little used as landing places (LRO DDIn 55/189). The population was growing, roads were gradually improving and Southport would soon be founded. Wreck lookers and the landlord's strong defence to his right of wreck, however, continued into the 19th century, as more ships were wrecked on the coast (Harrop 1985, 113; Glazebrook 1826, 90). That the

old practice of fishing with nets on the shore continued until the early 20th century is shown by the evidence of the plan shown (fig.4, above).

Regarding Sefton's coastal heritage, it is important to recognise two major factors discussed in this article. First, that this coast was of such importance in the history of smuggling. The total amount of goods smuggled into the country along the Lancashire coast was almost as great as that illicitly landed on the Kent and Sussex coasts – without the level of violence seen there. This difference, it is argued, is a direct result of the involvement of people from all levels of society in a trade which they deemed to be lawful, because of the status of the Isle of Man and the Earls of Derby as Lords of Man. Second, there was a system of fishing stalls that we have not so far found recorded in other parts of the country. The rights and usage of these stalls continued until the second half of the 19th century, when fishermen from the new and growing town of Southport began to fish from the Birkdale shore, mainly without permission, and caused trouble. More importantly, the new owner of Birkdale, Thomas Weld-Blundell, wanted to repossess the Birkdale shore – even though leases granting the holders rights over three of the stalls were still in force. Access to the shore was increasingly denied. Fishing stalls were part of the old economy, and vanished with it: the landowners wished to build new Birkdale, with no place for old practices (Harrop 1982, 163; 1985, 147-49).

Acknowledgements

I wish to thank Pat Perrins, the Secretary of the Birkdale and Ainsdale Historical Research Society and my husband, John, for reading this text and for their helpful comments.

I am also grateful to the Chetham Society for giving permission for the use of the map of south west Lancashire before the Industrial Revolution, and to Liverpool Record Office (Liverpool Libraries) for supplying the image of Yates' map.

A Dangerous Coast

Barbara and Reginald Yorke

INTRODUCTION

Historians of the Port of Liverpool agree on the extremely hazardous nature of the seaward approaches to the river in the past, particularly in the 18th and first half of the 19th centuries, when strenuous attempts were made to attract more shipping into the Mersey (Hyde 1971, 11). Accidents to ships occurred as often as not in the final approaches to the port, notably within Liverpool Bay itself (Jarvis 1998, 17). This was also the view of the port's first Marine Surveyor, Captain Denham. Writing in 1840 he says, '…Little does the merchant think of this in his calculations when stopping the insurance on learning his cargo is off Point Lynas; why 'tis then the risk commences' (Mountfield 1953, 134). J. H. Lawson Booth listed 304 sea casualties on the Sefton coast between 1740 and 1946 (Booth 1947). More recent work indicates 688 shipwrecks between 1740 and 1990 (Head 1990).

These difficulties were partially caused by the extreme tidal range (over 30 feet) and the fact that ships had to navigate through shifting channels between some 20,000 acres of sandbanks that dry out at low tide (Ritchie-Noakes 1984, 3). Except for a couple of hours either side of High Water, the tide would race at up to 7 knots. In addition the estuary is '…exposed to sometimes ferocious winds which in former times could make the simplest manoeuvre difficult or even hazardous' (Jarvis 1998, 24). These factors were reflected in the formerly high casualty rate of sailing vessels in the port. Here it should be noted that the 'port' was previously defined as extending from the Red Stones at Hoylake to Hesketh Bank in Lancashire (Woods 1945, 88). The seaward boundary was the Bar[1].

To understand further the navigational difficulties involved, the Mersey has been compared to a bottle with a narrow neck (Denham 1840, 126). On the ebb the upper estuary discharges through the neck of the bottle (between Liverpool and Birkenhead) a considerable volume of water in the general direction of Formby Point, which scours out the Formby Channel, the original true outlet of the Mersey. This channel was first accurately surveyed in 1689 by Greenville Collins, whose survey of British coastal waters was published as 'Great Britain's Coasting Pilot'. In this he described '…a channel near Formby to go into Liverpool where there is three fathoms at low water…but this place is not buoyed nor beaconed and so not known' (Collins 1693). The channel ran a somewhat twisting and dangerous course between the shoals of Burbo Bank and the appropriately named Mad Wharf on Sefton's lee shore. A number of westerly gullies flowed between the sandbanks in the general direction of deeper water. The alternative was the Rock Channel, which ran close along the Wirral shore towards Perch Rock (New Brighton) from Hoylake, where a deep pool provided safe anchorage for ships at all states of the tide. These two channels remained the only choices until the discovery and opening-up of the entrance to the Crosby Channel by Denham in 1839 (Denham 1840, chart opposite iv). It was imperative that the mouth of the Mersey be given a safer system of navigation. This first involved the placement of navigation beacons at strategic points at the mouth of the estuary and the marking of the more dangerous sandbanks (Hyde 1971, 13).

In obtaining the first Liverpool Dock Act in 1709 Liverpool Town Council had already stated a desire not only to provide an enclosed 'dock or basin' for merchant shipping but also to improve the safety of the port. The preamble to the Act recognised that the entrance into the port, '…has been found so dangerous and difficult that great numbers of strangers and others have frequently lost their lives as well as ships and goods for want of proper land-marks, and buoys to direct them into the said harbour and that when such ships have entered the Port they have been exposed to great dangers for want of a convenient wet dock or basin for their safety'.

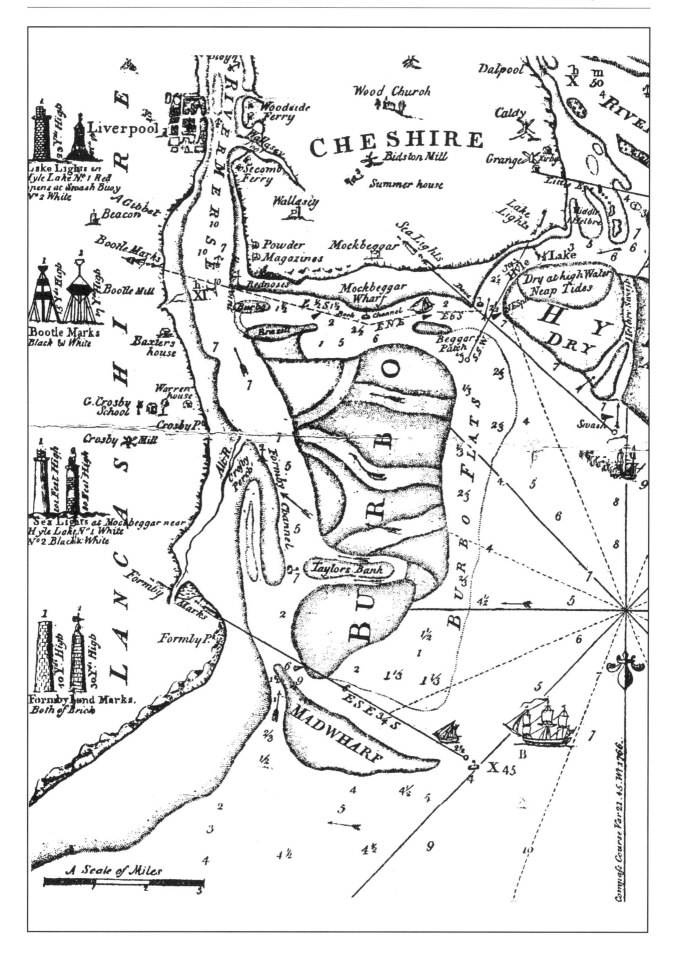

Fig. 1: Williamson's Chart 1766, North is at the bottom. This shows the Formby Channel (leading line – Formby's two brick Formby towers) and the Rock Channel (leading line – Bootle's two wooden marks). (FCS Archives)

To improve safety they undertook to place at least three buoys and '...erect land-marks as shall be necessary near or in the said Port by and through the channel called Formby Channel'.

Liverpool's second Dock Act in 1715 re-authorised the building of landmarks[2] on the Lancashire coast '...for direction of Ships coming into the Formby Channel from the sea' (Statutes 1715). Two years later, in 1717, the Liverpool Common Council elected Thomas Steers as Dock Master '...to take care of the Dock...and of the buoys and land marks that are or shall be placed and made for direction of ships into the harbour' (Picton 1907, 50).

Further important improvements in the navigational safety of the Mersey came between 1759 and 1793, the period of office of William Hutchinson as Dock Master. He published his remarkable 'Treatise on Practical Seamanship' in which he set out his findings, concerns and proposals. In this he described the Formby Channel as,

Fig. 2: Formby Lighthouse, 1931
(Courtesy of E. Chambre Hardman Trust)

'...far more dangerous than the Rock Channel though there is at present two fathoms more water through it, but then it is a Lee Shore with a strong Westerly wind, which makes the waves run very high here, and besides that the Sand Banks on both sides are very often shifting – but a Northerly wind, and want of water in the Rock Channel may oblige a ship to come this Way' (Burdett 1776, footnote Hutchinson 1777). Burdett's chart of 1771 (corrected 1776) was bound in with Hutchinson's book and illustrated those navigational aids, which by then had been erected. Amongst these were some of the earliest on our coast.

LANDMARKS AND LIGHTHOUSES

Only three nautical landmarks now survive on the Sefton coast. These are at Formby, Crosby (Hall Road) and at the mouth of the Alt. In order to understand their function it is necessary to review the history and positioning of the more important of these interesting structures. Some of the earlier ones are illustrated in Williamson's chart 1766. (fig. 1).

a. The Formby Landmarks

On 15 May 1717, Liverpool Common Council '...Ordered that Mr Mayor have power to contract with Mr Mollinex of Mossborough for ground to build the Landmarks at Formby for direction of ships coming into Formby Channel' (Picton 1907, 50). Thus from 1719 the entrance to this important but dangerous channel was marked by the erection of a brick landmark 120 feet high, situated at Alt Grange near the mouth of the Alt (position Lat 53"32'N; Long 3"04'W). This was known subsequently as the Formby Upper Landmark or Formby South East Landmark. Its construction was noted in Nicholas Blundell's Diary (Tyrer 1970, 271) '...Pat Gillibrond, my Wife and I rode out to see the Land Mark as is building at the Grange' (fig. 2).

At first it worked in conjunction with a lower mark, which was a wooden perch (pole) (Fearon and Eyes 1737). When these were in line, vessels would be led on an ESE course into the channel between Mad

Wharf to landward and Burbo Bank to seaward. By 1767 the perch had been replaced by another lower tower, 90 feet high (Eyes 1767) this being the Formby Lower Landmark. Both are clearly depicted on Burdett's chart of 1771.

Unfortunately, the continually changing courses of the natural channels though the estuarine delta of sandbanks, meant that the positioning of landmarks also frequently needed changing. There were regular complaints that they were in the wrong position. In October 1811 it was reported that the Old Formby Landmark '...being in the wrong position was therefore highly dangerous to navigation and should be immediately taken down' (LDCM 1/10/1811). By 1813, the Lower Landmark had been moved one and a half miles further north to stand beside the Formby Lifeboat House (Thomas 1813). This was subsequently shown as a wooden 'frame-work beacon' (Denham 1840, figure between x and xi).

Later the North West Mark was moved again about one mile further north to Freshfield. A pair of marks was then constructed, the upper just above Mean High Water Line (MHWL), the lower midway between Mean High and Low Water Lines. The last upper North West Mark was a wooden 'diamond' structure, 64 feet high, which blew down in the late 1960s. The lower beacon was originally shown as 'stone tower' but, after 1944, simply as 'remains' on the beach below MHWL (Admiralty 1944).

Early in the 1830s the deterioration in the Formby and Rock Channels prompted the Liverpool Dock Trustees to seek help from the Admiralty: as a result Lieutenant Henry M. Denham was seconded to survey the outer harbour and make recommendations (Mountfield 1953, 124). Following a diligent survey carried out between 1834 and 1838 Denham produced what was immediately agreed to be 'an excellent chart', (Denham 1840), for which he was rewarded with the Freedom of the Borough of Liverpool and, in 1835, was appointed to the newly created post of Marine Surveyor of the Port (Mountfield 1953, 127). Following this appointment Henry Denham then

discovered and deepened a new and safer outlet channel in 1834, which eventually opened up the Crosby Channel of today (Denham 1840, 31). This was so successful that Denham was able to report '...12,000 vessels passed through the channel every year and that the Rock and Formby Channels were closed'. As always there were still '...considerable changes taking place on the twelve square miles comprising the Formby, Burbo and Jordan Flats' (Mountfield 1953, 129). These necessitated further changes to the navigation beacons ashore.

Denham rose to the challenge by arranging, in 1831, for the Formby Upper Landmark to be converted into a lighthouse which, working in conjunction with a new Formby Floating Light-Vessel, guided shipping through the new channel (Woods 1945, 111). The bill for the elevation of the landmark to a lighthouse came to £300 for an attached dwelling and £40 for the light and reflector. A Keeper was to be appointed at a salary of £20 per annum; running costs in the form of oil, cotton wick and maintenance were calculated at £100 per annum (LDCM 20/6/1829).

Fig. 3: Formby Landmark, at Formby Point (Photo, authors)

After further changes to the channels it ceased as a lighthouse for a period, in 1839, when the Victoria Channel was opened. It was however lit again between 1851 and 1856, after which the light had to move to a new lighthouse at Crosby (Woods 1945, 111-112). The 'Old Lighthouse', continuing simply as a landmark but recognised as '...the Methuselah of local nautical structures', was demolished in 1941 as it was feared it might act as a useful beacon to enemy bombers during the Second World War (Woods 1945, 111).

Standing slightly south of the remains of Formby Lifeboat House, the present day Formby Landmark is shown as a 'flag staff with triangle' on modern Admiralty charts and indicates the site of the North West Beacon prior to its move one mile further north to Freshfield (fig. 3).

The Victoria Beach Mark replaced the Formby Lower Landmark and stood above MHWL due west of Formby Old Lighthouse on the Formby boundary and on the line between the two former Formby landmarks (LDCM 5/5/1830).

Fig. 4: Crosby Beacon - (Photo, authors)

b. The Crosby Marks

Hutchinson describes how, having entered the Formby Channel with the Lower Landmark bearing ESE, '...you should then change course to bring the two North End Marks "in one" to go past Taylors Bank' (Burdett 1776, footnote Hutchinson 1777). These stood south of the Formby Old Landmark. The upper one would have been situated where Hightown is today, which was probably at the later site of the first Crosby lighthouse. The lower one would correspond to the position of the Crosby Beacon that, remarkably, still survives. (fig. 4).

This is the last remaining true navigation beacon in the Mersey approaches and its predecessor here seems to have been the first. An order of Liverpool Common Council of 8 January 1683 stated that the perch from Crosby '...be brought, or a new one set up at Black Rock' (Woods 1945, 89). Collins' Chart of 1689 does show a perch at Black Rock and nothing at Crosby. In practice the only navigational aids on the adjacent coast at that time were the small spire of the original Formby Chapel which, like its successor 150 years later, must have been just visible above the dunes, and the spire of Sefton Church, some four and a half miles inland. Williamson's Chart of 1766 shows a perch near Mean Low Water Line adjacent to the mouth of the Alt. A new beacon was ordered to be placed 'on the shore at Crosby' in connection with the new Crosby Lighthouse in 1839 (LDCM 24/10/1839) and, in 1847, this was moved half a mile to the NNE when the lighthouse was itself moved the same distance in that direction (LDCM 18/2/1847). A perch or beacon appears to have remained at about that position, marking the passage through the Formby Channel. It is still there today, a triangular framework structure showing 'a ball over a diamond'. Around it now are what appear to be the anchoring points of several earlier beacons (authors' observation).

The Crosby Lighthouses situated one and a half miles SSW of the old Formby Lighthouse, the first of these was a wooden flat-faced, shaft-like structure (Denham 1840, between x and xi). This came into service in 1839 with the opening of the Victoria

Channel and worked in conjunction with the Formby Floating Light to lead vessels through the new channel (Woods 1945, 111). The Formby Light being then extinguished, John Christopherson vacated Formby and took over Crosby Lighthouse. He resigned in September 1840 and his position was taken by the former master of Formby Light Vessel (LDCM 15/10/1847). In 1847, because of continuing changes in the channels, the Master Pilots recommended that the Crosby Light be re-sited half a mile NNE, and the Crosby Shore Beacon should also be moved half a mile NNE (LDCM 18/2/1847).

The continuing changes in the channels made Captain Denham even consider having a 'moveable' light. In fact a second Crosby Lighthouse was erected in 1847 (Rees 1949, 180). This was a square brick tower 90 feet high, situated about half a mile north of the first Crosby Lighthouse. This became serviceable on 2 November 1847 (Notice to Mariners, Gore's General Advertiser 23/9/1847). It was extinguished on 16 October 1851 when Formby was again relit, operational until 1856. It was again relit when the light returned to Crosby (Notice to Mariners, Gore's General Advertiser 15/9/1856). A painting by J. Harry Williams, dated 1856, of the mouth of the Alt looking south clearly shows the two Crosby lights (Walker Art Gallery 1978, 222).

The second Crosby Lighthouse was destroyed by fire with the loss of three lives, including the Keeper, in the night of 2 February 1898 during strong winds. The lighthouse had a powerful paraffin-fuelled lamp with five mirrors, visible for 12 miles. It had caught fire four years previously when a window of the lamp-room blew in: that fire was put out by sand. The final conflagration in 1898 was described as like a 'huge furnace in full blast'. Because of its remote situation the Crosby fire engine was unable to reach it (Crosby Herald 12/2/1898, 12).

With the introduction of lightships and improved buoyage of the Crosby Channel, lighthouse provision on the Lancashire coast was no longer necessary.

The Hall Road Beach Mark is the last survivor of the two pairs of beacons situated north and south of Crosby, one nautical mile apart and marking a 'measured mile' They were known as the North and South, Inner and Outer Marks and were placed to assist with steamship trials, rather than serve a navigational function.

Denham had thought that the use of the Formby Channel would cease, except for small local craft, after his discovery of the New Channel. However, a comprehensive and informative book on the Port of Liverpool produced by the United States Shipping Board in 1929, described the Formby Channel as four miles in length and 400 yards wide with a 16 feet depth at half-tide, and still usable by coastal vessels (Cotter 1929, 7).

c. The Bootle Landmarks

Two wooden landmarks appear at Bootle on 18th century charts, such as that of Williamson, 1766. Somewhat surprisingly on Mackenzie's 1776 Chart they are shown as 'lights'. These provided a leading-line[3] for vessels using the Rock Channel. The lower one of these was described as 'ancient' in 1820 (Troughton 1820, no page number). It was moved into a better position as a leading mark in 1811 (LDCM 10/9/1811). (fig. 5).

Fig. 5: Bootle Landmark. Wood engraving by Henry Hole. Described by Denham (1840) as the Inner Bootle Mark. (From Troughton's 'History of Liverpool' 1820')

The Marine Surveyor requested authority to remove the lower Bootle landmark in 1827 because the recently erected church was 'serving the purpose of the mark' (LDCM 7/8/1827). This mark was replaced on 1 September 1829 by twin stone obelisks (Denham 1840, 84). A fine painting of them by Samuel Austin hangs in Liverpool (Walker Art Gallery 1978, 29 and 91). The proposal to erect these seems to have alarmed Lord Derby as the Secretary to the Dock Committee and the Harbour Master were directed to '…wait upon the Earl and explain the necessity for their erection and to solicit his lordships permission for them to be placed in the situation fixed by the committee' (LDCM 30/6/1829). When erected the obelisks stood side-by-side, 100 feet high, just below HWL on the site of what is now Alexandra Dock. The Bootle Upper Land Mark situated much further inland towards Walton Church was 'sighted' through the twin lower marks from the Rock Channel. Most leading-line marks are arranged in a straight line: this was a most unusual arrangement. The obelisks were finally removed to make way for the construction of the Alexandra Dock, which opened in 1881. The leading-line for the approach to the Mersey via the Rock Channel was then marked by a red and white flashing light.

Summary

Man-made navigational aids in the form of landmarks have been provided on this coast at least since the 18th century. Their positions had to be altered very frequently due to changes in the navigable channels. Four pairs existed at various times at Bootle, Crosby, Formby and Freshfield. One of these landmarks was for two periods a lighthouse. In addition there were two other purpose-built lighthouses at Crosby.

BRITAIN'S FIRST LIFEBOAT[4] STATION

The first published evidence of a 'boat and station for saving lives' at Formby Point is contained in a footnote to the Chart of the Harbour of Liverpool, originally surveyed by Burdett in 1771 but updated in 1776. The footnote reads:

'NB: On the strand[5] about a mile below Formby Lower Land Mark there is a boathouse, and a boat kept ready to save lives from vessels forced on shore on that coast, and a guinea, or more, reward is paid by the Corporation for every human life that is saved by means of this boat.'

The exact date of the establishment of Formby's lifeboat station remains uncertain, as the minute book of the Liverpool Dock Committee prior to 1793 has long since been destroyed. However a minute of the Liverpool Common Council dated 5 March 1777 indicates that the boat and boathouse had already been there long enough to need repair, so it must have been built between 1771 and 1776:

'It is ordered that the boat and boathouse which was formerly ordered to be built and kept at Formby in readiness to fetch any shipwrecked persons from off the banks, be repaired and kept up for these purposes but that Mr Gerrard [the treasurer] do go over and agree with any person for such purpose and what the same will have by the year to take care of the said house and boat and doing this humane and good service and report it to the Council' (LCCM 5/3/1777).

At the next meeting of the Council on 2 April 1777 it was ordered that:

'Richard Scarisbrick of Formby, sailor, be appointed to take care of the boat and boathouse erected and provided to be built and stationed at Formby to assist and save shipwrecked persons and goods on this coast. And that Mr Gerrard do pay him the sum of five guineas for the good services by him already done herein and that he have a salary of two guineas a year from henceforth for such service. And that he and the boat's crew shall be handsomely rewarded hereafter for such good service done herein and not less than one guinea per head for every life or person they shall save and to be further rewarded as the Council shall on enquiring find he or they merit to be paid out of the dock duties' (LCCM 2/4/1777).

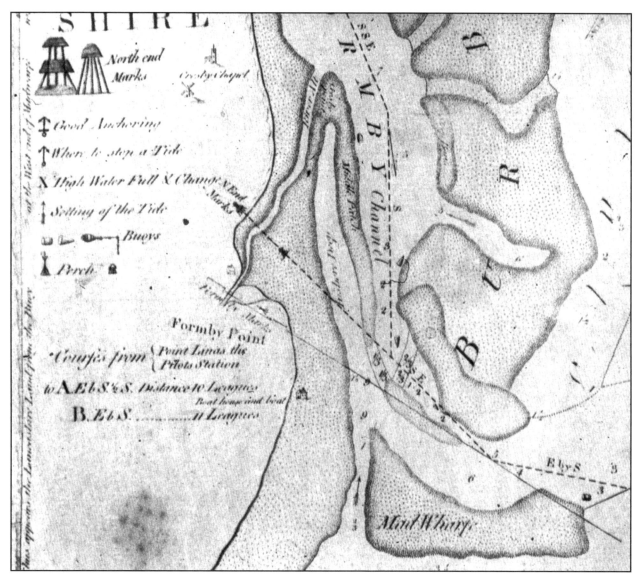

Fig. 6: Burdett's Chart 1781. North is at the bottom. This as the first chart to show the position of the Formby lifeboat station. (Courtesy of Liverpool Record Office, Liverpool Libraries).

Burdett's chart was updated and reprinted in 1781 and, in addition to the footnote, the position of the boathouse and boat was shown at Formby Point (fig.6).

Although little is known about this boat or her service, we may assume that she was a local fishing craft, possibly of the type known as a Mersey Gig, a useful and seaworthy, two or three-masted spritsail-rigged vessel, requiring a crew of three or four, and capable of being rowed or sailed. This type of boat probably developed in the Mersey in the 18th century (Stammers 1975, 283).

We hear little more about this boat until 1799 when the Dock Committee appointed William Brown to look after her '…in room of Robert Whitfield,

deceased, with the like allowances as enjoyed by his predecessor' (LDCM 1/2/1799). Then on 9 April 1800 Robert Neale, the Riding Officer at Formby, was appointed to the care of the boat and boathouse '…in the room of William Brown' (LDCM 9/4/1800). Whether the boat was adapted in any special way for its purpose is not known.

The original boathouse was rebuilt in 1793 on the same site at the end of what subsequently came to be known as Lifeboat Road (LDCM 9/2/1793). According to Eyes's 1828 survey of the bay the lifeboat house was situated 100 yards inland, well above the high tide line, on land belonging to the lord of the manor, the Reverend Richard Formby (Boult 1870, 246). This gentleman was the incumbent of St

John's Church, Liverpool, from 1784 to 1792 and later of Holy Trinity Church, St Anne's Street, Liverpool. He seems to have had a local beneficial influence and interest in lifesaving, somewhat akin to that of Dr John Sharpe at Bamburgh (Kipling 1982, 10). In 1798, he was honoured with the Freedom of the Borough of the Town of Liverpool '…as a mark of respect for his unwearied and compassionate attention in a variety of instances to the unfortunate who have suffered shipwreck on the coast near Formby, both with regard to their person and property' (LCCM 2/5/1790).

This boat was the only one serving the entire Liverpool Bay until 1803. In 1801, however, the Dock Committee directed the Marine Surveyor '…to obtain the best information and particulars he can from North Shields respecting the construction, expense and management of the boat called the "Lifeboat"' (LDCM 14/8/1801). The following year it was ordered '…that a boat (upon the improved principle) be built by Mr Henry Greathead to be used as occasion may require in this harbour' (LDCM 9/2/1802). Arriving in 1803, this was the first boat on the newly established Hoylake Lifeboat Station. In the meantime another lifeboat was built in Liverpool

at the instigation of the Collector of Excises, Jonathan Scott, and placed to the northward of the Fort, near the North Shore Coffee House (LDCM 7/2/1803).

In February 1802 the Formby boathouse was reported to have been destroyed by '…late tempestuous winds' but was ordered to be immediately rebuilt (LDCM 9/2/1802). By 1809 the rebuilding of the Formby Lifeboat Station was completed. It then received a boat from Liverpool, built by Richard Bushell, under William Croft as Coxswain[6], who was allowed to reside in an adjoining cottage (Boat House Cottage) (LDCM 28/11/1809). This building, which was also capable of receiving a limited amount of goods and merchandise '…that may be rescued from any vessel' is that which survived – with minor modification – up to the time of its final demolition in 1965 (fig.7).

Unfortunately, from a minute of the Dock Committee dated 5 April 1809, it must be inferred that the performance of the Formby Station in the early years of the 19th century had left much to be desired, its supervision perhaps having been neglected, (following the retirement of Hutchinson in 1793) in favour of the newer stations, particularly Hoylake (LDCM 5/4/1809). The work in 1809 represented a new start, but problems remained.

Fig. 7: Formby Lifeboat House, 1916. (FCS Archives)

In September 1816 the Liverpool Underwriters Association subscribed 25 guineas to a fund for a new boat at Formby, which the Dock Committee allowed to be placed on station in 1818 (LDCM 22/9/1818) but the Underwriters and the Reverend Richard Formby continued to express anxieties due to '...depredations by the sea'. The Surveyor reported to the Dock Committee in July 1817 that he had found the Formby Lifeboat House to be in a very '...hazardous state in consequence of the great encroachment of the sea' (LDCM 12/8/1817). Five years later, in 1822, the Surveyor reported that the sand-hill near the boathouse had been washed away to '...allow the tide to surround it and to be a danger to the building'. Repairs and protective measures at a cost of £25 were then approved (LDCM 10/4/1822).

In 1825 following public disquiet, the whole subject of the 'Recovery of Persons Apparently Drowned' and the state of the lifeboats in Liverpool Bay was referred to a sub-committee '...with power for them to provide and establish such boats as they may deem best and with a request that they will report their opinion upon the most effectual means of rendering prompt assistance in the Saving of Life and Property in case of Shipwreck on these coasts'. The ensuing report was presented to the Council on 1 November 1825 (LDCM 1/11/1825).

This comprehensive document laid the foundation for the future and more satisfactory operation, not only of the Formby boat, but also boats at the Point of Ayr, Hoylake and at the Magazines (Wallasey). New boats were built for each station and boathouses constructed at the Point of Ayr and the Magazines. Rules were drawn up explicitly dealing with the manning of the boats, each Master's remuneration and housing, and pay of the crew. The need for constant lookout by telescope (which was provided) and the exercise of the boat once a month under the superintendence of the Harbour Master were also stressed.

In view of the distance of the boathouse from Formby Village, the Master of the Formby Boat was to be paid £12 a year (and 5 tons of coal) as distinct from £7 10s 0d

elsewhere. The men were to be paid five guineas a year retainer and five shillings each day for exercising the boat, together with '...such further remuneration as may be determined by the Dock Committee for going out to vessels in distress in proportion to the risk incurred and the services rendered'. Thus in 1825 at the time of the foundation of the National Institution for the Preservation of Life from Shipwreck, the forerunner of the Royal National Lifeboat Institution (RNLI), the Formby Station quietly celebrated its first half-century of existence (Kipling 1982, 10).

The contribution of Denham to the navigational safety of the western approaches to the Mersey has already been referred to. This was based on his careful survey, excellent chart and published 'Sailing Directions' (Denham 1840). His description of a passage through the Formby Channel in the 1830s and 1840s makes interesting reading. Particularly poignant is his comment:

'To such as are in distress and are craving assistance, ere nightfall, in this region, it will be comfort to know that a life-boat station is established close to the NW Mark, where, or at the SE Mark, or Crosby Lighthouse, a blue flag will be hoisted, in recognition of your case; and if a telegraph, at Crosby, which I have repeatedly urged, be established, three hours will be saved in communicating your difficulties to the town' (Denham 1840, 77).

The first Keeper of the Formby Lighthouse in 1834 was Lieutenant Joseph Walker RN, and his duties also included the supervision of the Formby lifeboat. For a long time the boat had been in the charge of a succession of Coxswain/Keepers who actually lived with their families in the boathouse. To make the Coxswain responsible to the Lighthouse Keeper as his immediate superior was an idea that had been introduced at Hoylake in 1809. The Keeper was also made a 'Constable' with respect to the shore. Thus a chain of command was established via the Lighthouse Keeper to Lifeboat Coxswain.

The career of Lt Walker was to end on 13 January 1836, less than eighteen months from his appointment. The lifeboat under his command capsized and he was drowned, together with four of his crew (Liverpool Courier 20/1/1836). On seeing a vessel, the *Bryades*, in distress he had left a servant girl to 'mind the light', hoisted the distress flag and fired the signal gun to summon the crew. Unfortunately insufficient crew reported, but the lifeboat was launched with Walker as an additional member. Meanwhile the crew of the stricken vessel had got themselves to safety. Attempting to return to the shore the lifeboat capsized. Five crew members drowned, including the Lighthouse Keeper. Three were saved, two under the boat and one on top. Subsequently it was found that, instead of having been worn, newly issued cork life-jackets (the latest safety equipment) were still tied to the thwarts because the crew had found them cumbersome and they made rowing difficult. Meanwhile, a fund was set up for the widows and orphans (LDCM 19/1/1836).

This accident had an unfortunate sequel in 1839 when a further destructive gale hit the river. On Monday 7 January, at 11am, Mr Christopherson, the Lighthouse Keeper, saw through the haze a vessel with fore-and main-mast gone, about three to four miles south of the lighthouse; but he could not persuade the crew to launch. The next day, the gale still blowing, two further wrecks occurred. The first, on Burbo Bank, was judged to be within reach of the Magazines' lifeboat but the next, the brig *Harvest Home* outward bound for St Thomas's, struck on Mad Wharf. Attempts were made to launch the lifeboat without success as she repeatedly became swamped and had to return to shore to be bailed out. Finally conditions improved on the Thursday, the survivors being rescued from the wreck. The boat at that time, presumably the one built in 1825, was described by the Marine Surveyor as '...very old, heavy and unwieldy', with her freeboard low amidships. In 1841 she was replaced by a new boat specially built by Thomas Costain, a Liverpool boat builder, at a cost of £128 8s 10d. She measured 30 feet long, with a beam of nine feet three inches, and depth of four feet; she had 12 oars double-banked, two spritsails and a jib (LDCM 18/11/1841).

Another interesting report on the 'Lifeboat Establishment of the Port' was produced by Denham's successor, William Lord, in 1843. This gave a detailed and illuminating insight into the difficulties facing the lifeboat crews in Liverpool Bay, the seaworthiness of the boats and how the boats were constructed, supervised, crewed and operated (LDCM 16/10/1843). William Lord reported:

'There are 9 Life Boats, stationed as follows: Liverpool, Magazines, Hoylake, Point of Ayr, and Formby; (1 Master and 12 Men). Nearly all the Boats have been built since 1839, they pull double banked, are rigged with 2 Sprit Sails and a Jib, are of large size, possess great strength and are constructed on the most approved principles, with air-tight Casks inside, and a broad band of Cork running round the whole length of the boat, above the waterline, to resist violent shocks and give increased buoyancy enabling the boat to float although loaded with a considerable number of persons and filled with water, as many as 50 individuals having on one occasion been rescued from a wreck at one trip, making, with the Boat's crew of 11, sixty one persons in the boat at one time.

'The Boats are kept on Carriages in the Boat House near the Shore and horses are provided to enable them to proceed to the most advantageous spot for launching. A Gun is placed at the Station to summon the Crew, as also distress flags at each Lighthouse, Light ship, and Telegraph Station for the same purpose. The arrangements in these respects being such, that in many instances the Life Boat has been manned, launched and on her way to the Wreck in 17 or 18 minutes from the time of the distress signal being seen.

'The Masters and Crews of the Hoylake, Magazines and Formby Boats are composed of picked Fishermen intimately acquainted with the Banks, Swashways, Tides and Currents in Liverpool Bay: They reside in the immediate vicinity of the boat houses. The whole of the Crew is kept in constant and permanent pay; they are regularly mustered and exercised once a month: and no expense and been spared in rendering the boats, their equipments and Crews as perfect as possible. The Formby Boat is under the Direction of the Keeper of Crosby Lighthouse.'

In his report Lord referred graphically to the practical difficulties in launching a boat from the beach at Formby in the teeth of a gale:

'Many Patches of all the Banks dry; and some of them to a considerable height above the low water level: but in heavy on shore gales of wind owing to the shelving nature of the Sand Banks, and the shallowness of the water, a continuous line of heavy breakers extends far to Seaward on the weather side of them, rendering it extremely difficult, and at times perfectly impracticable (however advantageously the boats may be placed, and however near they may attain the position) to penetrate to a wreck so situated, without the certain and inevitable destruction of the Life Boat and her Crew.'

In 1874 the Formby Lifeboat Station was given a new boat. It was also constructed by Thomas Costain (MDHB DCM 1874) who continued building lifeboats for the Liverpool Dock Committee for many years and, in 1851, entered a life boat design for the 'Duke of Northumberland's Premium'. This was a competition for an improved lifeboat design: Costain won third place (Report of Committee 1851). A scale model of his boat entered for the competition is still on display at the National Maritime Museum, Greenwich (Exhibit No. F2945-2).

Costain built a total of nine lifeboats for the Liverpool Dock Committee. They had a length of 25 feet 6 inches and beam of seven feet six inches, and were described as being similar to a ship's pinnace in shape but with a bow and stern alike. Buoyancy was secured by a dozen airtight casks, but the boats were not self-righting and had no means of freeing themselves from water apart from bailing (Report of Committee 1851, 54). Nevertheless it was stated in the Report that these 'Liverpool' type lifeboats '…have been the means of assisting 269 vessels and saving 1,128 lives during the

Fig. 8: Formby's penultimate lifeboat. (FCS Archives)

Fig. 9: Last Launch c1916 (Courtesy of Liverpool Record Office, Liverpool Libraries)

last eleven years, so this boat must be a fine sea-boat and which perhaps has a great deal to do with it, must be efficiently manned and well managed.'

After 1850, the boats were improved by the introduction of relieving tubes and valves beneath a deck set a few inches above their waterline, and the fitting of side air-cases in place of casks. The clinker hull was also improved with the introduction of double-diagonal planking, which provided a lighter and stronger hull (fig. 8).

In 1889, the Mersey Docks and Harbour Board, despite local opposition, closed Formby Lifeboat Station and removed the boat to the Point of Ayr. Mr Aindow, one of the survivors of the 1836 disaster, who by then had become Coxswain, was invited to stay on in the boathouse to read and record the tidal measurements from the 'tide poles'[7], two of which can still be seen today from the remains of the Lifeboat Station (MDHB DCM 4/5/1889).

In 1891 there was a disaster in which all the crew of a coastal vessel, the steamer *Hawarden Castle*, were lost in Formby Channel (Liverpool Mercury 13/11/1891). Highly critical comments were made by

the Coroner, regarding the closure of the station (Journal of Commerce 20/11/1891), resulting in it being re-opened (MDHB DCM 11/1/1892).

In 1896 the RNLI took over responsibility from the Mersey Dock Committee for all Liverpool Bay lifeboats (RNLI 1897, 2) and in the same year gave the Formby Station its final boat, the *John and Henrietta* (RNLI 1897, 197). This boat was still powered by 'sail and oars'. The rig consisted of two standing lugsails and jibsail, and the boat had two steel drop-keels. It was crewed by 12 men and a Coxswain, and launched on a special carriage pulled across the sands by six horses.

The station remained on 'active service' until the First World War when there were difficulties in finding suitable horses for the launch, as the Army had requisitioned most of them. The *John and Henrietta*'s last (practice) launch took place with the aid of horses and men from a Royal Artillery regiment then stationed at Altcar (RNLI 1916 23, 140) (fig. 9).

By the early 20th century the great difficulty in launching from Formby, graphically described by Lord in 1843, meant that powered lifeboats stationed in deeper water at the northern tip of the Wirral peninsula were better able to reach distressed vessels in the approaches to the port. The Formby Station was finally closed in 1918 with the agreement of the MDHB (RNLI 1918, 9). Thus ended this heroic chapter in lifeboat history, but once again the former Keeper was invited to stay on in Lifeboat Cottage, in order to read and record the tide readings for the Mersey Docks and Harbour Board. During the 1930s the Formby Lifeboat Station became surrounded by dunes and in 1935 had to be 'dug out', but the boathouse and cottage continued as a café.

Having served as a popular café for many years the building remained standing until 1970 when it became derelict and was then demolished, leaving only its foundation platform remaining. This now, due to continuing erosion, stands in MHWL and is swept by the sea during high Spring tides.

Fortunately however, a remarkable film, 'The Launching of Formby Lifeboat', survives of the final practice launch, carried out around 1916 with the aid of the Royal Artillery and with (one might say) 'military honours'. It is preserved at the North West Film Archive, in Manchester.

TIDAL MEASUREMENT AT FORMBY

William Hutchison was not the first to start tidal measurements in the UK (Woodworth 1999, 12). However he was a pioneer in the recognition of the importance of being able to predict accurately the height and strength of the tide, in the port, from hour to hour and day to day. His records are not only the first known systematic measurements for Liverpool but indeed for the UK as a whole (Woodworth 2003, 19).

He stated '...our utmost endeavours should be used to get the greatest knowledge of the tides that is possible in all our tide and bar harbours that lie near the sea, by observing and remarking the time, and how much they flow... which, if it was made public, might contribute greatly to a more perfect theory of the tides, as well as preventing the loss and damage that may be occasioned' (Hutchinson 1777, 139).

Measurements started in 1764 '...on the time and height of the tides flowing at the old dock gates in Liverpool'. He refers to the work of '...the ingenious mathematicians Messrs Richard and George Holden [who] from observations here, and some from Bristol have formed a theory and an accurate method, whereby they calculate and publish yearly tide tables to show not only the time, but the height of the tides flowing at Liverpool old dock gates, which I can say from experience agrees surprisingly near to observations' (Hutchinson 1777, 142). This was, in effect, the beginning of the famous series of Holden's Tide Tables for Liverpool Bay, which continued until 1974 (Woodworth 2003, 42).

Not only did Hutchinson record the height and fall of the tide at the dock gate, he also realised the importance of measuring low waters, if he could. He stated, '...But to observe more exactly the whole rise of one of our middling tides, I had a board fixed upright at low water in the river marked with six inch marks each foot, high enough to observe by till the tide reached the dock gates, and remarked the time it flowed to each foot the rise of the whole tide...' (Hutchinson 1777, 140). Also he would have realised the importance of measurements elsewhere in the river, such as at Formby.

These observations recorded over a 25-year period, were summarised in a report, a bound copy of which was presented to the Liverpool Lyceum. It was later transferred to the Picton Library and is now in the Liverpool City Record Office. Its data have recently been analysed by the Proudman Oceanographic Laboratory using sophisticated computerised mathematical methods. Added to the later tidal records of the port, it now provides one of the longest series of near continuous tidal records for any where in the world – approximately 230 years (Woodworth 1999, 1).

These tidal observations were later extended to include outlying positions on the river and estuary. Denham developed a very clear understanding of the importance of the scientific study of the hydrography of the estuary and introduced self-registering gauges in about 1834. His data were entered into a 'fine leather-bound book' but unfortunately did not record the exact location of the measurements (Woodworth 1999, 17). They were presented to meetings of the British Association for the Advancement of Science in 1837 (Mountfield 1953, 128). In particular he demonstrated the importance of knowledge of Mean Water Level, his work being recognised by the then experts Whewell and Franklin as '...one of the most important points on physical geography yet submitted' (quoted in Denham 1840, appendix, 129). Its scientific importance was recognised by his election to Fellowship of the Royal Society on 28 February 1839 (Mountfield 1953, 132).

We do not know when tide poles were installed at Formby but many tide gauges were operated by the MDHB at various times in different parts of the River Mersey and surrounding area (Woodworth 1999, 20). Visual readings continued over a long period using a set of tide poles set in a line between Formby Lifeboat Station and low water line. Each of them was marked in feet and inches up to 32 feet, carefully maintained free from barnacles and repainted as necessary. From their position it may be deduced that they were intended to gather data particularly on low and mid tide levels. In 1889 the Keeper of the Tide Gauge, who was also the Lifeboat Coxswain, was paid an allowance of 3/6d per day '...to keep the tide gauge when ever it is required' (MDHB DCM 4/5/1889). In the 1970s the MDHB continued to require the resident of Lifeboat Cottage to keep a continuous telescopic sighting record every 15 minutes from 9am to 4pm and send these observations to the Mersey Docks and Harbour Board (Aindow 1978 personal communication). (fig. 10).

Even after Lifeboat Cottage was abandoned the 15-minute readings continued to be taken during daylight hours and forwarded to the MDHB. The last Formby 'tideman', interviewed in 1972 described how he read off the depths using high-powered binoculars. In poor visibility he had to walk to the edge of the water every quarter hour. The Proudman Oceanographic Observatory has listings of Formby levels between 1948 and 1972 (Woodworth 2005 personal communication).

*Fig. 10: Formby Lower Tide pole
(Photo, authors)*

The Chart of Liverpool Bay for 1948 shows three tide poles close to the low water line at Formby Pool, the lowest at one kilometre in a straight line 120° SW of the Old Lifeboat House. These poles are still marked on the Admiralty Chart of 1980. Two survive in the inter-tidal zone in front of the former lifeboat house: approximate apparent height above beach, 20 feet (fig. 10): the 'middle' pole, 3°6.65" west of Greenwich 53°32.5" latitude, the 'easterly' pole, 3°6.3" west of Greenwich, 53°32.7" latitude. The 'westerly' pole, 3°6.85" west of Greenwich, 53°32.4" latitude, is no longer there (Mersey Docks and Harbour Board 1988). Their measuring scales are no longer visible, the poles themselves being encrusted with barnacles. So far as is known these surviving tide poles at Formby are unique in Liverpool Bay[8]. They are a reminder of the tradition of meticulous tidal recording (established by Hutchinson) and of the importance (established by Denham) of detailed knowledge of tidal flow in the estuary, and at low and mid-water levels.

Accurate tidal measurements in Liverpool Bay are today as important as ever and it is noteworthy that tidal currents and waves are still being recorded at Formby by the Proudman Oceanographic Laboratory, Liverpool, using an array of specialised radar antennae situated on the Ravenmeols dunes.

CONCLUSION

This study has focussed on aspects of the human consequences of life with the sea on this 'dynamic' and continually changing coastline. Well-motivated and enlightened attempts to improve the safety of navigation in Liverpool's seaward approaches 'led the way', as William Hutchison himself claimed, between the mid-18th and mid-19th centuries. That period saw the wild and untamed estuary carefully surveyed, its tides and currents measured, and its trends plotted.

In addition to the construction of the country's first enclosed commercial dock, the enlightened Liverpool civic leaders furthered efforts to save life from drowning, not only in the vicinity of the docks themselves but also from the many casualties occurring in the outer harbour. Before specialist modifications such as built in buoyancy and 'self-righting', and before the term 'lifeboat' had been invented by Lukin and others, the Liverpool Dock Committee arranged for Britain's first dedicated 'boat and station for saving lives' to be established at Formby, overlooking this very dangerous approach to the port. With knowledge of Hutchinson's other achievements it seems likely that it was he who produced the initial idea. The background to this lies beyond the boundaries of Sefton so will not be dealt with here; a full account is provided by the present authors (Yorke and Yorke 1982).

The inherent dangers of the river and estuary were increasingly tamed by another remarkable man, Captain (later Admiral) H. M. Denham RN, FRS, Liverpool's first Marine Surveyor and the only one to be elected a Fellow of the Royal Society. Having been seconded by the Admiralty to help Liverpool in its attempt to avoid becoming silted-up, like the Dee, he diligently explored and charted the outer channels and recognised that a new and safer 'middle' channel could be opened up. This was the New Channel, later to become the Victoria and today's Crosby Channel. He not only developed a truly scientific understanding of the Mersey tidal processes but proceeded to discover the New Channel and devise a way of deepening it by using a steamer to tow '...a flexible harrow made of lengths of old chain cable spiked at intervals and spread on a beam of African Oak'. This was the only mechanical means of 'channel deepening' used in the estuary until 1890 (Mountfield 1953, 124).

Early attempts to provide land-based navigational aids in the form of perches, beacons and lighthouses, had been continually thwarted by the constantly changing course of these channels. Denham resolved the problem by stabilising the main approach.

The human endeavour in all this has hardly been touched on in this brief account – but is evident in the scatter of coastal landmarks, lighthouses, perches and beacons, now mainly lost and forgotten but still represented by the few which remain. It is apparent that, before the days of port radar and global positioning, these structures were often the subjects of much anxious scrutiny, frequently in poor visibility and dreadful sea conditions, perhaps particularly by those who were leaving our shores for the last time en route to new lives elsewhere.

Together with the remaining traces of Britain's first lifeboat station it is suggested that these structures now merit preservation as potent reminders of our coastal and cultural heritage. In particular the coastal area, which includes the surviving tide gauges, the surviving landmarks and the remains of Formby's lifeboat station, should be considered a 'historic heritage site' locating – as it does – much evidence of human interaction with the sea.

ACKNOWLEDGEMENTS

Our interest in the progressive improvement to the nautical safety of the Mersey estuary stemmed initially from our researches on the Formby Lifeboat Station. Mike Stammers and colleagues at the Liverpool Maritime Museum, Gordon Read at the Merseyside Record Office and the staff of the Liverpool City Record Office particularly helped us at that time. We were also encouraged by lifeboat historian Graham Farr and staff of the National Maritime Museum, Greenwich.

In our latest researches on tidal measurement on the Mersey we are grateful to Phillip Woodworth, (a co-admirer of the pioneering Captain William Hutchinson) who has recently published his own excellent account of Mersey tidal measurement and prediction.

For this paper we owe our thanks for patient support and editorial advice to Dr Jen Lewis; also Mike Stammers, Dr Phil Smith and our daughter Diana, for reading and constructive comments on early drafts.

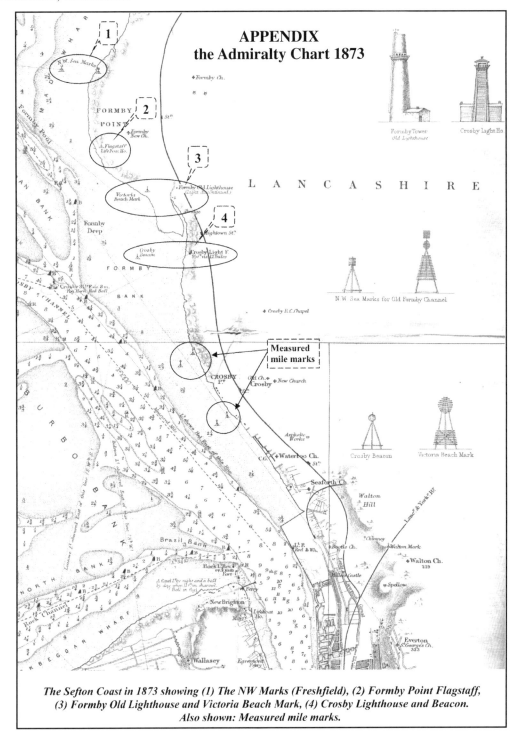

**APPENDIX
the Admiralty Chart 1873**

*The Sefton Coast in 1873 showing (1) The NW Marks (Freshfield), (2) Formby Point Flagstaff,
(3) Formby Old Lighthouse and Victoria Beach Mark, (4) Crosby Lighthouse and Beacon.
Also shown: Measured mile marks.*

ENDNOTES

1 The submerged sand bank extending across the outlets of the natural channels at the mouth of the estuary.

2 A nautical landmark, or more correctly 'seamark', is defined as '...an artificial or natural object of easily recognizable shape or colour or both, situated in such a position that it may be identified on a chart or related to a known navigational instruction' (Naish 1985, 14, quoting *The International Dictionary of Aids to Marine Navigation*).

3 Prominent objects visible from the sea such as trees, spires, buoys and marks which kept in line or transit, guide the pilot, while working into port.

4 This term, for a boat specially dedicated or constructed for saving lives at sea, does not appear to have been used until 1801.

5 That part of the shore that lies between the tide-marks.

6 The steersman and senior member of a lifeboat crew.

7 This carries a measured scale by means of which the height of the sea may be ascertained visually as the tide rises and falls.

8 According to recent information from Michael W. Bankes a Formby resident and formerly hydrographic draughtsman for the MDHB, the meticulously kept readings were telephoned daily (as soon after 4pm as possible) to the Marine Surveyor and Water Bailiffs Department. The written sheets of measurements were sent in at the end of each week. Their purpose was to provide continuous 'real time' measurements of sea-level in the Bay which was not always the exact level predicted. They were then correlated with the ongoing and concurrent echo-sounding depth measurements carried out from the MDHB Survey vessel, particularly in the several extremely important estuarine channels, the beds of which could 'shoal up' within a month with potential hazard to shipping despite being within the navigation buoys, training bank and revetment.

Pine Trees and Asparagus –
the development of a cultural landscape

Reginald and Barbara Yorke

'The cultivation of the waste lands in this county, is undoubtedly the first object that ought to be attended to. A county like that of Lancaster, distinguished for the opulence and spirit of its inhabitants, should never rest, whilst a single acre remains, that does not yield some valuable production. There is scarcely a rood in it, that might not yield some species of grain, or some sort of useful pasture, or some kind of valuable timber' (Holt 1795, 233).

INTRODUCTION

The history of human activity on the Sefton Coast was discussed very fully by Jones, Houston and Bateman in 'The Sand Dunes of the Sefton Coast', published following an important conference with the same title held in Liverpool in 1991 (Atkinson and Houston 1993). Much further work has been published since then. This paper is an attempt to examine the impact on the natural landscape of the Sefton coast of two important, mainly 19th century, developments – estate forestry and asparagus cultivation – and to consider the rationale, motivation and development of these important forms of land-use in this often hostile environment.

Our coastline consists entirely of a considerable depth of blown sand, exposed to strong westerly winds, high tides and salt spray. The hollows between the dunes, known locally as 'slacks'[1], formerly collected considerable sheets of water especially during the winter months because of the high water table. In the mid 19th century the newly conceived Liverpool, Crosby and Southport Railway was carefully constructed to run along the eastern edge of this wild coastal area, described then as 'waste' or at best as 'warren'[2].

The 'natural' features and wildlife of the Sefton Coast are now greatly valued, but a great deal of what we see today owes as much to man as nature. In this paper we would like to specifically examine two

aspects of human involvement on the coast during the last two centuries – one very well known but often misunderstood, the other much less in evidence today but of great historical interest – which together have contributed to a special 'cultural landscape'.

The character of the natural coastal landscape has been frequently described in literature (see below); recently in more objective and analytical ways using 'Historic Landscape Characterisation' methods (Sefton Council 2003, 6). The 'cultural landscape', which reflects the long-term impact of human presence and use of the natural wild landscape over time (thousands of years), is what we now see and need to understand.

SEFTON COASTAL WOODLANDS
(a) *The Formby Plantations*

For many people the pine plantations situated in a 6.5 km stretch between Ravenmeols and Ainsdale are considered to be one of the coast's great attractions (fig. 1). However maps, such as those of Yates in 1786, show no woodlands of any extent (Harley 1968, 19, 24-25). Even by 1848 the first Ordnance Survey maps show very little tree cover (Ordnance Survey 1848). They first re-appeared here as a result of the 'Age of Improvement' (Briggs 1979, 39), now defined as '…the century after 1760 which saw the Agricultural Revolution and much enclosure and reclamation of "Waste"' (Winchester 2006, 93).

Writing in 1795 Holt graphically described the conditions on the Sefton coast,

'…Towards the coast it is with great difficulty that wood of any kind can be raised: the tops of the trees, hedges, and even the corn in the fields in general bend towards the east, as if shrinking from the Western gale, brought over the Atlantic Ocean'.

Fig. 1: Aerial photo Sefton Coast (Formby Point) (Courtesy Sefton Council)

However he notes with approval, '…On the sea-coast there are some acres of land planted with forest-trees, which are flourishing and ornamental to the country. They were originally placed in holes (with a mixture of sea Slutch and broken pieces of turf at their roots) four inches beneath the surface of the ground; and sods were raised round them, to guard their tender shoots from the wintry blast' (Holt 1795, 84-85). (Sea-slutch was the footprint-bearing silt, exposures of which are still to be found in the inter-tidal zone).

Due credit is then given for this interesting experiment to '…the Reverend Mr Formby, of Formby, who has succeeded in raising plantations so near the sea, that it was hardly thought practicable till he effected it'. Although as Atkinson and colleagues point out, Nicholas Blundell at Little Crosby had carried out regular small scale planting on his estate earlier in the century, notably around Crosby Hall, at the Sniggery and other small coverts, to provide shelter (Greenwood 1999, 96). This however was not, as at Formby, on dune, and not therefore nearly so remarkable.

Fig. 2: The Rev. Richard Formby
(From Catherine Jacson's, 'Formby Reminiscences', courtesy Sefton Libraries)

The Reverend Richard Formby (1760-1832) of Formby Hall, Curate of Formby Chapel, and incumbent of Holy Trinity Church, St Anne's Street, Liverpool, was then also joint Lord of the Manor of Formby (Yorke and Yorke 1982, 22-23) (fig. 2) An educated and well-connected man he started his first experimental planting at Formby. In this he followed in the steps of his father John (1721-1776) who apparently planted most of the woodland adjacent to the Hall, at the centre of the Formby Hall estate (Tithe Map 1845; Ordnance Survey 1848). This was three kilometres inland in an area now characterised as 'dune backland'[3], SB05 in the Sefton Landscape Character Map (Formby 1903).

What was his motivation to plant trees on the Formby sandhills? He had an understandable desire to provide extra shelter for his tenant farmers from the western gales. His granddaughter Ann Lonsdall Formby thought that he might also have been following the example of his old college friend Thomas Lobb Chute, 1721-1791, who had planted a similar wood at his home in Hampshire; he was a cousin and successor of John Chute, 1706-1776, and a friend of Horace Walpole, 1717-1797 (Formby 1876, 9; Jacson, 1897, 74). It may also however have been connected with the national timber shortage following the Seven Years War, 1756-1763. It is known that the Reverend Formby was a most forward looking, philanthropic and enlightened man. He provided land for the establishment of Britain's first Lifeboat Station at Formby in 1776 (Yorke and Yorke 1982, 23). He also gave land adjacent to his woodland at Formby Hall for the cultivation of willow for the pioneering Liverpool Institute for the Blind, of which he was a patron (Royden 1991, 76).

Although the Royal Navy had triumphed in the Seven Years War it had also sustained heavy losses and, by the end of the war, was struggling to find timber for hulls and masts. In 1755 Edward Wade presented the Royal Society for the Encouragement of the Arts with a Memoir encouraging mass tree planting (Schama 1995, 168). The Society then offered prizes '...to those proprietors who had sown the most acorns or planted other trees, like Spanish Chestnut or Scotch Fir deemed useful by the Navy'.

In 1763, at the end of the war, Roger Fisher a Liverpool shipwright testified to a Parliamentary Committee that in south Lancashire, Cheshire, Shropshire, Staffordshire and Flint, most of the timber had been cut down in the previous 30 years (Stewart-Brown 1932, 24,55).

Reacting to this national concern the Royal Society for the Encouragement of the Arts offered prizes to encourage land-owners, large and small, to grow more trees.

In 1757 it was decided to offer prizes for the planting of oak, elm and chestnut. The Society stated that '...a continual supply of useful Timber being absolutely necessary, as well as for the Ornament and Conveniency as for the Security of these Kingdoms', a Premium would be awarded, in particular for sowing acorns and planting oak, chestnut and elm, soon followed by Scotch fir and Weymouth pine, these being '...the properest for masts'. Annual awards for tree planting continued until 1835 (Allen, Archivist RSA, pers.comm. 2004). During this period the Society awarded 178 medals and prizes, and many were for small plantations (Rackham 2006, 451).

Until wooden-hulled ships started to be replaced by iron, the necessity for tree planting remained a pressing issue. John Formby's planting interests had been to screen the manorial demesne but his son Richard's experiment with planting on the periphery of his sandy coastal domain at Firwood, in the mid-18th century, clearly reflected the national interest, bolstered by the Royal Society for the Encouragement of the Arts.

This experimental planting, deemed by Holt to be surprisingly successful by 1795, still survives in private ownership – not under the aegis of the Sefton Coast Partnership, nevertheless with some of the oldest and most interesting trees on the Sefton Coast (fig. 3).

Fig. 3: Firwood (Photo, authors)

After Richard Formby's death in 1832 his fourth son the Reverend Hesketh Formby inherited Firwood; however the area around St Luke's Church, the site of a medieval chapel that had been '…overcome by sand' and abandoned in the early 18th century (Lewis 1978, 73), went to his third son Dr Richard Formby. The main part of the Formby estate was divided (rather surprisingly) mainly between his daughters, and little further planting took place until the end of the century. By 1885 however the Formbys had planted woodland at Shorrocks Hill and this was clearly well established, as evidenced by a letter to the local newspaper from a Birkdale resident, W. A. Wright, who had visited Formby Point. The writer had been impressed by the '…Austrian Pines, grown in thousands, close to the sea' and suggested that a visit to see them was well worth the journey. At Shorrocks Hill he described '…pleasant little glades sheltered by acres of unique looking pine trees'. Further away (at Firwood) '…another mansion' was surrounded by older dense pines of another variety

(Scotch pine), planted at an earlier time. The writer thought that the landowner responsible '…was a public benefactor for sandy waste has been made wonderfully attractive, so close to the storm swept seashore'. He hoped that one day Birkdale '…may possess a few acres at least as attractive' (Southport Guardian 9/5/1885). It was not to be.

More of the area around Shorrocks Hill was planted between 1894 and 1900. The belt of trees on the Ravenmeols dunes, today being overcome by blown sand from a massive 'blow-out', was planted with Austrian Pines, a few Scotch Firs and *Pinus montana* between 1901 and 1902; the belt down the south side of Lifeboat Road with Corsican Pine from 1905 to 1910 (Gresswell 1953, 78).

The Formby family's planting slowly extended north to Greenloon's Farm, at which point it reached the boundary with the lands of the other joint Lords of the Manor, the Weld-Blundells of Ince Blundell. Agreed in

1667, the boundary in the dune warrens was indicated by a line of iron markers, some visible to this day (LRO DDFo/34/1). The Weld-Blundells subsequently, in the late 1880s, followed the Formby example and commenced their own tree-planting programme.

In general the Formby family planted along the 50-foot ridge of rear dunes running parallel to the coast about two thirds of a mile inland from the sea. The effect of this was to provide a more efficient windbreak for the cultivated area inland. As the trees grew they doubled the height of the ridge. This was particularly important for the asparagus fields being developed at about that time. The pines also reduced the tendency to 'blow-outs', but were also undoubtedly intended to provide a supply of timber after 30 to 40 years' growth. It is interesting to see today that the Formbys planted their trees in regularly spaced rows, whereas the Weld-Blundells planted in a more haphazard manner.

The frontal dunes[4] to the west of the plantations were in general left as warren. Later sand-winning[5] was to occur in Ravenmeols, starting at Cabin Hill and Range Lane in the 1930s, then at Beacon Hill west of St

Luke's, finally in the 1960s close to Wicks Lane path. It is said that when a later Formby had to find death duties in the 1930s, the Beacon Hill area became known locally as 'Death-duty Hill'. The Formby family did little further planting after that time.

(b) *The Weld-Blundell plantations*

We would now like to turn to the work of the other manorial family, the Blundells – or Weld-Blundells as they became, when Thomas Weld succeeded to the estate in 1847 after a long lawsuit. Almost immediately, in 1848, he helped promote a Private Act of Parliament which enabled work to start on the Liverpool, Crosby and Southport Railway, '…and to improve 3475 acres of Sandhills and Rabbit Warrens in Birkdale, Ainsdale and Formby for agricultural and other purposes… whereas the lands or grounds consist of considerable tracts of waste land, remaining at present uncultivated' (Statutes 1848 Weld-Blundell, T.).

Thomas Weld-Blundell, however, was not a tree-planter. It was left to his son Charles Joseph Weld-Blundell (1845-1927) who was equally energetic when he succeeded his father in 1887. Charles

Fig. 4: Victoria Road, National Trust entrance, (Jubilee Wood). (Drawing by Muriel Sibley 1975 FCS Collection.

immediately started planting, at first in an area near where the National Trust red squirrel reserve is today but then called by him 'Jubilee Wood', in honour of Queen Victoria's Golden Jubilee (fig. 4).

For our knowledge of the development of the Weld-Blundell plantations we are very indebted to former Estate Manager, Mr I. Walmesley-Cotham. In December 1934 he gave an interesting account, 'Forestry in Formby', of the planting and management north of Wicks Lane, to the Liverpool Botanical Society. At that time active planting had almost finished and he was able to provide a comprehensive review. We also have useful notes from Charles's successor (Weld-Blundell 1934).

The first Blundell planting, like that of the Formby family, was on the rear dune ridge, 'In 1887 ... Victoria Road was merely a grass track. In the same year Charles Weld-Blundell planted the first of the larger woods with Scots Pine, and called this the Jubilee Wood. It is situated west of Larkhill Lane, between Victoria Road and the continuation of College Path known as Blundell Avenue. At the time of the planting of Jubilee Wood there were no ditches or drains in the whole area, whereas there are now about 6 miles of ditches and long lengths of piping' (Walmesley-Cotham, 1934).

At first, Scotch pine and maritime pine were planted but the 'Scots' in most cases failed to thrive or grew stunted. It was six years later (about 1893) that, following a visit to Les Landes on the Atlantic coast of France, Charles Weld-Blundell discovered that Corsican pine *(Pinus nigra)* grew '...astonishingly well' – if planted as three year old seedlings about four feet apart. He met the Head of the French Forestry Department at Arcachon and Boulogne, and discovered they had successfully planted Corsican pine, and heard about the use of the French hybrid, black poplar ('Frenchmen') as 'nurse-trees'. The Corsican seed was bought from various places but eventually seedlings were raised in the estate nursery from seed obtained from Copenhagen (Weld-Blundell 1921) and later in the 1920s from France. At that time

'broadcast' seeding was used but, as the results were uncertain, Charles Weld-Blundell suggested sowing in raised beds, four feet wide. The ground had to be previously prepared by reducing the slope of the steeper dunes, draining the slacks and planting lines of marram (star-grass) as wind-breaks.

He further suggested that at least 30 pounds of seed '...should be carefully sown end of April in four-foot raised beds (and gutters to carry off rain) anywhere under shelter of a bank or hedge and so placed as not to get a southerly aspect as sunburn is the worst danger and moisture lying close under them is the next'. The sand should be '...mixed with plenty of broken peat to encourage better roots, and boughs had better be stuck in the gutter between the beds to shade the young plants from sun'. Although away from his estate a lot he kept closely in touch, even to the extent of sending much practical advice such as this handy hint, '...get a woman to put into small bits of soft clay as big as a shilling 3 or 4 seeds and prick them into the sand 2 inches deep with a stick. It answers well on hill sides or bank sides. You can use the same plan or merely dibble in Corsican seeds'.

According to Captain E. J. Weld-Blundell, the secret of his predecessor's success was in planting a great number of trees at one time; they then '...helped each other up". The area was prepared the year before by planting star-grass. E. J. Weld-Blundell also noted that the planting was '...greatly helped by the natural growth on the black or Arctic willow (*Salix repens*) which runs along below of the surface of the sand and forms a network which holds the sand in place'.

After further planting between Wicks Lane and Victoria Road he extended towards Ainsdale. He planted close to the railway, except for the land originally leased by Thomas Fresh (see below) and now occupied by the Formby Golf Club. He also often planted closer to the sea than the Formbys had done. Much of this frontal woodland has been lost to the sea and sand-blow, as well as ageing (fig. 5).

Fig. 5: Gypsy Wood remnant. (Courtesy Dr P. H. Smith)

Because of the extent of the area, the Estate Manager sometimes had difficulty in knowing exactly where he was, when viewing the trees or finding the workmen. He overcame this by having many numbered concrete posts set out to form an extensive grid. Some of these may still be found at Ainsdale. A hand-drawn map of these in 1934 survives (Foster 2000, 111).

Problems however were many. Great difficulty was experienced due to gales cutting 'great holes' in the hills and necessitating continual attention with grading down of inclines and renewed planting of 'starr'. Considerable help had been obtained in the planting due to the fact that the electric railway line between Southport and Liverpool made access difficult for the general public, but fires were started by sparks from the steam trains that also continued to run on the tracks. The solution to this had been to plant a mile long strip of asparagus along the railway line. Fires were also attributed to motorists using the shore. The pine shoot beetle (*Myelophylus piniperda*)

was a more intractable problem. The only answer was the removal of dead trees and branches (with the beetles) and burning them.

It was partly to discourage beetles that in 1905 Charles Weld-Blundell took measures to stop the killing of birds on his land. (This apparently had been a '…pursuit of local farmers and labourers' using a very long hooked line known as a 'pantle'[6], by means of which large numbers of larks and plovers were caught and sent to Liverpool Market and sold at 5d to 1/- per dozen). Rabbits were a worse problem. All measures including gassing were tried. The most effective was to give all estate employees permission to catch rabbits with traps, snares and ferrets. This was much cheaper than erecting wire netting fences.

Charles Weld Blundell died in August 1927 and was succeeded by Captain E. J. Weld-Blundell, but the planting was continued on the same lines until 1932. It was then halted for reasons of economy and because of fears of taxation of site values, taxation of improvements and an 'alarming clause' in the Town and Country Planning Act 1932 by which all trees were to be registered, and felling would require permission from the Local Authority, thus restricting commercial felling. The Estate Manager, then '...reluctantly advised the owner that it was unwise to continue planting northwards towards Ainsdale' (Walmsley-Cotham 1934).

By the 1930s the Weld-Blundell plantations had reached the stage when large scale thinning was required but doubts were expressed as to how it should be tackled (Weld-Blundell 1934). Were more 'rides' required and if so where? What should the final tree density be? 40 to the acre? Should it be different on the weather side as distinct from the lee side?

In addition to conifers, sycamores had recently been planted as 'fire-screens' but the possible planting of other more exotic species was being considered, such as *Robinia pseudoacacia*. Also known as Black Locust, this was one of the earliest North American trees to have reached Europe in the early 1800s after William Cobbett, author of 'The English Gardener', journalist and rural reformer, returned from a trip to the New World full of missionary zeal about its excellence.

Diversification was evidently in mind. It was clearly stated at this time that the main object of the plantations was to 'fix the sand' and protect the sites where it was hoped to install 'small holders'. Two such had started on asparagus and poultry holdings and '...potatoes appear to do excellently well'. A small silver fox farm was also started, later to be destroyed by a stray bomb during the Second World War. With the object of preparing the land someone had suggested the '...growing of mustard crops and ploughing them in'. It was thought that with '...cheap colonial houses there might be a future for small-holders here' which might possibly eventually '...realise the ambition of the "originator" and create a new estate' (Weld-Blundell 1934).

During the Second World War German planes were to inflict much damage on Sefton plantations, dropping incendiary and other bombs, perhaps confused (as was the intention) by the 'Starfish' decoy at Ravenmeols. During the war all planting stopped, but much clear felling took place. The thousands of wooden posts placed all along the Sefton coast to prevent enemy planes landing probably came from these the nearest plantations.

By 1952 Mr Walmesley-Cotham, (in reply to an enquirer), summarised the position at that time as follows, 'The Corsican Pine had proved the most successful on sand. Other species such as Sitka Spruce, Maritime Pine, Weymouth Pine and Pinaster had failed ...There had been financial and maintenance problems. The high dunes had to be levelled, the area then planted with "Starr-grass" to fix it. Corsican Pine transplanted badly and had to be put in when extremely small, (1-2 year seedlings), which owing to heavy losses, had to be planted close together (about 4 foot apart) and this produced a high density of plants per acre' (Walmesley-Cotham 1952a).

The Corsican pine is unfortunately subject to many pests and diseases, especially when grown in these harsh conditions and a very large number of seedlings died out even when established. The pine weevil (*Pissodes notatus*) was a particular problem, which could only be dealt with by trapping. It was found that Austrian pine appeared to stand the harsh conditions better than the Corsicans and '...if further planting is carried out' the Austrians would be planted on the outer fringes. Finally the only commercial use of the woodlands for timber had been for pit props, '...of which a large quantity were supplied during the late war' (Walmesley-Cotham 1952a).

With regard to *Pissodes notatus*, by 1952 the Forestry Commission was then informed that in certain areas the pest was 'quite out of control' and the Estate Manager wondered whether '...something might be done by encouraging parasites and predators' (Walmesley-Cotham 1952b).

Giving evidence to a Government Commission as early as 1911, Weld-Blundell even then already deplored his efforts as '…Planting with fir trees by my highly trained and skilled staff conducted at very great expense and heavy loss' (Royal Commission 1911). From the estate correspondence it is clear that a financial return was originally hoped for from the plantations, with some profit expected 30 years after planting. Whilst providing a shelterbelt, and helping to prevent sand-blow, the woodlands were certainly intended to be a cash crop. Even 'thinnings' were marketed but most of the rather poor quality timber was sold for pit props.

Just as the Formby tree-planting had started at a time of national concern, so the later Blundell planting starting in the 1880s coincided with another national concern – a severe and prolonged period of agricultural depression. It then seemed that plantations could financially compete with agriculture for land. Landowners with money '…began to think of trees as an investment. Although markets for oak bark and timber had declined, oaks were still planted but were overtaken by conifers…' (Rackham 2006, 455).

Whatever the financial or social reasons, planting did provide shelter to the area inland of the dunes with the idea of their eventually being brought into cultivation, asparagus the intended crop being very susceptible to wind blow. The 'amenity' of the district and possible future development of this portion of the estate for building was also in mind. Otherwise Weld-Blundell considered '…the experiment has proved an outstanding success' (Walmsley-Cotham 1934). It was not expected, particularly in this environment, that the trees would live to be over 100 years old, despite the loss of much of the seaward planting due to erosion which had defeated all Weld-Blundell's attempts to control.

Following the death in 1958 of the last manorial owner, Captain E. J. Weld-Blundell, the estate trustees began to negotiate the sale of the plantation to the Forestry Commission. In 1959 this resulted in a formal offer of £26,600 to purchase approximately

1,378 acres (Forestry Commission 1959). Sporting rights were to be let back at a peppercorn rent. A lease to the Nature Conservancy, who had already expressed great interest in the scientific value of the 'unimproved' open dunes, would also be considered; but the sale would be agreed only up to the Southport boundary as there was a proposal for sand-winning beyond that boundary and '…the value of the sand may be very substantial' (Weld and Weld 1959). In the end Captain Weld-Blundell had calculated that the income derived from the enterprise had been negligible compared with the cost of planting and maintaining. Forestry had not been a commercial success on the Sefton coast due to the poor quality of the timber and changes in demand.

The Formby and Weld-Blundell families had however changed the landscape forever.

A correspondent in the Manchester Guardian newspaper, writing before 1897, described the view from the railway thus, 'The ordinary traveller who journeys by the Lancashire and Yorkshire Railway will be surprised at the poetry which mere sand hills can inspire. Within the broadest portion of the range of sand hills, shut out entirely from the outer world, lies a series of fresh water lakes, many acres in extent, which are most charmingly wild and picturesque. The fantasy of nature has here described, in wildest beauty, all the geographical features of seas, bays, islands, and peninsulas, with a delightfully broken surface of irregular hills and plains, where mosses and aquatic plants revel... The water, which is most pellucid, is the haunt of waterfowl, which are seldom disturbed in this beautiful solitude.' (Jacson 1897, 122).

In 1934 Mr Walmesley-Cotham said, 'If one stands on a high sand hill near the boundary line between the Townships of Ainsdale and Formby, and looks north-east towards Ainsdale, one sees a stretch of sand hills unimproved by tree planting; but on turning to the south-west a vast forest meets the eye, commencing with the small trees a few inches high, planted last year, then belts a few feet high, and beyond that to the west and south, larger trees stretching away to the sailing mark at Victoria Road, some two miles away. The plantations south of that cannot be seen. It is really remarkable what a difference there is between the planted and unplanted portions of the hills' (Walmesley-Cotham 1934).

ASPARAGUS CULTIVATION
(a) *Cultivation history and local methods*

A taste for asparagus seems to have arrived in France during the Gallo-Roman period and then spread to England, possibly even during the Iron Age (Uglow 2004, 8). Its ancient cultivation was described by both Pliny the Younger in his Natural History (455, 515) and Columella, in his work on agriculture (155), both writing in the first century AD. In 1597 Gerrard described it growing wild in Essex, Harwich and Lincolnshire (Gerrard 1636, 255). It was later found in its prostrate form on the cliffs of the Lizard in 1667, and cultivated asparagus was grown in Tudor gardens (Grigson 1987, 401). By the mid-17th century, it was grown on the outskirts of London and in Worcester; also at Levens Hall, Westmorland, in 1694. (Bagot and Munby 1988, 142).

In northwest England Holt relates that asparagus grew wild on Bidston Hill, Wirral, in 1795 but the greatest quantity was in the 'rich vale of Kirkdale', two miles from Liverpool (Holt 1795, 80). In Sefton, there are numerous references by Nicholas Blundell, in his diary, to its cultivation at Little Crosby (for domestic consumption), in the early 18th century (Tyrer 1968/1970/1972). In 1902 'considerable quantities' were recorded growing 'wild' in Formby by Green, but then correctly regarded as having escaped from cultivation (Green 1902, 130).

The best account of Formby cultivation methods is given in a special government bulletin produced in 1969 (Ministry of Agriculture, Fisheries and Food 1969a, 12). The first step was for an area to be 'reclaimed' from the dunes. This was achieved in the early days almost entirely by spadework. The process was first to level the dunes and protect from wind, and then to open up deep trenches and to completely bury the top layer of 'turf' (often including dwarf

willow) by covering it with two spits of sand and ensuring the same level throughout the reclaimed area. The final process was to 'ridge' (as for potatoes and at similar row distances), but as deeply as possible. Dung was then spread along the furrows at about 30 tons per acre and two year old crowns planted out 12 inches apart in rows. These would then take between two and three years to develop.

The provision of large amounts of manure was critical to the growth of this crop. This was recognised by Columella and repeated by Holt in the 18th century (Holt 1795, 80). The secret of local success was the abundant supply of 'night-soil' from Liverpool which suddenly became available along this coast following the construction of the Liverpool, Crosby and Southport Railway in 1848, coinciding with increasingly active measures then being introduced to improve the sanitation of central Liverpool.

(b) *'Liverpool Dung' and Thomas Fresh*

By the mid-19th century, the public health of Liverpool had become an extremely serious issue. In 1844 there were 138,334 people per square mile in the town. The lack of sanitation and accumulation of 'cess' posed severe health problems, evidenced by the death rate, the highest in England (Hope 1931, 43). The Liverpool Sanitary Act of 1846 (published 1854), endeavoured to improve this situation. Thomas Fresh, a former police inspector, was appointed Inspector of Nuisances (Fresh 1851). This was one of the historic Liverpool trio of pioneer public health appointments, the others being Dr Duncan, the first Medical Officer of Health, and James Newlands, the first City Engineer (Borough of Liverpool, Health Committee 1851). Working from his office at 2 Cornwallis Street, (Gore 1855, 248) Fresh's responsibility was to deal with the accumulation of human waste ('night soil') in the oldest and poorest area of the town. The 1846 Act gave responsibility to the Council for emptying ash pits and cesspools. Fresh set to with a will but, coincidentally, helped provide a much needed impetus to the agricultural development and prosperity of this area, as the manure from the cleansing of the middens was disposed of by the contractors by being sold to local farmers.

At one time this waste had been discharged into the river, then transported to the outlying areas by canal (Coney 1995, 16). By the mid 19th century the availability of rail transport meant that other surrounding rural areas could benefit. Cost of transport was as low at one penny per ton per mile. After the opening of the Liverpool, Crosby and Southport Railway in 1848 a 'manure-siding' (not at first a station), was sited north of Formby at Fresh's request on land leased from Thomas Weld-Blundell (Liverpool, Crosby and Southport Railway 1845-55).

The early records of the railway reveal abundant evidence of Thomas Fresh's activities. He first appears in 1852 when '...having leased a quantity of land about a mile to the north of Formby station is desirous of having a siding for the purpose of conveying manure and clay to his property.' He argued that '...as there was a scheme for establishing a watering place in the vicinity, his depot could be used for other purposes besides the deposit of manure'. The Board agreed, and within days instructed the railway's

engineer to proceed with the new siding. Soon afterwards Fresh leased a house and some land adjacent to the siding and, in order to facilitate his personal transport into Liverpool, he then requested the railway directors to construct a station. The Board accepted an estimate of £132 for the station and shed, and it was opened in 1854 after the Board's Secretary reported in January 1854 '...Mr Fresh is very anxious to have it opened as soon as possible. Some few building plots have been sold and Mr Fresh seems very confident that the place will increase' (Liverpool, Crosby and Southport Railway 1845-55).

One plot was referred to in the 1845 tithe schedule as 'Poverty' and to this day is called 'Poverty Fields' (Tithe Map 1845). Further acquisitions can be traced in a lease book (Blundell of Ince Blundell). Three leases date from 1 January 1853. One is for 147 acres of land described as 'waste and rabbit warrens', now mainly occupied by Formby Golf Club. The second is for land intended for building; Fresh was to erect a house to the value of £500 on the west side of the

Fig. 6: Thomas Fresh's house, Freshfield Road. (Photo by Muriel Sibley, FCS Collection)

railway and on the north side of the intended road leading from the sea to Formby Church (i.e. St Peter's). This is now Victoria Road. The third lease is also intriguing; this was a 99-year lease from 1 January 1853 of a plot of land and '…old dwelling house thereon known as Bradshaws'. A condition of the lease was that Thomas Fresh had to enlarge the existing house by erecting a new front, kitchen and pantry, out offices, stable and shippon; all these improvements to cost not less than £400. This house or cottage was occupied by John Bradshaw and appears on the tithe map of 1845 and again in the census return of 1851. It stands east of the railway line to the south of Freshfield Station (fig. 6) and has a date stone on it with lettering as follows:

F

T   M

1855

The letters, of course, stood for Thomas Fresh and his wife Martha. In 1855, the year of the date stone, there is a reference to '…a field in the centre of Mr Fresh's farm'. The context shows that this relates to other fields near to Freshfield Station. The same year the Weld-Blundell's solicitor was '…requested by Mr Fresh and many of your tenants at Formby' to accompany them in a deputation to the Railway Board for additional services. Fresh is the only tenant mentioned by name; he was becoming a leader in Formby affairs.

Fresh is not however listed among the residents of Freshfield three years later (Kelly 1858). By 1859 he is shown in Gore's Liverpool Directory as living at 13 Chester Street, Toxteth Park. Had he given up his farming venture or was the Liverpool Health Committee concerned about his dual activities? Certainly in 1859 there was a reorganisation of his department and he ceased to be employed there. He moved to Glasgow where he died 1861. His will was proved by his widow; she was the sole beneficiary and his effects were valued at under £600.

What of Thomas Fresh as a person? No portrait survives but he was described by one of the century's great writers, Nathaniel Hawthorne, at that time American Consul in Liverpool (Hawthorne 1856-7, 172). He recounts meeting the Inspector of Nuisances on a train and describes him as, '…a rather puffy and consequential man as Englishmen in whatever official station, seldom fail to be… A very racy and peculiarly English character… having his life concerned wholly with the disagreeables of a great city [who] spent, apparently, his whole life in Liverpool, and long occupied the post of Inspector of Nuisances… He seemed to be a good and kindly person, too, but earthy – even as if his frame had been moulded of earth impregnated with the draining of slaughter-houses and moistened with the rank liquid of common sewers'.

This was the man who founded Freshfield; he had a relatively brief association with the area but he certainly took a major part in its early development. On 31 January 1854 the Railway Board resolved that the new station should be called 'Freshton'. However, an addition to this minute states '…afterwards changed to Freshfield at the request of the solicitor of Thomas Weld-Blundell esquire'. The company planned to stop two trains per day in each direction but this was not good enough for Thomas Fresh. He asked for the 8.55am from Southport and the 5.10pm from Liverpool to be stopped at Freshfield. This request was declined, presumably foiling Fresh's plan to be the first commuter from Freshfield to Liverpool.

(c) "Bringing fertility to waste"

Henry Grazebrook, also a frequent early user of the line, wrote in 1853, 'But there is still something better worth notice by a mind attached to progress, namely that in numerous instances, observable along the line, and especially on its Eastern side, patches of cultivation and of abundant produce already showing themselves, where previous to the opening of the railway, not yet a year ago, nothing but neglect and consequent barrenness prevailed around. Food for man and beast may now be seen springing from hitherto waste sandlands and bog, and value reigns where all was valueless before. The railway has brought fertility to the fields within reach of the market. This gives a charm to an otherwise monotonous half-hours ride and realises expectations which many assigned as their reason for siding in the construction of the line. Two blades of grass will now grow where none grew before. Vive, le Chemins de fer!' (Gahan 1985, 34).

In a paper to the Historic Society of Lancashire and Cheshire in 1865 the Reverend A. Hume was one of the first to attribute credit, '…Cultivated land … has been recovered from the sand, especially by the late Mr Fresh of Freshfield. A stratum of vegetable soil is placed over the sand and on this upper surface stand some modern villas and gardens.' He apparently misunderstood the source of the 'soil' (Hume 1866, 35).

Inspection of serial maps of the areas benefiting from this cheap fertiliser does in fact indicate how the asparagus fields developed from tree-less rabbit warren to the enclosed fields of the 20th century. Maps, such as the Ordnance Survey 6 inch to 1 mile in 1955, reveal a mosaic of open dune, woodland and asparagus fields (fig. 7). The key to the geography is the distribution of drainage ditches. Asparagus was grown where it was originally too wet for conifers and probably best in areas that had originally been slacks. Closer scrutiny reveals scattered 'bunching' sheds, a summer bungalow in the case of Pinetree Farm and a specially built farmhouse at Sandfield Farm. Public access developed from one or two isolated footpaths in the mid 19th century to busy (if still narrow) roads in the 20th century. These areas have been levelled, drained and surrounded by trees to provide shelter.

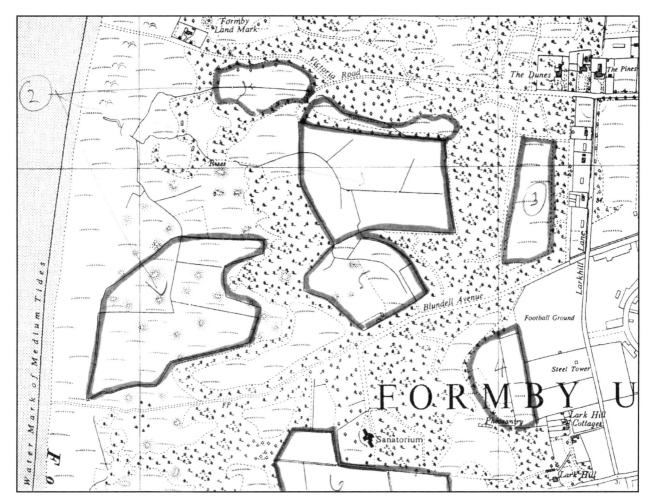

Fig. 7: Four asparagus farms, 1955. Note the 'mosaic' of pine woodland and asparagus fields. (Reproduced from OS map (6 inch - 1 mile) 1955, sheet SD20 NE. ©Crown Copyright. All rights reserved Sefton Council Licence no. 100018192 2008)).

Fig. 8: Aerial photo Pine Tree and Sandfield Farms
(Courtesy of Sefton Coast Partnership)

An aerial photograph in the 1960s shows parts of the Pinetree Farm subdivided by neat hedging into approximately 14 smaller, probably seed-bed, areas (fig. 8). There is now a large bare area at the shore end of Victoria Road where increasing numbers of visitors have destroyed the marram grass cover. To the north of this, a former asparagus field is now a caravan site. A surviving footpath runs from the end of Victoria Road, southwards, with a branch towards Sandfield Farm, another large area of asparagus cultivation.

Asparagus cultivation also occurred in the 'dune backland' area between Hoggs Hill (Ravenmeols) and north almost as far as West Lane, Ainsdale, along the west side of the railway, covering a total of some 100 hectares at its peak, declining to 60 hectares in the 1950s, 16 hectares in 1966 and only 10 hectares by the early 1980s (Smith 1999, 61).

Fig. 9 : 'Jimmy' Lowe
(Courtesy Mrs J. Castle)

(d) *Local Growers*

The asparagus fraternity produced a number of interesting families and characters: two will serve to illustrate this.

James Hunter Lowe was born 1872. He became a well-remembered and colourful local figure and died in August 1944 in Formby. It was at Devon Farm that Jimmy started growing asparagus. Later (c.1925) he took over Pinetree Asparagus Farm, Victoria Road, on the Weld-Blundell Estate. He had six children. One son (Stanley) went to America where he also became a successful large-scale asparagus grower.

The Lowe family had a four-bedroom timber 'bungalow' on the Pinetree Farm fields, which provided a very useful base, particularly during the harvesting season and summer months. During these months his mother remained as matriarch in residence. (Castle pers.comm. 2004). Jimmy enjoyed competition more than other Formby growers, and for

many years regularly competed at the Vale of Evesham Asparagus Championship, winning in 1930-32, 1934 and again in 1936-37 (fig. 9).

John Brooks came to Larkhill Farm, Wicks Lane, with his father about 1907, when he was 14 (Brooks pers.comm. 2004) (fig. 10). His sons and grandsons continue asparagus cultivation there to this day. Some of the land was taken over for the building of Harington Barracks in 1940; this was replaced by a large housing development in the 1960s. About 2 hectares of the remainder of the farm are still cultivated, but the Brooks family have now relinquished their original home. Larkhill Farm is, at the time of writing, about to be demolished. This house (at one time the residence of the Weld-Blundell Estate Manager) now physically represents the decline of asparagus cultivation here in the last half century. The reasons for this decline are not hard to find. Firstly, with the introduction of piped sewage disposal, finally being completed in Formby by the

Fig. 10: John Brooks (Courtesy of Brooks family)

1950s, the supply of cheap but highly valuable manure came to an end. For a while it was replaced by the so-called 'Oldham shoddy', similarly brought to Formby by rail. Shoddy consisted of cotton or woollen mill waste, mixed with human excrement. Increasingly sophisticated local residents living near Formby Station complained in the early 20th century of the smell of the uncovered wagons in the goods sidings, particularly during the summer months (Formby Ratepayers 1896, 20).

Asparagus cultivation did however bring useful seasonal employment opportunities to local residents. There are still many who remember this with pleasure (Morrice pers.comm. 2003). It also made the area famous for this seasonal delicacy (Kelly 1972, 102).

(e) *The decline of cultivation*

Unfortunately the asparagus crop is prone to beetle, 'rust', violet root rot, slugs, frost, wind and injudicious cutting, as well as long-term nutrient depletion (Rimmer 1986, 12). The traditional cultivation has depended on a 'shifting' pattern of land-use from worn-out fields to new areas as yields fell, but the area of unused land in Formby, not exposed to wind or with an unsuitable water-table, became limited by other land uses, particularly conifer plantation, urban development, tobacco-waste tipping and erosion. These, together with the sale of huge quantities of sand ('sand-winning') by the former landowners during the mid-20th century, have resulted in the physical loss of colossal areas of sand down to the water table. At this level the ground is too wet for asparagus cultivation. Re-using the previous fields was found to be unsatisfactory.

Fig. 11: Asparagus ridges. (Photo, authors)

The most obvious remaining evidence of asparagus cultivation is the still-persisting ridge and furrow of the old asparagus fields (Yorke in preparation) (fig.11). These ridges, dating back to the days of horse-drawn implements, are only 0.58 to 0.64 metres from ridge to ridge and, where best preserved, are now about 80 millimetres deep. These are an unusual form of 'field monument'. They are perhaps comparable with the 'cord-rig' of the Scottish machair – a very narrow ridge and furrow pattern created in late prehistoric times, but which still survives in some upland areas (Muir 2004, 46) and are just as worthy to be protected as a reminder of our cultural past.

CONSERVATION AND THE CULTURAL LANDSCAPE

Both Ainsdale and Freshfield dunes were included in the first-ever reserves list, the 1915 survey of areas worthy of protection, carried out by the Society for the Promotion of Nature Reserves (Rothschild and Marren 1997); and Ainsdale in particular appeared in a number of national surveys from that time on. Ainsdale was one of the top 22 sites listed by the Nature Reserves Investigation Committee in 1944 and its value on Merseyside was outlined (Merseyside Plan 1944, 37). This was largely on account of its importance as a wet dune habitat providing one of the few remaining strongholds of the vanishing sand lizard, whilst the marshy slacks behind the dunes are the spawning places of the uncommon Natterjack toad.

Since then most of the natural Sefton coast has been designated as a 'Special Area of Conservation'. In the Sefton dune system we possess not only important protected natural habitats and species in an area of special conservation but we also recognise that here we have a 'cultural landscape'; which the the Cultural Landscape Foundation defines as '…a geographic area that includes cultural and natural resources associated with an historic event, activity, person, or group of people'.

It thus requires protection. Indeed the conservation strategy now being discussed, takes account of the necessity to safeguard features of historic and archaeological interest Amongst these we need to some extent to protect the special 'cultural landscape' which has resulted from the difficult and only partly successful former attempts of our predecessors to cultivate the dune system on this wild, exposed and still semi-natural coast.

ACKNOWLEDGEMENTS

Having enjoyed Sefton's natural coast for very many years we are grateful to the many friends and colleagues who have helped us to understand aspects of its development. The topics discussed in this paper have a comparetively short history but nevertheless have involved some interesting and rewarding research. In understanding the pine woodland development we have drawn considerably on the accounts provided by Mr I. Walmesley-Cotham to the Liverpool Botanic Society in 1934 and again to the Formby Society twenty years later. For the historic sequence of planting we are indebted to the publications of Gresswell who, in turn, recorded information direct from the families concerned. For our knowledge of asparagus cultivation history, techniques and problems we are grateful for information from Andrew Brockbank (National Trust), who allowed us access to the Trust's invaluable sound archive; and several growers including, outside our area, Mr Ron Rigby of Lydiate. The unravelling of the Thomas Fresh story was greatly assisted by the late Neville Carrick, former Librarian, Liverpool City Record Office.

In our preparation of this account we are grateful for helpful advice from Dr Phil Smith and Dr Jen Lewis; for loan and permission to use photographs, Mrs Joan Castle and Mr Garry Brooks, Dr Phil Smith and John Houston; for other illustrations by Muriel Sibley, the Formby Civic Society. We acknowledge, for digitising photographs, Alex Watson of Formby Photographic Group and, for help with the maps, Sefton MBC staff Paul Wisse (Technical Services Department) and John Gramauskas (Leisure Services Department).

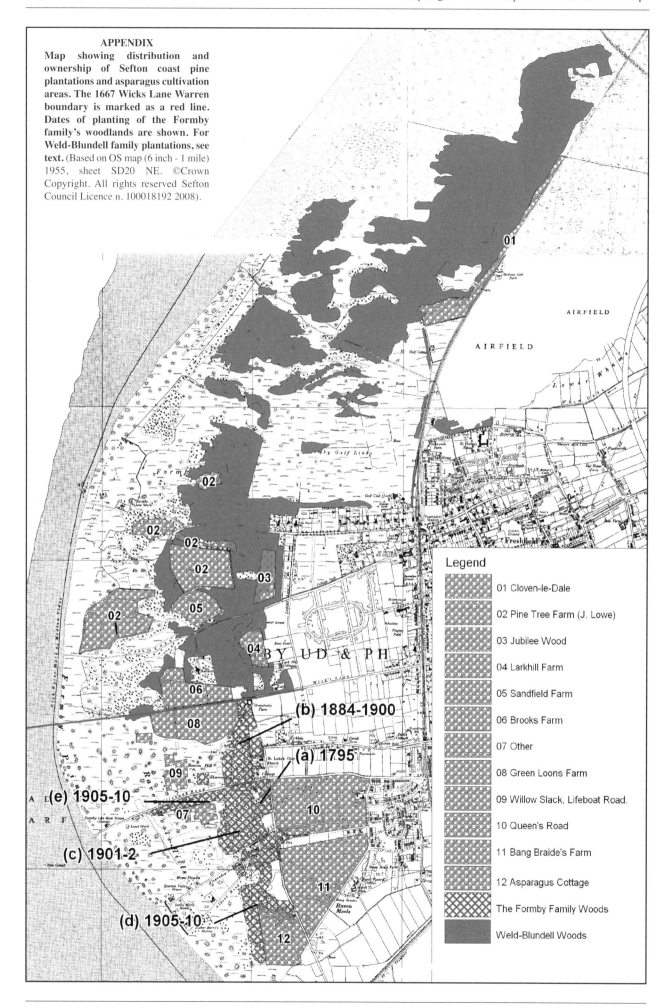

APPENDIX
Map showing distribution and ownership of Sefton coast pine plantations and asparagus cultivation areas. The 1667 Wicks Lane Warren boundary is marked as a red line. Dates of planting of the Formby family's woodlands are shown. For Weld-Blundell family plantations, see text. (Based on OS map (6 inch - 1 mile) 1955, sheet SD20 NE. ©Crown Copyright. All rights reserved Sefton Council Licence n. 100018192 2008).

Legend

01 Cloven-le-Dale

02 Pine Tree Farm (J. Lowe)

03 Jubilee Wood

04 Larkhill Farm

05 Sandfield Farm

06 Brooks Farm

07 Other

08 Green Loons Farm

09 Willow Slack, Lifeboat Road.

10 Queen's Road

11 Bang Braide's Farm

12 Asparagus Cottage

The Formby Family Woods

Weld-Blundell Woods

END NOTES

[1]   Slacks: formed by wind erosion; when down to the water table, further deflation is impossible and a level area is produced.

[2]   Warrens: areas (often with protected boundaries) set aside for the raising of rabbits; in this district their purpose-built accommodation is known as 'rabbit cops'.

[3]   Dune backland: 'A small scale settled pastoral landscape closely associated with a low-lying zone of blown sand to the rear of the coastal dune belt' SPG note 2003.

[4]   Frontal dunes: relatively young, unstable, 'yellow' dunes, closest to the sea.

[5]   Sand-winning: the physical quarrying and removal of sand from the dune-system for industrial use.

[6]   Pantle: described by Mr I. Walmsley-Cotham as 'a long length of cord sometimes 3,000 yards long, to which nooses of horse hair were fastened at frequent intervals, grain being sprinkled along the line of nooses.'

Turning the Tide: Managing the Coastal Environment

Sarah-Jane Farr

The full paper presented at the Conference in 2004 is not available for publication. However, the following short summary provides a brief introduction to the guidelines for managing, protecting and preserving the archaeological resource.

The management of our coastal and maritime historic environment is the responsibility of a number of national and local agencies that cover a range of environmental issues. Whereas the identification, protection and enhancement of terrestrial archaeological sites and landscapes are clearly defined in planning legislation, policy, and professional practice, the management of our coastal heritage is a comparatively new and emerging discipline. The identification of our rich coastal and maritime heritage is particularly challenging as information can be revealed and lost with the changing tides. In recognition of the threats and opportunities afforded by development and access to our coasts, English Heritage has produced guidance promoting the full integration of historic environment issues into coastal management. The key to successful management is ongoing documentation and research to build up data in the local authority Historic Environment Records so that archaeological information is considered alongside other competing activities such as nature conservation and economic considerations and public access.

Aberg, Alan and Lewis, Carenza (eds) 2000 *The Rising Tide: archaeology and coastal landscapes*, Oxbow, Oxford.

Davidson, Andrew (ed) 2002 *The Coastal Archaeology of Wales*, (Council for British Archaeology research report 131), Council for British Archaeology, York.

English Heritage 1996 *England's Coastal Heritage: a statement on the management of coastal archaeolog*y, English Heritage, London.

English Heritage 2003 *Coastal Defence and the Historic Environment: English Heritage Guidance*, English Heritage, Swindon.

Fulford, M., Champion, T. and Long, A. 1997 *England's Coastal Heritage: a survey for English Heritage and the Royal Commission on Historical Monuments of England*, (English Heritage archaeology report 15), English Heritage, London.

Hunter, J. and Ralston, I. 2006 *Archaeological Resource Management in the UK: an introduction* (2nd edition), Sutton Publishing, Stroud.

Roberts, P. and Trow, S, 2002 *Taking to the Water: English Heritage's initial policy for the management of maritime archaeology in England*, English Heritage, London.

Sefton Metropolitan Borough Council *The Sefton Coast Management Plan. Second Review. 1997-2006*, Sefton Council.

Biographical notes

Ron Cowell

Ron Cowell is Curator of Prehistoric Archaeology for National Museums Liverpool and has been involved in the prehistory of the region for 27 years. He was responsible for the Merseyside element of the North West Wetlands Survey, which provided the evidence for human settlement and land use context of prehistoric people using the coast. He has undertaken small prehistoric excavation projects and survey work on the coast at Hightown and Formby. He works closely with various University colleagues on sediments, pollen analysis, and interpretation associated with prehistoric vegetation, freshwater and marine deposition and sea level change. Ron is currently directing the long-term excavation and survey project of Iron Age and earlier sites at Lathom, south west Lancashire.

Sarah-Jane Farr

As Merseyside's Archaeological Officer, Sarah-Jane Farr manages the Merseyside Archaeological Service and provides the five local authorities of Merseyside with advice on a range of archaeological development planning issues associated with the investigation, protection and management of the historic environment. She has a particular interest in promoting an improved understanding and protection of our coastal and marine archaeology and is currently the Secretary of the Maritime Committee of the Association of Local Government Archaeological Officers: UK. Contact details: DTO, Albert Dock, Liverpool L3 4AX. Tel: 0151 478 4258.
Email: sarahjane.farr@liverpoolmuseums.org.uk
http://www.liverpoolmuseums.org.uk/mol/archaeology/mas/

Sylvia Harrop

Now retired from the University of Liverpool, Sylvia Harrop was Senior Lecturer in Education and served as Dean of the Faculty of Education. A Fellow of the Royal Historical Society, she is currently Vice-President of the Historic Society of Lancashire and Cheshire, and Chairman of the Birkdale and Ainsdale Historical Research Society, whose members have been working on the history of the local coast for over 30 years. Her book *Old Birkdale and Ainsdale: life on the south-west Lancashire coast 1600-1851* dates from 1985, and she edited *Families and Cottages of Old Birkdale and Ainsdale*: both are Research Society publications.

John Houston

John Houston has been associated with the Sefton coast since he was appointed Project Officer for the Sefton Coast Management Scheme in 1979. He has been involved in all aspects of management and has developed a life-long interest in dunes as natural and cultural landscapes. His knowledge of the dune systems of north west Europe helps John place the Sefton coast in a wider context in terms of current management and research interests. He enjoys walking the beach, especially after westerly gales, to see what the changing coast can reveal about past landscapes.

Jennifer Lewis

Jen Lewis first became involved in recording Sefton's archaeology in the late 1970s, the outcome being published by Merseyside Archaeological Society in 2002. Until her retirement she was Academic Organiser for the Archaeology and Classics programme for the University of Liverpool's Centre for Lifelong Learning. During her career she has undertaken work commissioned by English Heritage, the National Trust and various local authorities in Merseyside and Cheshire. Since 2005 Jen has been Chairman of Sefton Coast Partnership's Archaeology and History Task Group.

Robert Philpott

Now Head of Archaeology at National Museums Liverpool, Rob Philpott has worked on the archaeology of the north west since the early 1980s. His latest publication is a collaborative volume on

Meols with nearly 20 contributors, published by Oxford University School of Archaeology in December 2007. This catalogues the 19th-century collections and sets the site in a wider context. Rob has excavated a number of sites in the north west, prehistoric to post-medieval, and also carries out research projects in the Falkland Islands and Caribbean.

Gordon Roberts

Retired, former Head of Languages at Formby High School 1968–1985, since when Gordon Roberts has been a committed National Trust Volunteer and Sefton Volunteer Ranger. A lifelong, passionate interest in archaeology, backed by a little amateur, practical experience, enabled him in 1989 to devise a strategy for identifying, recording and researching the origins of the imprints preserved in the erosion-uncovered Holocene sediment strata on Formby Point.

Jennifer Stanistreet

Before retirement in 2007, Jenny Stanistreet was a principal manager with Sefton's library service. With credentials in local history and librarianship, 'and printing ink in the blood', she was well placed to reform and develop the service's publications programme. From 1992 she edited all titles, and co-authored two, under the 'Sefton Libraries' imprint.

Ann Worsley

Annie Worsley is Reader in Physical Geography at Edge Hill University. She lectures primarily in environmental change and physical geography, taking students to a range of field locations in the UK and Europe. A Chartered Geographer and Fellow of the Royal Geographical Society, her research includes major collaborative work such as the Coastal Flooding from Extreme Events (CoFEE) project, funded by the Natural Environment Research Council (NERC), and the innovative Liverpool/Halton project investigating records of atmospheric pollution in urban lake sediments, funded by the NHS. Working for several years alongside Gordon Roberts studying the sediments

bearing the human and animal footprints at Formby, she and Gordon appeared in the BAFTA award winning first series of BBC2's *Coast* programme.

Barbara Yorke

Barbara Yorke has been Secretary of the History Group of the Formby Civic Society continuously since 1981. Prior to that she researched Formby Lifeboat Station and was amazed to discover that it was (until then unrecognised) Britain's First. She has written – or, with her husband, co-authored – several local history publications.

Reg Yorke

A retired medical practitioner, Reg Yorke has been interested in landscape and farming history since school summer holidays spent working on old farms in the West Riding. Later he became interested in aspects of Liverpool history, in particular the 18th century 'Institution for the Recovery of the Apparently Drowned' and the subsequent efforts to improve Liverpool's sanitary conditions in the mid-19th century.

Abbreviations

BP	Before Present (in radiocarbon citations, taken as AD1950)
Crosby Lib.	Crosby Library, Waterloo, Liverpool
FCS	Formby Civic Society
GIS	Geographic Information Systems
HER	Historic Environment Record
LCCM	Liverpool Common Council Minutes
LDCM	Liverpool Dock Committee Minutes
L'poolRO	Liverpool Record Office
LRO	Lancashire Record Office, Preston
MDHB	Mersey Docks and Harbour Board
MDHB DCM	Mersey Docks and Harbour Board, Dock Committee Minutes
MHWL	Mean High Water Line
MLWL	Mean Low Water Line
MMMA	Merseyside Maritime Museum Archives and Library
MRO	Merseyside Record Office, Liverpool
NMGM	National Museums and Galleries on Merseyside
NML	National Museums Liverpool
OE	Old English
ON	Old Norse
OS	Ordnance Survey
PAS	Portable Antiquities Scheme
POL	Port of Liverpool
RNLI	Royal National Lifeboat Institution
RSA	Royal Society for the Encouragement of the Arts
SMR	Sites and Monuments Record
TNA	The National Archives (formerly Public Record Office), London
VCH	Victoria County History

Bibliography

Adams, M. H. and Philpott, R. A. (forthcoming) *Excavations on a Romano-British and Early Medieval Site at Court Farm, Halewood, Merseyside*, National Museums Liverpool monograph, Liverpool

Admiralty 1873, 1944, 1948, 1980 [Charts] *Liverpool Bay*

Aikin, J. 1795 *A Description of the Country from Thirty to Forty Miles round Manchester*, reprinted 1968 David and Charles

Aitken, M. J. 1990 *Science-based Dating in Archaeology*, Longman, London/New York

Ashton, W. 1909 *The Battle of the Land and Sea on the Lancashire, Cheshire and North Wales Coasts and the Origin of the Lancashire Sandhills*, W.Ashton and Sons Ltd, Southport

Ashton, W. 1920 *The Evolution of a Coastline*, E.Stanford Ltd, London/W.Ashton and Sons Ltd, Southport

Atholl Papers, Manx Museum Library, Isle of Man: X14-14, X40B/24

Atkinson, D. and Houston, J. (eds) 1993 *The Sand Dunes of the Sefton Coast*, National Museums and Galleries on Merseyside/Sefton Metropolitan Borough Council

Aughton, P. 1988 *North Meols and Southport: a history*, Carnegie, Preston

Bagot, A. and Munby J. (eds) 1988 *'All Things Is Well Here': letters from Hugh James of Levens to James Grahme, 1692-5*, Cumberland & Westmorland Antiq & Archaeol Soc, Record Series **10**

Bailey, F.A. 1953 'The Modern Period' in W. Smith (ed) *A Scientific Survey of Merseyside*, British Association, Liverpool

Bailey, F. A. 1955 *A History of Southport*, Downie, (reprinted to mark the bi-centenary of Southport 1792-1992, Sefton Libraries)

Baines, E. 1825 *Lancashire* **II**

Barraclough, G. 1953 'The Mediaeval Period' in W. Smith (ed) *A Scientific Survey of Merseyside*, British Association, Liverpool

Bayon, C. and Politis, G. 1998 'Las Huellas del Pasado. Pisadas Humanas Prehistorícas en la Costa Pampeana' *Ciencia Hoy* Volumen **8**, 48

Beck, J. 1954 'The Church Brief for the inundation of the Lancashire coast in 1720', *Trans Hist Soc Lancashire and Cheshire* **105**, 91-106

Bell, M. 1995 'Field Survey and excavation at Goldcliff 1994' in M. Bell (ed) *Archaeology in the Severn Estuary 1994*, Annual Report of the Severn Estuary Levels Research Committee, 115-144

Binford, L. R. 1983 *In Pursuit of the Past*, Thames and Hudson, London

Bland, E. 1903 *Annals of Southport*, Southport

Blundell of Ince Blundell family, papers, LRO DDIn

Blundell, F. O. 1924 'Crannogs', *Trans Hist Soc Lancashire and Cheshire* **75** (for 1923), 203-7

Blundell, M. (ed) 1952 *Blundell's Diary and Letter Book*, Liverpool University Press

Booth, J. H. L. 1947 *The Sea Casualties on the Southport Coast 1745-1946*, Botanic Gardens Museum, Southport

Borough of Liverpool, Health Committee 1851 *Report to the Health Committee by the Borough Engineer, Inspector of Nuisances and the Medical Officer of Health*

Borough of Liverpool, Health Committee 1854 *The Liverpool Sanitary Act 1846 as amended by the Liverpool Sanitary Amendment Act 1854*

Boult, J. 1870 'A Littoral Survey of the Port of Liverpool', *Trans Hist Soc Lancashire and Cheshire* **22** (**10** n.s.) 171-246

Brennand, M. (ed) 2006 *The Archaeology of North West England. An Archaeological Research Framework for North West England* **1**: Resource Assessment. Archaeology North West **8** (issue 18 for 2006)

Brennand, M. (ed) 2007 *Research and Archaeology in North West England. An Archaeological Research Framework for North West England* **2**: Research Agenda and Strategy. Archaeology North West **9** (issue 19 for 2007)

Briggs, A. 1979 *The Age of Improvement 1783-1867*, 1st (corrected) edition

Brownrigg, W. 1748 *The Art of Making Common Salt, as now Practised in Most Parts of the World*, C. Davis, London

Bullock, H. A. 1816 *History of the Isle of Man*, London

Bulman, J. 2003 *My Hightown 1897-1969, being personal reminiscences*, 3rd (revised) edition, Sefton Libraries

Bulpit, W. T. 1908 *Notes on Southport and District*, Southport Visiter [Press]

Burdett, P. 1771 *A Chart of the Harbour of Liverpool* (corrected 1776) bound in with W. Hutchinson, *A Treatise on Practical Seamanship* 1777

Carrick, N. 2001 *Thomas Fresh of Freshfield* [parish newsletter article, St Peter's Church, Formby] FCS Archives

Carson, E. 1972 *The Ancient and Rightful Customs: a history of the English Customs Service,* Faber and Faber, London

Cartwright, J. J. (ed) 1888 *The Travels through England of Dr. Richard Pococke* **1**, Camden Soc

Charteris, J., Wall, J. C. and Nottrodt, J. W. 1981 'Functional reconstruction of gait from the Pliocene hominid footprints at Laetoli, Northern Tanzania', *Nature* **290**, 496-498

Cheetham, F. H. and Sparke A. (eds) 1934 *The Parish Registers of North Meols 1732-1812*, Lancashire Parish Register Soc **72**

Clarke, M. 1994 *The Leeds & Liverpool Canal: a history and guide*, Carnegie Press, Ashton

Clutton-Brock, J. 1986 'New dates for old animals: the reindeer, the aurochs and the wild horse in prehistoric Britain' *Archaeozoologia, Mélanges publiés à l'occasion du 5e congrès international d'archéologie, Bordeaux, août 1986*, 111-117

Collins, G. 1693 *Great Britain's Coasting Pilot. The first part. Being a new and exact survey of the sea-coast of England, from the River of Thames to the Westward, with the Islands of Scilly, and from thence to Carlile.* Liverpool University Library Special Collection SPEC Q2.13

Columella, Lucius Junius Moderatus n.d. *On Agriculture,* Book XI, English translation by E.S. Forster and E. H. Heffner

Coney, A. 1992 'Fish, Fowl and Fen: landscape and economy in seventeenth-century Martin Mere', *Landscape History* **14**, 51-64

Coney, A. 1995 'Liverpool Dung: the magic wand of agriculture', *The Lancashire Local Historian* **10**, 15-26

Cook, A. L. M. 1989 *Altcar: the story of a rifle range,* Territorial, Auxiliary & Volunteer Reserve Association for the North West of England & The Isle of Man

Cotter, E. P. 1929 *The Port of Liverpool*, Foreign Port Series no.2, United States Department of Commerce

Cowell, R. W. 1981 Knowsley Rural Fringes Survey, Archaeological Survey of Merseyside, Merseyside County Council/Merseyside County Museums, unpublished report, Liverpool

Cowell, R. W. 1991 *Interim Report on the Survey of the Wetlands in Merseyside: 1990-91.* North West Wetlands Survey Annual Report 2. Lancaster University Archaeological Unit, 13-20

Cowell, R. W. 1992 'Greasby, North Wirral, Merseyside: interim report on the excavation of an early Mesolithic site', *Archaeology North West*, **4**, 7-15

Cowell, R. W. 2000 'The Early Prehistoric Period in Southern Merseyside' in R. W. Cowell and R. A. Philpott *Prehistoric, Romano-British and Medieval settlement in Lowland North West England: archaeological excavations along the A5300 road corridor in Merseyside,* National Museums and Galleries on Merseyside, Liverpool, 165-8

Cowell, R. W. 2005 'Late Prehistoric Lowland Settlement in North West England' in M. Nevell and N. Redhead (eds) *A Regional Study of an Iron Age and Romano-British Upland Settlement,* Manchester Archaeological Monographs, **1**, Manchester, University Manchester Archaeological Unit/Greater Manchester Archaeological Unit/Mellor Archaeological Trust, 65-76

Cowell, R. W. and Innes, J. B. 1994 *The Wetlands of Merseyside,* North West Wetlands Survey **1**. National Museums and Galleries on Merseyside/ Lancaster University Archaeological Unit

Cowell, R. W., Milles, A. and Roberts, G. 1993 *Prehistoric footprints on Formby Point beach, Merseyside* in R. Middleton (ed) North West Wetlands Survey Annual Report 1993, 43-48

Cowell, R. W. and Philpott, R. A. 2000 *Prehistoric, Romano-British and Medieval Settlement in Lowland North West England: archaeological excavations along the A5300 road corridor in Merseyside,* National Museums and Galleries on Merseyside, Liverpool

Cox, E. W. 1895 'Traces of submerged lands on the coasts of Lancashire, Cheshire and North Wales', *Trans Hist Soc Lancashire and Cheshire* **46** (**10** n.s.) (for 1894), 19-56

Crosby, A. G. 1998 'The roads of county, hundred and township 1550-1850', in A.G. Crosby (ed) *Leading the Way: a history of Lancashire's roads,* Lancashire County Books, Preston

Crosse of Shaw Hill family, papers, LRO DDSh

Cultural Landscape Foundation www.tclf.org/whatis.htm

Day, M. H. 1991 *Bipedalism and prehistoric footprints*, Origine(s) de la bipédie chez les hominidés (cahiers de la paléoanthropologie), Editions du CNRS, Paris

De Rance, C. E. 1869 *Geology of the country between Liverpool and Southport: explanation of sheet 90 SE*, Memoirs of the Geological Survey of England and Wales, HMSO, London

De Rance, C. E. 1877 *The Superficial Geology of the country adjoining the coast of south-west Lancashire*, Memoirs of the Geological Survey of England and Wales, HMSO, London

Denham, H. M. 1840 *Sailing Directions from Point Lynas to Liverpool: with charts, coast-views, river sections, tidal courses and tide gauge table, for navigating the Dee and Mersey, including the latest alterations* [surveyed 1832-1839], J. and M. Mawdsley, Liverpool. LpoolRO Hf 912.LIV

Dickinson, J. R. 1996 *The Lordship of Man under the Stanleys: government and economy in the Isle of Man, 1580-1704*, (for) Chetham Soc, Carnegie, Manchester

Dodgson, J. McN. 1972 *Place-Names of Cheshire Part IV*, English Place-Name Soc **47**, Cambridge University Press

Dolley, R. H. M. 1966 *The Hiberno-Norse Coins in the British Museum*, British Museum, London

Duncan H. 1812 'On the Mode of Manufacturing Salt from Sea-sand or Sleech' in W. Singer, *General view of the Agriculture of Dumfries*

Ecroyd Smith, H. 1866a 'Coins at Otterspool', *Trans Hist Soc Lancashire and Cheshire* **18**, 197-8

Ecroyd Smith, H. 1866b 'A Second Find of Coins at Otterspool', *Trans Hist Soc Lancashire and Cheshire* **18**, 199

Ecroyd Smith, H. 1868 'Archaeology in the Mersey District, 1867', *Trans Hist Soc Lancashire and Cheshire* **20** (**8** n.s.), 87-130

Edwards, B. J. N. 1992 'The Vikings in North-West England: the archaeological evidence' in J. Graham-Campbell (ed) *Viking Treasure from the North West: the Cuerdale Hoard in its context*, National Museums and Galleries on Merseyside, Liverpool, 43-62

Ekwall, E. 1922 *The Place Names of Lancashire*, Chetham Soc **81**

Ekwall, E. 1960 *The Concise Oxford Dictionary of English Place-names*, 4th edition, Oxford University Press

Eyes, J. 1767 [Chart] *Chester-bar to Formby Point*, 3rd edition, L'poolRO Hf 386.35 FED

Fairbanks, R. G. 1989 'A 17,000-year glacio-eustatic sea level record: influence of glacial melting rates on the Younger Dryas event and deep-ocean circulation', *Nature* **342**, 637-642

Farrer, W. 1903 *A History of North Meols*, Henry Young and Sons

Farrer, W. (ed) 1900 *The Chartulary of Cockersand Abbey* 2 part 2, Chetham Soc **43** n.s.

Farrer, W. (ed) 1909 *The Chartulary of Cockersand Abbey* 3 part 3, Chetham Soc **64** n.s.

Farrer, W. and Brownbill, J. 1906 *The Victoria History of the County of Lancaster* **1**, London

Farrer, W. and Brownbill, J. 1907 *The Victoria History of the County of Lancaster* **3**, London

Farrer, W. and Brownbill, J. 1908, *The Victoria History of the County of Lancaster* **2**, London

Fearon, S. and Eyes, J. 1737 *Chart of Liverpool Bay, Chester-bar to Formby Point, with proper directions to sail into any harbour … according to an actual survey thereof made in the years 1736 and 1737*, 2nd edition 1755, L'poolRO Hf 912 LIV

Fellows-Jensen, G. 1992 'Scandinavian Place-Names of the Irish Sea Province' in J. Graham-Campbell (ed) *Viking Treasure from the North West: the Cuerdale Hoard in its context*, National Museums and Galleries on Merseyside, Liverpool, 31-42

Fenwick, C. (ed) 1998 *The Poll Taxes of 1377, 1379 and 1381 Part 1 Bedfordshire-Leicestershire*, Records of Social and Economic History, New Series **27**, British Academy. Oxford University Press

Feudal Aids 1904 *Feudal Aids III, Kent to Norfolk*, Public Record Office, London

Finberg, H. P. R. 1975a 'Ingimund's Invasion' in F. T. Wainwright, *Scandinavian England: collected papers by F. T. Wainwright* (ed by H. P. R. Finberg), Phillimore, Chichester, 131-161

Finberg, H. P. R. 1975b 'The Scandinavians in Lancashire' in F. T. Wainwright, *Scandinavian England: collected papers by F. T. Wainwright* (ed by H. P. R. Finberg), Phillimore, Chichester, 181-227

Fisher, R. 1763 *Heart of Oak the British Bulwark. Shewing I. Reasons for paying greater attention to the propagation of oak timber …II. The insufficiency of the present laws, etc*, London

Fishwick, H. (ed) 1879 *Lancashire and Cheshire Church Surveys, 1649-1655,* Rec Soc Lancashire and Cheshire **1**, Part 1

Fishwick, H. (ed) 1896 *Pleadings and depositions in the Duchy Court of Lancashire, 1.* Rec Soc Lancashire and Cheshire **32**

Fishwick, H. 1898 'Places in Lancashire destroyed by the sea', *Trans Hist Soc Lancashire and Cheshire* **49** (**13** n.s.) (for 1897), 87-96

Forestry Commission (Conservator) 11 May 1959 Letter to O.Williams and Sutcliffe (Agents), MRO 920 WBL/8/4

Formby of Formby family, papers, LRO DDFo

Formby, Ann Lonsdall 1876 *A Sketch of the Life of R. Formby MD FRCP of Liverpool and Formby, and of his family* [Typescript] L'poolRO Bickerton Collection, H 920 FOR

Formby, John 1903 Letter to Mrs C. Jacson, Lytham, FCS Archives

Formby Ratepayers 1896 [Submission] *For the formation of an Urban District Council* FCS Archives, Box A13

Foster, H. 1995 *New Birkdale: the growth of a Lancashire seaside suburb, 1850-1912,* Birkdale and Ainsdale Historical Research Soc

Foster, H. 1998 *Don E Want Ony Srimps?: the story of the fishermen of Southport and North Meols,* Birkdale and Ainsdale Historical Research Soc

Foster, H. 2000 *New Ainsdale: the struggle of a seaside suburb, 1850-2000,* Birkdale and Ainsdale Historical Research Soc

Foster, H. 2002 *Crossens: Southport's Cinderella suburb,* Birkdale and Ainsdale Historical Research Soc

Fraser, S. M., Gilmour, S. and Dawson, T. 2003 'Shorewatch: monitoring Scotland's coastal archaeology' in T. Dawson (ed) *Coastal Archaeology and Erosion in Scotland,* Historic Scotland, Edinburgh, 197-202

Fresh, T. 1851 *Report to the Health Committee of the Town Council of the Borough of Liverpool comprising a detail of the sanitary operations in the Nuisance Department from 1st Jan 1847 to 31 March 1851*

Frey, C., Smith, J., Sanders, M. and Horstman, H. 1993 'American Orthopaedic Foot and Ankle Soc Women's Shoe Survey', *Foot & Ankle* **14**, 78-81

Gahan, J. W. 1985 *Seaport to Seaside: lines to Southport and Ormskirk – 13 decades of trains and travel,* Countyvise, Birkenhead

Gaskell, Mrs. 1857 *Life of Charlotte Bronte,* 2nd edition, Smith Elder and Co, London

Gerrard, J. 1636 *The Herball or Generall Historie of Plantes,* T. Johnson (ed) republished 1985 Bracken Books, London

Gibson, T. E. 1876 *Lydiate Hall and its Associations,* Ballantyne Hanson and Co

Gladstone, R. 1932 *Notes on the History and Antiquities of Liverpool,* Liverpool

Glazebrook, T. K. 1826 *A Guide to Southport, North Meols, in the County of Lancaster,* Southport

Godwin, H. 1984 *History of the British Flora: a factual basis for phytogeography,* 2nd edition, Cambridge University Press

Gonzalez, S. and Huddart, D. 2002 'Formby Point' and 'Hightown' in D. Huddart and N. F. Glasser *The Quaternary of Northern England,* Geological Conservation Review Series No. **25**, Joint Nature Conservation Committee, Peterborough, 569-588

Gonzalez, S., Huddart, D., and Roberts, G. 1996 'Holocene development of the Sefton coast: a multidisciplinary approach to understanding the archaeology' in A. Sinclair, E. Slater and J. Gowlett (eds) *Archaeological Science 1995,* Oxbow Books, Oxford, 289-299

Gore, J. *Directory of Liverpool and environs* 1855 <u>and</u> 1859

Green, C. T. (ed) 1902 *The Flora of the Liverpool District,* D. Marples and Co, Liverpool

Greenwood, E. F. (ed) 1999 *Ecology and Landscape Development: a history of the Mersey Basin: proceedings of a conference held at Merseyside Maritime Museum, Liverpool, 5-6 July 1996,* Liverpool University Press

Gresswell, R. K. 1953 *Sandy Shores in South Lancashire,* Liverpool University Press

Griffiths, D. W. 1992 'The Coastal Trading Ports of the Irish Sea' in J. Graham-Campbell (ed) *Viking Treasure from the North West: the Cuerdale Hoard in its context,* National Museums and Galleries on Merseyside, Liverpool, 63-72

Griffiths, D. W., Philpott, R. A. and Egan, G. 2007 *Meols: the archaeology of the north Wirral coast: discoveries and observations in the 19th and 20th centuries, with a catalogue of collections,* Oxford University School of Archaeology Monograph **68**, Oxford University School of Archaeology

Grigson, G. 1987 *The Englishman's Flora: illustrated with woodcuts from sixteenth-century herbals*, Phoenix House, London

Hale, W. G. 1985 *Martin Mere, Its History and Natural History*, Causeway Press Limited Editions

Hall, B. R. and Folland, C. J. 1967 *Soils of the south-west Lancashire coastal plain*, Soil Survey of Great Britain: England and Wales, Harpenden

Hall, B. R. and Folland, C. J. 1970 *Soils of Lancashire*, Bulletin no.5, Soil Survey of Great Britain: England and Wales, Harpenden

Harland, J. (ed) 1856 *The house and farm accounts of the Shuttleworths of Gawthorpe Hall, in the county of Lancaster, at Smithills and Gawthorpe, from September 1582 to October 1621*, 1, Chetham Soc **35**

Harley, J. B. 1968 *A Map of the County of Lancashire, 1786, by William Yates*, Hist Soc Lancashire and Cheshire, Liverpool

Harris, A. 2003 *Byzantium, Britain and the West: the archaeology of cultural identity AD 400-650*, Tempus Publishing, Stroud

Harrop, S. A. 1982 'Fishing stalls on the south west Lancashire coast', *Trans Hist Soc Lancashire and Cheshire* **131**, 161-164

Harrop, S. A. 1985 *Old Birkdale and Ainsdale: life on the south-west Lancashire Coast 1600-1851*, Birkdale and Ainsdale Historical Research Soc

Harrop, S. A. (ed) 1992 *Families and Cottages of Old Birkdale and Ainsdale*, Birkdale and Ainsdale Historical Research Soc

Hawthorne, N. 1856-7 *The English Notebooks*, republished 1962 Russell and Russell

Head D. 1990 *The Lawson Booth List of Wrecks, lying off the West Coast, 1740-1990, revised, enlarged and corrected*, [typescript] Sefton Libraries (Southport Local History Collection) S910.4

Higham, M. 1998 'The roads of dark age and medieval Lancashire' in A.G. Crosby (ed) *Leading the Way: a history of Lancashire's roads*, Lancashire County Books, Preston

Higham, N. J. 1992 'Northumbria, Mercia and the Irish Sea Norse, 893-926' in J. Graham-Campbell (ed) *Viking Treasure from the North West: the Cuerdale Hoard in its context*, National Museums and Galleries on Merseyside, Liverpool, 21-30

Fiennes, C. 1983 *The Journeys of Celia Fiennes*, introduction by J. Hillaby, Macdonald and Co, London/Sydney

Holt, J. 1795 *General View of the Agriculture of the County of Lancaster With Observations on the Means of Its Improvement*, reprinted 1969 David and Charles

Holt, G. 1796 Gentlemen's magazine **66**, 549-551. Quoted by G.H. Morton 1871 'The progress of the geological research in the connection with the geology of the country around Liverpool', *Proc Liverpool Geol Soc*, **2**, 3-33

Hope, E. W. 1931 *Health at the Gateway: problems and international obligations of a seaport city*, Cambridge University Press

Howard-Davis, C. 1996 'Seeing the Sites: survey and excavations on the Anglezarke Uplands, Lancashire', *Proc Prehist Soc*, **62**, 133-166

Huddart, D, 1992, Coastal environmental changes and morphostratigraphy in southwest Lancashire, England, *Proc Geologists' Assoc*, **103**, 217-236

Huddart, D., Gonzalez, S. and Roberts, G. 1999a 'The Archaeological Record and Mid-Holocene Marginal Coastal Palaeoenvironments Around Liverpool Bay' in Edwards, K. J. and Sadler, J. P. (eds) 1999 *Holocene environments of prehistoric Britain*, J Quaternary Science **14** (Quaternary Proceedings No. **7**), Chichester, 563-574

Huddart, D., Roberts, G. and Gonzalez, S. 1999b 'Holocene human and animal footprints and their relationships with coastal environmental change, Formby Point, NW England' *Quaternary International* **55**, Issue 1 (March 1999), 29-41

Hulton, W. A. (ed) 1847 *The Coucher Book or Chartulary of Whalley Abbey*, Chetham Soc **X**, **XI**

Hume, A. 1863 *Ancient Meols: some account of the antiquities found near Dove Point on the sea coast of Cheshire*, J. Russell Smith, London

Hume, A. 1866 'Changes in the sea coast of Lancashire and Cheshire', *Trans Hist Soc Lancashire and Cheshire* **18** (**6** n.s), 1-82

Hutchinson, W. 1777 *A Treatise on Practical Seamanship*, reprinted 1979 Scolar Press, London

Hyde, F.E. 1971 *Liverpool and the Mersey: an economic history of a port 1700-1970*, David and Charles, Newton Abbot

Innes, J. B. and Tooley, M. J. 1993 'The age and vegetational history of the Sefton Coast Dunes' in D. Atkinson and J. Houston (eds) *The Sand Dunes of the Sefton Coast*, National Museums and Galleries on Merseyside/Sefton Metropolitan Borough Council, 35-40

Jacson, C. 1897 *Formby Reminiscences*, 2nd edition (centenary 1997), Sefton Libraries

James, R. 1636 *Iter Lancastrense: a poem*, (ed) by T. Corser 1845, Chetham Soc, **VII**, lines 305-320

Jarvis, A. 1998 'Safe Home in Port? Shipping Safety within the Port of Liverpool', *The Northern Mariner* **4**

Jarvis, R. C. 1945-46 'Illicit trade with the Isle of Man', *Trans Lancashire and Cheshire Antiq Soc* **58**, 245-267

Jarvis, R. C. 1954 *Customs Letter Books of the Port of Liverpool*, Chetham Soc, Third Series, **VI**

Jones, C. R., Houston J. A. and Bateman, D. 1993 'A History of Human Influence on the Coastal Landscape' in D. Atkinson and J. Houston (eds) *The Sand Dunes of the Sefton Coast*, National Museums and Galleries on Merseyside/Sefton Metropolitan Borough Council, 3-20

Kelly, E. 1973 *Viking Village: the story of Formby*, 3rd (revised) edition 1982, The Formby Soc

Kelly's Directory of Lancashire 1858

Kenna, R. 1978 'Early Settlement on the North Wirral Coastal Area', *J Merseyside Archaeol Soc* **2**, 27-34

Kenna, R. 1986 'The Flandrian Sequence of North Wirral (N.W. England)', *Geol J* **21**, 1-27

Kipling, R. 1982 *A Source Book of Lifeboats*, Ward Lock, London

Lamb, H. H. 1982 *Climate, history and the modern world*, Methuen, London

Lamb, H. H. 1991 *Historic Storms of the North Sea, British Isles and Northwest Europe*, Cambridge University Press

Latham, R. *Account book of Richard Latham of Scarisbrick, farmer, 1723-67*, LRO DP385

Launching of Formby Lifeboat c1916 North West Film Archive, Film and Video Catalogue, film no. 58, http://www.nwfa.mmu.ac.uk/

Leigh, C. 1700 *Natural History of Lancashire, Cheshire and the Peak in Derbyshire, with an Account of the Antiquities in Those Parts*, Oxford.

Lewis, J. M. 1978 'An Abandoned Church at Formby' *J Merseyside Archaeol Soc* **2**, 73-74

Lewis, J. M. 1982 Sefton Rural Fringes Survey Report, Archaeological Survey of Merseyside, Merseyside County Council/Merseyside County Museums, unpublished report, Liverpool

Lewis, J. M. 2002 'Sefton Rural Fringes', *J Merseyside Archaeol Soc* **11**, 5-88

Liverpool Common Council Minutes 1776-1792, L'poolRO 352/COU

Liverpool, Crosby and Southport Railway 1845-55 Committee Minutes, TNA GB/NNAF/B11686/Rail 372

Liverpool Dock Committee Minutes 14/1/1793-April 1848, L'poolRO 352MIN/DOC

Lumby, J. H. 1936 *Calendar of deeds and papers in the possession of Sir James de Hoghton, Bart*, Record Soc Lancashire and Cheshire **88**

Lumby, J. H. 1939 *Calendar of the Norris Deeds (Lancashire) 12th to 15th century*, Record Soc Lancashire and Cheshire **93**

McAvoy, F. 1994 'Marine Salt Extraction: the excavation of salterns at Wainfleet St Mary, Lincolnshire', *Medieval Archaeology* **38**, 134-163

McGrail, S. 1997 *Studies in Maritime Archaeology*, British Archaeological Reports (British Series) **256**, Oxford

McGrail, S. and Switsur, R. 1979 'Medieval logboats of the River Mersey – a classification study' in S. McGrail (ed) *The archaeology of ships and harbours in Northern Europe*, British Archaeological Reports (International Series) **66**, Oxford, 93-115

Mackenzie, M. 1776 [Chart] *The Coast adjacent to Chester and Liverpool, from Orme's Head to Formby Point*, L'poolRO Hf 912 LIV

McNulty, J. (ed) 1933 *The Chartulary of the Cistercian Abbey of St Mary of Sallay in Craven*, Yorkshire Archaeol Soc Record Series **87**

Maddock, A. 1999 'Watercourse management and flood prevention in the Alt Level, Lancashire, 1589-1779' *Trans Hist Soc Lancashire and Cheshire* **148**, 59-94

Matthews, K. J. 1999 'The Iron Age of North-west England and Irish Sea Trade' in B. Bevan (ed) *Northern Exposure: interpretative devolution and the Iron Ages in Britain*, Leicester Archaeology Monographs **4**, Leicester, 173-95

Mayer, J. 1871 *History of the Art of Pottery in Liverpool*, 2nd edition, D. Marples and Co, Liverpool

Mersey Docks and Harbour Board 1988 [Chart] *Approaches to Liverpool, England – West Coast*, International Chart Series

Mersey Docks and Harbour Board, Dock Committee Minutes 1874, 1889, 1892

Metcalf, D. M. 1992 'The Monetary Economy of the Irish Sea Province' in J. Graham-Campbell (ed) *Viking Treasure from the North West: the Cuerdale Hoard in its context*, National Museums and Galleries on Merseyside, Liverpool, 89-106

Middleton, R and Tooley, M. J, (forthcoming) *The Wetlands of West Lancashire*, North West Wetlands Survey **7**, Lancaster University Archaeol Unit

Mills, D. 1986 *The Place Names of Lancashire*, Batsford, London

Ministry of Agriculture, Fisheries and Food 1969a *Asparagus*, Bulletin 60, HMSO

Ministry of Agriculture, Fisheries and Food 1969b *The Asparagus Handbook*, 5th edition

Molyneux, Earls of Sefton family, papers, LRO DDM

Moore, A. W. 1900 *A History of the Isle of Man*, T. F. Unwin, London, reprinted Manx Museum 1977

Moore, P. D. and Webb, J. A. 1978 *An Illustrated Guide to Pollen Analysis*, Hodder and Stoughton, London

Moore Papers 1889 'Selections from the Ancient Papers of the Moore Family, formerly of Liverpool and Bank Hall' *Trans Hist Soc Lancashire and Cheshire* **39** (for 1888), 159-174

Morrice, G. 2003 *Personal Memories* [audio recording] FCS Archives

Morris, E. L. 1985 'Prehistoric Salt Distributions: two case studies from western Britain', *Bulletin of the Board of Celtic Studies* **32**, 336-79

Morton, H. 1871 'The progress of the geological research in the connection with the geology of the country around Liverpool', *Proc Liverpool Geol Soc* **2**, 3-33

Mountfield, A. S. 1953 'Admiral Denham and the Approaches to the Port of Liverpool', *Trans Historic Soc Lancashire and Cheshire* **105** (for 1952)

Muir, R. 2004 *Landscape Encyclopaedia: a reference guide to the historic landscape*, Windgather, Bollington

Naish, J. M. 1985 *Seamarks, Their History and Development*, Stanford Maritime, London

Nash, R. C. 1991 'Liverpool Trade and Shipping in the Atlantic Economy of the late 17th and 18th centuries', lecture to Hist Soc Lancashire and Cheshire

Neal, A. 1993 'Sedimentology and morphodynamics of a Holocene coastal barrier complex, Northwest England' (Unpublished PhD thesis, University of Reading)

Ordnance Survey 1848 *Lancashire* 6 inches to 1 mile; sheet 90, surveyed 1846

Ordnance Survey 1955 *Lancashire* 6 inch to 1 mile; sheet SD 20 NE

Parham, K. R., Gordon, C. C. and Bensel, C. K. 1992 *Anthropometry of the foot and lower leg of US Army soldiers: Fort Jackson, SC - 1985*, US Army Natick Research, Development and Engineering Centre Report, Natick, MA

Patton, M. A. 1993 'Neolithic and later archaeology' in D. H. Keen (ed) *Quaternary of Jersey: field guide*, Quaternary Research Association Field Guide **51**, London, 48-56

Pennant, T. 1801 *A Tour from Downing to Alston-Moor*, London

Philpott, R. A. 1999 'Three Byzantine Coins found near the North Wirral Coast in Merseyside', *Trans Historic Soc Lancashire and Cheshire* **148**, 197-202

Philpott, R. A. and Adams, M. H. (forthcoming) *Irby, Wirral: excavations on a late Prehistoric, Romano-British and Medieval site, 1987-96*, National Museums Liverpool

Picton, J. A 1907 *City of Liverpool Municipal Archives and Records from AD 1700 to the passing of the Municipal Reform Act 1835*, Edward Howell, Liverpool

Plater, A. J., Huddart, D., Innes, J. B., Pye, K., Smith, A. J. and Tooley, M. J. 1993 'Coastal and Sea-level Changes' in D. Atkinson and J. Houston (eds) *The Sand Dunes of the Sefton Coast*, National Museums and Galleries on Merseyside/Sefton Metropolitan Borough Council

Plinius Secundus, Caius c77 *Naturalis historia*, Book XX, 245. Bohn's Classical Library IV, English Translation by J. Bostock and H. Riley

Plot, R. 1686 *Natural History of Staffordshire*, Oxford. (Facsimile ed. 1973, E. W. Morten, Manchester)

Potter, C. 1876 'Observations on the Geology and Archaeology of the Cheshire Shore', *Trans Hist Soc Lancashire and Cheshire* **38** (**4** n.s.) (for 1875-6), 121-42

Potter, C. 1893 'Agricultural and Mechanical Implements found on the Meols Shore', *Trans Hist Soc Lancashire and Cheshire* **43-44** (for 1891-2), 233-44

Proudman Oceanographic Laboratory, Liverpool http://cobs.pol.ac.uk/cobs/radar/

Pye, K. and Neal, A. 1993a 'Late Holocene dune formation on the Sefton coast, northwest England' in K. Pye (ed) *The Dynamics and the Environmental Context of Aeolian Sedimentary Systems*, Geological Survey Special Publications No **72**, Geological Survey Publishing House, Bath, 201-217

Pye, K. and Neal, A. 1993b 'Stratigraphy and age structure of the Sefton dune complex: preliminary results of field drilling investigations' in D. Atkinson and J. Houston (eds) *The Sand Dunes of the Sefton Coast*, National Museums and Galleries on Merseyside/Sefton Metropolitan Borough Council, 41-44

Quarter Sessions petitions, LRO QSP

Rackham, O. 2006 *Woodlands*, Collins, London

Raemaekers, D. 2003 'Cutting a long story short? The process of neolithization in the Dutch delta re-examined', *Antiquity* **77** (298), 740-749

Reade, T. M. 1871 'The geology and physics of the post-glacial period, as shown in the deposits and organic remains in Lancashire and Cheshire', *Proc Liverpool Geol Soc* **2**, 36-88

Reade, T. M. 1881 'On a Section of the Formby and Leasowe Marine Beds and Superior Peat Bed, disclosed by Cuttings for the Outlet Sewer at Hightown', *Proc Liverpool Geol Soc* **4**, 269-77

Rees. J. S. 1949 *History of the Liverpool Pilotage Service, mentioning the local Lighthouses and Lightships*, Southport Guardian [Press]

Renfrew, C. & Bahn, P. 2000 *Archaeology: theories, methods and practice*, Thames and Hudson

Report *of Committee Appointed to Examine the Life-boat Models Submitted to Compete for the Premium Offered by His Grace the Duke of Northumberland*, 1851, W. Clowes, London

Rimmer, J. 1986 *The Changing Countryside: the decline of asparagus farming on the Formby Coast, Merseyside* (Unpublished thesis, Open University) FCS Archive

Ritchie-Noakes, N. 1984 *Liverpool's historic waterfront: the world's first mercantile dock system*, HMSO, London

Roberts, E. J. 1995 The Height Distribution of a Stone Age Population compared with that of a Modern Population, (Unpublished 'A' Level [Oxford] Mathematics and Statistics project)

Roberts, G., Gonzalez, S. and Huddart, D. 1996 'Intertidal Holocene footprints and their archæological significance', *Antiquity* **70**, 647-651

Roberts, O. T. P. 2002 'Accident not Intention: Llyn Cerrig Bach, Isle of Anglesey, Wales – site of an Iron Age Shipwreck', *Int J of Nautical Archaeology* **31.1**, 25-38

Robinson, F. W. 1848 *A Descriptive History of Southport*, Arthur Hall and Co. (reprinted to mark the bi-centenary of Southport 1792-1992, Sefton Libraries)

Rothschild, M. and Marren, P. 1997, *Rothschild's Reserves: time and fragile nature*, Balaban, Israel

Royal Commission on Coast Erosion, Report 1911 *The Reclamation of Tidal Lands and Afforestation in the UK*, 111 pt.1, HMSO Cmd 5708

Royal National Lifeboat Institution 1897 for 1896 *Annual Report*

Royal National Lifeboat Institution 1916 *The Lifeboat or Journal of RNLI*, **23**

Royal National Lifeboat Institution 1918 *Annual Report*, Port of Liverpool Branch

Royden, M. W. 1991 *Pioneers and Perseverance: a history of the Royal School for the Blind, Liverpool 1791-1991*, Countyvise, Birkenhead

Rylands J. P. (ed) 1896 'The Exchequer Lay Subsidy Roll of AD 1332', *Miscellanies relating to Lancashire and Cheshire*, vol. **II**, Record Soc of Lancashire and Cheshire

Scarisbrick of Scarisbrick family, papers, LRO DDSc

Schama, S. 1995 *Landscape and Memory*, Harper Collins, London

Schulting. R. J. and Richards, M.P. 2002 'Finding the coastal Mesolithic in southwest Britain: AMS dates and stable isotope results on human remains from Caldy Island, south Wales', *Antiquity* **76**, no.294 Oct, 1011-1026

Sefton Metropolitan Borough Council 2003 *Landscape Character Assessment of Sefton*, Supplementary Planning Guidance

Shaw, R. C. 1956 *The Royal Forest of Lancaster*, Guardian Press, Preston

Sheppard, B. 1978 'Aerial Photography aiding Landscape Studies on Merseyside', *J Merseyside Archaeol Soc* **2**, 83-90

Shorter Oxford English Dictionary 1978, Clarendon Press, Oxford

Smith, G. 1980 *Something to Declare: 100 years of Customs and Excise*, Harrap, London

Smith, P. H. 1999 *The Sands of Time: an introduction to the sand dunes of the Sefton coast*, National Museums and Galleries on Merseyside/Sefton Metropolitan Borough Council

Stammers, M. 1975, 'The Mersey Boatmen and their Gigs', *Mariner's Mirror*, **61**, 283-288

Stanistreet, J. E. and Farthing, A. 1995 *Crosby in Camera: early photographs of Great Crosby and Waterloo*, Sefton Libraries

Statutes 1709 *An Act for making a convenient Dock or Basin at Liverpool, for the Security of all Ships trading to and from the said Port of Liverpool*, 8 Anne, Cap XII; 83-90

Statutes 1715 *Liverpool Dock Act*, 3 George I, Cap I

Statutes 1847 *An Act for making a railway from the Liverpool and Bury Railway near Liverpool, through Crosby to the Town of Southport, to be called "The Liverpool, Crosby and Southport Railway"*, 10 and 11 Victoria, Cap CV

Statutes, Private 1848 Weld-Blundell, T. An Act to authorise the granting of Building Lease for Ninety-nine years of Parts of the Trust Estate of the Will of the late Charles Robert Blundell, Esquire, situate in the Parishes of Sefton, Walton on the Hill and North Meols in the County of Lancaster, and to lease waste Lands and Coal and other mines and to exchange certain detached and intermixed Lands, other parts of the said Trust Estate, 11 and 12 Victoria, Cap XV, 8-9

Statutes 1854 An Act to make further provision for the Sewerage, Sanitary Regulation and Improvement of the Borough of Liverpool, 17 and 18 Victoria, 1316-1357

Stewart-Brown, R. 1932 *Liverpool Ships in the Eighteenth Century: including the King's ships built there with notes on the principal shipwrights*, Liverpool University Press

Tait, J. 1923 *The Chartulary or Register of the Abbey of St Werburgh Chester, Part II*, Chetham Soc **82**

Thomas, G. 1813 *Admiralty Survey; Sea Chart, Liverpool Harbour* L'poolRO Hf 912 LIV

Thompson, F. H. 1956 'Pilgrim's Flask from Meols', *J Chester Archaeol Soc* **43**, 48-9

Thompson, F. M. Longstreth (ed) 1945 *Merseyside Plan 1944*, HMSO

Tithe Map and Schedule, Formby 1845, LRO DRL

Tooley, M. J. 1970 'The peat beds of the southwest Lancashire coast', *Nature in Lancashire* **1**, 19-21

Tooley, M. J. 1974 'Sea-level changes during the last 9,000 years of north-west England', *Geogr J* **140**, 18-42

Tooley, M. J. 1978 *Sea-level changes in north west England during the Flandrian Stage*, Oxford Research Studies in Geography, Clarendon Press, Oxford

Tooley, M. J. 1980 'Theories of Coastal Change in North-West England' in F. H. Thompson (ed) *Archaeology and Coastal Change*, Occasional Paper (New Series) **1**, Soc of Antiquaries, London

Tooley, M. J, 1982 Sea-level changes in northern England, *Proc Geologists' Assoc*, **93**, 43-51

Tooley, M. J. 1985 'Sea-level changes and coastal morphology in northwest England' in R. H. Johnson (ed) *The Geomorphology of Northwest England*, Manchester University Press, 94-121

Travis, C. B. 1926 'The peat and forest bed of the South-West Lancashire Coast', *Proc Liverpool Geol Soc* **14**, 263-273

Troughton, T. 1820 *History of Liverpool*

Turner, E. 1992 'A Tudor Map from Lancashire: Downholland, Altcar and Formby', *The Lancashire Local Historian* **7**, 19-26

Tyrer, F. 1953 'The Harkirk', *Trans Hist Soc Lancashire and Cheshire* **104**, 153-158

Tyrer, F. (ed) 1968 *The Great Diurnal of Nicholas Blundell of Little Crosby, Lancashire 1, 1702-1711*, Record Soc of Lancashire and Cheshire **110**

Tyrer, F. (ed) 1970 *The Great Diurnal of Nicholas Blundell of Little Crosby, Lancashire 2, 1712-1719*, Record Soc of Lancashire and Cheshire **112**

Tyrer, F. (ed) 1972 *The Great Diurnal of Nicholas Blundell of Little Crosby, Lancashire 3, 1720-1728*, Record Soc of Lancashire and Cheshire **114**

Uglow, J.S. 2004 *A Little History of British Gardening*, Chatto and Windus, London

Van Vuure, C. 2003 *'De Oeros, Het spoor terug'*, Ministerie van de Vlaamse Gemeenschap, Afdeling Natuur, Brussel, 218

Wainwright, F. T. 1975 *Scandinavian England: collected papers by F.T. Wainwright* (ed by H. P. R. Finberg), Phillimore, Chichester

Walbank, F. W. 1953 'The Roman Occupation' in W. Smith(ed) *A Scientific Survey of Merseyside*, The British Association, University of Liverpool Press, 214-20

Waldron, T. 1989 'The effects of urbanisation on human health: the evidence from skeleton remains' in D. Serjeantson and T. Waldron (eds) *Diets and Crafts in Towns*, British Archaeological Reports (British Series) **199**, 63

Walker Art Gallery 1978 *Merseyside Painters, People & Places: catalogue of oil paintings – plates and text*, Merseyside County Council, Liverpool

Walker, F. 1939 *The Historical Geography of Southwest Lancashire before the Industrial Revolution*, Chetham Soc, New Series, **103**

Walmesley-Cotham, I. 1934 *Forestry in Formby*, a paper given to Liverpool Botanical Soc, MRO 920 WBL/8/4

Walmesley-Cotham, I. 1952a Letter to R. A. Shaw, Liverpool University, MRO 920 WBL/8/4

Walmesley-Cotham, I. 1952b Letter to Secretary, Forestry Commission, MRO 920 WBL/8/4

Weatherill, L. (ed) 1990 *The Account Book of Richard Latham 1724-1767*, (for) British Academy, Oxford University Press

Weld-Blundell, C. 10/1/1921 Letter to James Wright, Estate Manager, MRO 920 WBL/8/4

Weld-Blundell, E. J. 1934 Correspondence and other papers, MRO 920 WBL/8/4

Weld and Weld (Solicitors) 1959 Letter to O.Williams and Sutcliffe (Agents), MRO 920 WBL/8/4

Whitehaven and the origins of rum butter [leaflet] n.d.

Wilkins, F. 1992 *The Isle of Man in Smuggling History*, Wyre Forest Press, Kidderminster

Williams, M. (ed) 1990 *Wetlands: a threatened landscape*, Basil Blackwell, Oxford

Williamson, R. 1766 [Chart] *From Chester Bar to Madwharfe, Liverpool and Parkgate Harbours*, Bradley, Pass and Co, Liverpool, L'poolRO Hf 912 LIV

Winchester, A. J. L. 2006 'The Farming Landscape' in A.J.L. Winchester (ed) *The North West* (England's Landscape **8**), Collins, London

Woods and Plantations on the Ince Blundell Estate (n.d. 1930s) Memorandum, MRO 920 WBL/5/12

Woods, E. C. 1945-46, 'Some History of the Coastwise Lights of Lancashire and Cheshire, Part 1', *Trans Hist Soc Lancashire and Cheshire* **96** (for 1944) 81-103

Woodworth, P. L. 1999 *A Study of Changes in High Water Levels and Tides at Liverpool during the Last Two Hundred and Thirty Years with some Historical Background*, Proudman Oceanographic Laboratory, Report no.**56**

Woodworth, P. L. 2003 'Three Georges and one Richard Holden: the Liverpool tide-table makers', *Trans Hist Soc Lancashire and Cheshire* **151** (for 2002)

Yorke, B. and Yorke, R. 1982 *Britain's First Lifeboat Station, Formby 1776-1918*, Alt Press, Liverpool

Yorke, R. (in preparation) *The Formby Asparagus Project*, Formby Civic Soc

Index